THE MISSIONAL CHURCH

AND LEADERSHIP FORMATION

D0746212

MISSIONAL CHURCH SERIES

The missional church conversation continues to grow in importance in providing for many fresh ways to rethink what it means to be church in our rapidly changing context. The Missional Church Series, published by the Wm. B. Eerdmans Publishing Co., is designed to contribute original research to this critical conversation. This series makes available monographs as well as edited volumes produced from specially designed consultations.

The Missional Church
and Leadership Formation

Helping Congregations Develop
Leadership Capacity

Edited by

Craig Van Gelder

WILLIAM B. EERDMANS PUBLISHING COMPANY
GRAND RAPIDS, MICHIGAN / CAMBRIDGE, U.K.

© 2009 William B. Eerdmans Publishing Company
All rights reserved

Published 2009 by
Wm. B. Eerdmans Publishing Co.
2140 Oak Industrial Drive N.E., Grand Rapids, Michigan 49505 /
P.O. Box 163, Cambridge CB3 9PU U.K.

Printed in the United States of America

14 13 12 11 10 09   7 6 5 4 3 2 1

Library of Congress Cataloging-in-Publication Data

Mission Church Consultation (3rd: 2007: Saint Paul, Minn.)
      The missional church and leadership formation: helping congregations develop
      leadership capacity / edited by Craig Van Gelder.
            p.   cm.   — (Missional church series)
      Includes bibliographical references.
      ISBN 978-0-8028-6493-2 (pbk.: alk. paper)
      1. Mission of the church — Congresses.   2. Christian leadership — Congresses.
      I. Van Gelder, Cràig.   II. Title.

      BV601.8.M945   2007
      262'.7 — dc22

                                                                2009026541

www.eerdmans.com

Contents

Preface

This volume is the third in the Missional Church Series being published by the William B. Eerdmans Publishing Company. It utilizes the missional church conversation as a lens with which to engage an important dimension of U.S. church life: leadership formation. Leadership formation continues to emerge today as a topic of keen interest in the church. Numerous approaches to leadership and leadership formation are afoot in the church, and diverse sources seek to inform their practice. It is timely to bring the perspective of the missional church into conversation with this crucial dimension of church life, and that is the purpose of this book.

The "missional-church conversation" came on the scene in 1998 with the publication of the book entitled *The Missional Church: A Vision for the Sending of the Church in North America.* This conversation has now spread into many venues, and the missional language has been picked up by numerous denominations and faith traditions. However, it is clear that the use of the word "missional" means different things to different groups. Common today is the tendency by some to assume that being missional is just another way of framing the historical understanding of missions in the life of the church — that is, what the church *does.* Others assume that being missional is simply the latest fad geared to help grow the church. But the use of the word "missional" within the initial missional church conversation, as well as within this series, has something much more basic in view. Embedded in our use of this word are key insights into the very nature or essence of what it means to *be* the church, and how the *being* of the church provides the basis for the *doing* of the church.

This volume is intended to help bring further clarity to the word "missional" and to contribute to the ever-widening missional church conversation by engaging the issue of leadership formation. It is the result of the third annual Missional Church Consultation hosted by Luther Seminary in Saint Paul, Minnesota, in November 2007. The theme of that consultation was "The Missional Church and Leadership Formation: Helping Congregations Develop Leadership Capacity." The chapters of this book are the essays that were presented for discussion at that consultation.

Luther Seminary has been engaged in thinking about the missional church for over a decade, especially since it adopted its 2000 strategic plan, which was entitled "Serving the Promise of Our Mission." This plan envisioned the development of a strategic initiative in the field of congregational mission and leadership. Concentrations in this new field are now available in all degree programs, including Master of Arts, Master of Divinity, Doctor of Ministry, and Doctor of Philosophy. Part of the vision of this strategic initiative is to create an ongoing center for research on the missional church that is biblically and theologically framed while being informed by insights from the social sciences. The annual Missional Church Consultation is designed to contribute to this growing body of research.

The Wm. B. Eerdmans Publishing Company has graciously agreed to serve as the publisher for the Missional Church Series, which Luther Seminary is taking the lead in developing. This series will include both edited volumes that come out of the annual consultations and selected monographs. It is our prayer that the church of Jesus Christ will be more deeply informed, as well as built up and strengthened, as a result of the contributions made by this series.

CRAIG VAN GELDER
Editor, Missional Church Series

Contributors

Richard H. Bliese holds a Ph.D. from the Lutheran School of Theology in Chicago, where he served as professor of mission before taking the position of academic dean at Luther Seminary in 2003. Since 2005 he has served as the president of Luther Seminary. He is an ordained minister in the Evangelical Lutheran Church in America.

Sharon Henderson Callahan holds an Ed.D. from Seattle University. She joined the faculty of the Seattle University School of Theology and Ministry in 1996 and since 2006 has served as associate dean for academics and student life. She is a Roman Catholic laywoman who for many years served as lay minister in the archdiocese of Western Washington.

Scott Cormode holds a Ph.D. from Yale University. He taught at Claremont School of Theology in the field of church administration for a number of years before taking the position of principle of Fuller Theological Seminary's Max De Pree Center for Leadership in 2006, where he also serves as the Hugh De Pree Associate Professor of Leadership Development. He is an ordained minister in the Presbyterian Church (USA).

Dave Daubert holds a Ph.D. from the Graduate Theological Foundation. He is an ordained minister in the Evangelical Lutheran Church in America and between 2000 and 2008 served on the churchwide staff as Director for Renewal of Congregations. Presently he is serving as founding partner and

CEO of A Renewal Enterprise, which provides consulting services for organizational dynamics and missional leadership.

Terri Martinson Elton holds a Ph.D. in congregational mission and leadership from Luther Seminary. For ten years she headed up the Changing Church initiative of Prince of Peace Church (ECLA), focusing on congregational renewal and leadership development. Since 2008 she has served as director of the Center for Children, Youth, and Family at Luther Seminary.

Kyle J. A. Small holds a Ph.D. in congregational mission and leadership from Luther Seminary. He is an ordained minister in the Evangelical Covenant Church (ECC) and serves with his wife as co-pastors at Harbert Community Church in Harbert, Michigan.

Kristine M. Stache holds a Ph.D. in congregational mission and leadership from Luther Seminary. She served for many years in a parish as director of ministry development. Since 2007 she has been an assistant professor of youth and young adult ministries and also the director of the Center for Youth Ministries at Wartburg Theological Seminary.

Craig Van Gelder holds a Ph.D. in mission from Southwestern Baptist Theological Seminary and a Ph.D. in administration in urban affairs from the University of Texas in Arlington. He is an ordained minister in the Christian Reformed Church. Between 1988 and 1998 he was professor of domestic missiology at Calvin Theological Seminary, and since 1998 he has served as professor of congregational mission at Luther Seminary.

Engaging the Missional Church Conversation

What would it look like for a congregation to develop the capacity for forming missional leadership? This is the question that underlies all the essays in this volume, a question that is still very much in the process of being answered with regard to what is now known as the "missional-church conversation." We believe that this question can only be answered in the context of the United States today by engaging in a thorough critique and analysis of both theological education and the current leadership formation practices of congregations. We also believe that this question can only be answered by our drawing deeply on biblical and theological foundations that are, in turn, informed particularly by Trinitarian perspectives. These are the two orientations that are brought into conversation with the subject of leadership formation throughout this volume.

Some of the background information on the missional-church conversation in this introduction also appeared in the first and second volumes in this series: *The Missional Church in Context: Helping Congregations Develop Contextual Ministry* (Grand Rapids: Eerdmans, 2007) and *The Missional Church and Denominations: Helping Congregations Develop a Missional Identity* (Grand Rapids: Eerdmans, 2008). This introductory overview will be helpful to the reader who is new to or unfamiliar with the missional-church conversation.

A Changing Context and Changing Church

These are exciting yet challenging days for the church of Jesus Christ as it continues to face massive shifts that are taking place throughout the world. To those of us living in the United States, one of the more interesting shifts is the growing recognition by churches that they are now in their own mission location. This awareness is generating fresh opportunities for new ministry, but it is also introducing disruption into long-standing practices. For congregations to do business as usual is no longer possible. As a result, many historical denominations are now in serious decline. Alongside this development, significant new movements are coming into existence, such as: the rapid expansion of megachurches; a significant increase in the number of immigrant congregations; a dramatic expansion of the number of congregations being established along generational lines; and the rapidly growing emerging-church movement.

It is profoundly important, in the midst of such shifts, to keep returning to the foundations of what it means to be the church of Jesus Christ in the world. This involves the issue of ecclesiology (a theological term that refers to the "study of the church" [*ecclesia* = church; *ology* = study of]). In our encounter with our changing world, we need to continue to engage in the study of the church: to explore its nature, to understand its creation and continuing formation, and to examine carefully its purpose and ministry.

A very helpful discussion has emerged over the past several decades that is known as the "missional-church conversation," which is helping us focus our attention on this ongoing study of the church. It has a number of generative sources, but by far the most influential have been the contributions made by missiologist Lesslie Newbigin, whose writings began to gain wide circulation in the late 1970s and early 1980s.

The Influence of Lesslie Newbigin

In returning home to England from the mission field of India in the 1970s, Newbigin took up the challenge of trying to envision what a fresh encounter of the gospel with late-modern Western culture might look like. The issue he raised is probably best focused in his book *Foolishness to the Greeks,* where he asked this question: "What would be involved in a missionary encounter between the gospel and this whole way of perceiving, thinking, and living that we call 'modern Western culture'?"[1]

A movement emerged in England in the 1980s that was an effort to address this issue: it came to be known as the Gospel and Our Culture (GOC) conversation. While the GOC discussion first surfaced in England, it soon spread to the United States, where it was taken up by a new generation of American missiologists who focused their attention on seeking to address their context as its own unique mission location.

Newbigin's missiology was shaped largely by the mission theology given birth within the International Missionary Council (IMC) conferences during the 1950s through the 1970s. This involved a Trinitarian understanding of mission, or what is commonly referred to as the *missio Dei* (the mission of God). Influenced by the biblical theology movement of the 1930s and 1940s, a Trinitarian foundation for mission theology began to take shape at the Willingen Conference of the IMC in 1952. This understanding was later formulated as the *missio Dei* by Karl Hartenstein,[2] and then given fuller expression by Johannes Blauw in his 1962 publication *The Missionary Nature of the Church*.[3]

Newbigin articulated his own expression of this mission theology in his 1978 book *The Open Secret*.[4] Central to his understanding of mission is the work of the triune God in calling and sending the church through the Spirit into the world to participate fully in God's mission within all of creation. In this theological understanding, the church is understood to be the creation of the Spirit: it exists in the world as a *sign* that the redemptive reign of God's kingdom is present. It also serves as a *foretaste* of the eschatological future of the redemptive reign that has already begun. And it serves as well as an *instrument* under the leadership of the Spirit to bring that redemptive reign to bear on every dimension of life.[5]

---

1. Lesslie Newbigin, *Foolishness to the Greeks* (Grand Rapids: Eerdmans, 1986), 1.

2. H. H. Rosin, *'Missio Dei': An Examination of the Origin, Contents and Function of the Term in Protestant Missiological Discussion* (Leiden, Germany: Interuniversity Institute for Missiological and Ecumenical Research, Department of Missiology, 1972).

3. Johannes Blauw, *The Missionary Nature of the Church: A Survey of the Biblical Theology of Mission* (Grand Rapids: Eerdmans, 1962).

4. Lesslie Newbigin, *The Open Secret* (Grand Rapids: Eerdmans, 1978).

5. Newbigin, *Open Secret,* 124.

The British GOC Programme

The British version of the GOC conversation, as noted above, was a movement developed during the 1980s that came to be called a "programme." It was shaped largely by the writings of Newbigin during that period: *The Other Side of 1984* (1983), *Foolishness to the Greeks* (1986), and *The Gospel in a Pluralist Society* (1989).[6] Newbigin's intellectual leadership of the programme was joined by the administrative and organizational contributions of Dr. Dan Beeby and Bishop Hugh Montefiore. An occasional newsletter began publication in 1989, but the programme culminated in many ways with "The National Consultation" at Swanwick in 1992. A volume of essays entitled *The Gospel and Contemporary Culture,* edited by Montefiore, served as the agenda for discussion at that consultation.[7]

During the early 1990s the British GOC Programme floundered somewhat, due primarily to its failure to secure sufficient funding and to find an institutional home within the church. A move was made to merge the GOC programme with the C. S. Lewis Center in 1994, but this proved to be short-lived, and the GOC programme was disbanded in 1996.[8] The death of Lesslie Newbigin in 1998 brought an additional sense of closure to his substantive as well as symbolic leadership of the movement in England.

The GOC Network in the United States

As the British programme began to gain public recognition, a U.S. version of the Gospel and Our Culture conversation also began to emerge. Several consultations sponsored in the mid-1980s by the Overseas Ministries Study Center stimulated interest in the question Newbigin had posed in his Warfield Lectures at Princeton in 1984 (later published as *Foolishness to the Greeks*). Growing out of these early events, a "network" began to take shape in the mid-1980s under the leadership of George

6. Lesslie Newbigin, *The Other Side of 1984* (Geneva: World Council of Churches, 1983); Newbigin, *Foolishness to the Greeks;* and Newbigin, *The Gospel in a Pluralist Society* (Grand Rapids: Eerdmans, 1989).

7. Hugh Montefiore, ed., *The Gospel and Contemporary Culture* (New York: Mowbray/Cassell Academic, 1992).

8. A brief history of the British GOC Programme is available online at www .deepsight.org/articles/engchis.htm.

Hunsberger. By the early 1990s the Gospel and Our Culture Network was publishing a quarterly newsletter and also convening a yearly consultation. By the mid-1990s, the U.S. movement started to find its own voice beyond the influence of Newbigin as the Wm. B. Eerdmans Publishing Company began publishing a series of books under the moniker The Gospel and Our Culture Series. Included in this series to date are the following volumes:

George Hunsberger and Craig Van Gelder, eds., *The Church Between Gospel and Culture: The Emerging Mission in North America* (1996)
Darrel L. Guder, ed., *Missional Church: A Vision for the Sending of the Church in North America* (1998)
George R. Hunsberger, *Bearing the Witness of the Spirit: Lesslie Newbigin's Theology of Cultural Plurality* (1998)
Craig Van Gelder, ed., *Confident Witness — Changing World: Rediscovering the Gospel in North America* (1999)
Darrel L. Guder, *The Continuing Conversion of the Church* (2000)
James V. Brownson, ed., *StormFront: The Good News of God* (2003)
Lois Y. Barrett, ed., *Treasure in Clay Jars: Patterns in Missional Faithfulness* (2004)

This literature focused on understanding the United States as its own unique mission location and the church as being missional by nature; it continues to stimulate a very important conversation. A number of other books, from several different publishers, have also contributed to this conversation:

Craig Van Gelder, *The Essence of the Church: A Community Created by the Spirit* (Grand Rapids: Baker, 2000)
Richard H. Bliese and Craig Van Gelder, eds., *The Evangelizing Church: A Lutheran Contribution* (Minneapolis: Augsburg Fortress, 2005)
Alan J. Roxburgh and Fred Romanuk, *The Missional Leader: Equipping Your Church To Reach a Changing World* (San Francisco: Jossey-Bass, 2006)
Patrick Keifert, *We Are Here Now: A New Missional Era* (Eagle, ID: Allelon Publishing, 2007)
Craig Van Gelder, *The Ministry of the Missional Church: A Community Led by the Spirit* (Grand Rapids: Baker, 2007)

Richard W. Rouse and Craig Van Gelder, *A Field Guide to the Missional Congregation: A Journey of Transformation* (Minneapolis: Augsburg Fortress, 2008)

The strategic importance of the missional-church conversation is taking on increasing importance in the United States as the literature in this subject area continues to expand. Increasing numbers of denominational and congregational leaders are becoming aware of the need to explore more deeply the church's nature and identity. This awareness is coming largely from the increased recognition that the multiple late-modern strategies and programs being generated to make the church more effective have significant limitations in addressing systemic issues. This awareness and the need to continue to extend the missional-church conversation into new areas of exploration are the primary impulses that have given birth to this book, which is the third in the Missional Church Series being published by Eerdmans.

The Missional Church Series

The primary purpose of this series is to continue to generate original scholarship with regard to the missional-church conversation. Two previous volumes have been published in this series, both of which came out of the annual Missional Church Consultations at Luther Seminary (in 2005 and 2006):

Craig Van Gelder, ed., *The Missional Church in Context: Helping Congregations Develop Contextual Ministry* (2007)
Van Gelder, ed., *The Missional Church and Denominations: Helping Congregations Develop a Missional Identity* (2008)

This present volume builds on these previous publications by using the missional-church conversation to engage the subject of leadership formation. It is the result of the third annual Missional Church Consultation hosted by Luther Seminary in St. Paul, Minnesota, in November 2007, whose theme was "The Missional Church and Leadership Formation: Helping Congregations Develop Leadership Capacity." The essays from that consultation are the materials included in this volume and are organized into three sections (see the table of contents). Substantive developments in theology, especially the renewal of Trinitarian studies, continue to generate new insights for this conversation. In addition, efforts are now gaining traction to bring the missional-church conversation into more direct discussion with the variety of leadership theories and leadership formation processes that are present today — both in seminaries and in congregations.

How to Read and Use This Book

As noted above, the primary purpose of this book is to extend the conversation about the missional church by engaging the issues associated with leadership formation. The reader will find that the authors draw deeply on the missional church literature that has been generated to date. But in the midst of drawing on these resources, the authors also contribute some fresh insights and new research into thinking further about the missional church with regard to leadership formation.

The first section of three essays engages the subject of missional leadership formation and its relationship to theological education. The first chapter provides a historical overview of how seminaries and schools of theology have engaged in practices of leadership formation and how this has changed over time. The next chapter uses the present emphasis on missional theology to make an argument for the practice of a critical *paedeia* with respect to missional leadership formation. The third essay offers an extended case study of one school's journey through these developments, including identifying the gains made and the challenges encountered in making the missional move.

The second section of three essays engages the subject of missional leadership formation and its relationship to congregations. The first chapter of this section explores how mental models guide the decision-making processes for Christian leaders, and it offers the conception of an ecology of vocation to better understand the process of missional leadership formation within and through congregations. The second chapter explores such an ecology of vocation by utilizing an extended vignette of a particular congregation where the missional formation of both pastoral and lay leadership was developed around a theology of baptism. The final chapter argues theologically and theoretically for the involvement of all of God's people in a congregation to help shape and form vision as the more desirable approach to missional leadership in contrast to a vision developed by a singular leader.

The third section of two essays reports on missional leadership formation with regard to some recent field research that was conducted. The first chapter uses a grounded-theory methodology to identify common characteristics and practices among five ELCA congregations that have been successful in forming missional lay leadership. The second chapter uses a qualitative-exploratory methodology to identify the progress that is being made in four different denominational systems toward innovating missional leadership within their congregations and judicatories.

MISSIONAL LEADERSHIP FORMATION IN RELATION TO THEOLOGICAL EDUCATION

This first section of three essays brings the missional church conversation into discussion with the theological education that is being offered by seminaries and schools of theology. An energetic and somewhat contested debate about the character and content of theological education took place from the early 1980s to the mid-1990s. Numerous books and articles offering various proposals were published. But one fundamental question remained insufficiently answered: What is theological about a theological school? These essays pick up on the theological debate, in general, and on that question, in particular, and engage the discussion by bringing a missional perspective to bear on it.

Craig Van Gelder sets up this discussion in the first chapter by providing an overview of how leadership formation evolved within seminaries and schools of theology in the United States over the past 300 years. He lays out four historical patterns, from the colonial period through the 1960s, regarding leadership formation and then notes the emergence of several new patterns in recent decades. This chapter includes a helpful summary of the eight issues that surfaced within the theological education debate of the previous two decades. Van Gelder ends this chapter by offering some perspective on what it might look like for missional theology to begin to reshape leadership formation offered in theological education today by seminaries and schools of theology.

In the next chapter, Kyle Small builds on Van Gelder's essay by offering a helpful review of the extensive literature from the theological education debate that took place in the 1980s and 1990s. He notes how theological education is now caught to a large extent between the crossroads of Christian formation *(paideia)* and academic acumen *(Wissenschaft)*, or as David Kelsey labels the divide, between Athens and Berlin. Small constructs a proposal for a missional reframing of theological education by developing an approach that he calls *critical paideia.* This proposed approach takes seriously the challenge of dealing with the holistic formation of preparing persons for ministry while also attending honestly to the questions generated through research and scholarship.

In the final chapter in this section, Richard Bliese uses the case example of the history and experiences of Luther Seminary to illustrate the missional reframing of both the purpose and the process of theological education in that institution. Bliese carefully documents how the missional conversation has been engaged within Luther Seminary for the past several decades and how it has shaped and reshaped the school's approach to theological education. He provides a helpful typology of different approaches to the missional conversation that are offered by the Reformed, Roman Catholic, and Evangelical traditions. Then he advances a proposal for how Lutherans might best pursue their own framing of the missional discussion so that they can focus more directly on the development of evangelical public leadership for apostolic witness.

CHAPTER 1

Theological Education and Missional Leadership Formation: Can Seminaries Prepare Missional Leaders for Congregations?

Craig Van Gelder

Introduction

Significant changes are taking place in theological education today regarding the formation of church leaders. There have been previous periods of transition in this ongoing journey, but this present one represents what appears to be a strategic shift. The nature of this is quite complex, but in simple terms it involves the following: today new insights from an emerging missional theology are interacting within an expanding system of congregations to redefine the purpose, the method, and, to some extent, the location of theological education. This chapter uses a historical framework for understanding these changes and offers a proposal regarding how seminaries and schools of theology might better engage the opportunities now before them.[1]

---

1. Primary sources include the extensive literature generated in the theological education conversation since the early 1980s, and the substantive two-volume work by Glenn T. Miller, who breaks the Protestant theological education story into pre-1870 developments and developments between 1870-1970. Glenn T. Miller, *Piety and Intellect: The Aims and Purposes of Ante-Bellum Theological Education* (Atlanta: Scholars Press, 1990), and Glenn T. Miller, *Piety and Profession: American Protestant Theological Education, 1870-1970* (Grand Rapids: Eerdmans, 2007). The primary source for developing the Catholic side of the story is from the edited documents of a key conference at Marquette University in 1995: Patrick W. Carey and Earl C. Muller, S.J., eds., *Theological Education in the Catholic Tradition* (New York: Crossroad, 1997).

Argument of This Chapter

Significant developments have taken place in theological education in the United States over the past 250 years. It is helpful to identify the key institutional and cultural frameworks that shaped the various approaches to theological education that have emerged and morphed over time. The first part of this chapter maps the earlier stages of these developments through four somewhat distinct periods, with a time of transition occurring at the end of each period that in turn contributed to the formation of a changed framework in the next period. The second part of the chapter picks up the most recent transition, which took place during the last several decades of the twentieth century, and discusses the substantial conversation concerning theological education that emerged at that time. The final section offers perspective on a fifth period of development, the one we now appear to be in, and offers some suggestions about how a missional theology might help theological education better engage the opportunities that are present.

This analysis proposes that a key for understanding each of the five periods of theological education development is to explore the expansion of the system of congregations and the subsequent rise of new seminaries and schools of theology — as well as the changes taking place within them. This hermeneutic of reading the development of theological education through the lens of the expansion of the system of congregations suggests a crucial historical connection: *theological education as a system* tends to follow the development of *new congregations*. This premise is somewhat self-evident; however, if we take it seriously, it has profound implications for our understanding of what took place historically and also what is taking place today in the developments currently underway.

Historical Development of Theological Education in the United States

Period One — Foundations, 1600s to Late 1700s: Early Schools and Institutions and the Minister as Resident Theologian

The settling of the colonies in Northern America in the 1600s by European immigrants, especially those coming from England, marked the beginning of the extension of the Protestant church into the New World.[2] The earlier Spanish colonization had introduced the Catholic faith into territories to the south and southwest. But the vast majority of the new immigrants arriving on the Eastern Seaboard were Protestants, except for modest numbers of Roman Catholics settling in what became Maryland. Some of the newly arriving immigrants represented the established European churches, often referred to as "churches from the left."[3] They attempted to repeat in the more northern colonies the pattern of establishment that was initiated by the Anglicans in the southern colonies. Other immigrants represented the persecuted sects of the Protestant Reformation, such as the Quakers, Baptists, and Mennonites, that are often referred to as "churches from the right."[4] These groups came to the colonies primarily for the purpose of pursuing religious freedom. The Puritans in New England represented an interesting blend of these two traditions: while being persecuted as a sect by the Anglican Church in England, they proceeded to *establish* the Congregational Church in most New England colonies.

The development of Christian congregations in what eventually became the thirteen colonies — and later the first thirteen states — has been told numerous times.[5] It is not necessary to repeat the details of that story here, but a few things did have an impact on the development of theological education. These diverse, early-colonial congregations required qualified leadership, and different patterns emerged for supplying this leadership. Churches from the left initially continued to look to Europe to supply the necessary ministerial leadership for their congregations, but they often encountered problems in securing an adequate supply of qualified personnel. They soon recognized that schools needed to be built in the colonies to supplement the training of personnel, and they pursued this by drawing

---

2. "Northern American" has become the common usage today in referring to the United States and Canada, distinguishing it from "North America," which also includes Mexico.

3. Craig Van Gelder, "An Ecclesiastical Geno-Project: Unpacking the DNA of Denominations and Denominationalism," in *The Missional Church and Denominations: Helping Congregations Develop a Missional Identity,* ed. Craig Van Gelder (Grand Rapids: Eerdmans, 2008), 22-23.

4. Van Gelder, "An Ecclesiastical Geno-Project," 22-23.

5. See, e.g., John Corrigan and Winthrop S. Hudson, *Religion in America,* 7th ed. (Upper Saddle River, NJ: Prentice Hall, 2004); see also Sydney E. Ahlstrom, *A Religious History of the American People* (New Haven, CT: Yale University Press, 1972).

primarily on European approaches to theological education. For the Reformers, "[s]chools were the means of cultural change, and Protestants staked the future of their movement on the ability of teachers to transform habitual patterns of thought."[6]

The charter of the Virginia Company initially envisioned the establishment of a college to serve the colony. However, circumstances delayed the founding of the College of William and Mary in Williamsburg until 1693, when it finally became operational for the purpose of educating students in grammar, philosophy, and divinity. A number of those being educated were intended to serve as ministers in Anglican congregations.[7]

The churches from the right, especially the Puritans, also recognized early the need for training ministerial personnel. They established Harvard College in 1636 for the purpose of providing leadership for the expanding system and needs of the Congregational churches. More conservative elements in the Congregational Church founded Yale for that same purpose in 1701, having lost confidence in Harvard as it increasingly came under the influence of Unitarian thought.

These early schools were founded primarily for the purpose of training ministerial personnel, though they always had a broader mandate for educating leadership with a classical liberal education in the arts and sciences. Ministerial training involved primarily memorization via the reading of theology with a mentor-teacher, along with learning the classical languages for studying the Bible. Latin continued to be the common language of the scholar. Little attention was paid to the actual practice of ministry; it was largely assumed that an emerging minister, by forming his mind and character in the study of these disciplines, would be able to provide the necessary leadership for a congregation. Pastors were educated and formed primarily to serve as *resident theologians* in congregations and their broader communities.

These early approaches to the training of ministers were complemented by less formal efforts. The tradition of the log college in New Jersey established by William Tennent in the 1720s serves as an example. The Great Awakening also influenced the development of theological education: the emphasis on revival and personal conversion became a deep and enduring value within U.S. Christianity. Theological education was chal-

6. Miller, *Piety and Intellect*, 17.
7. See http://www.wm.edu/vitalfacts/seventeenth.php (accessed Sept. 12, 2007).

lenged with how to shape both the minds and the hearts of those being prepared for ministry. All too often, those two emphases became more of a dichotomy within the church and theological education rather than a complementary polarity.[8] The emergence of New Light and Old Light parties in the Presbyterian Church in the mid-1700s, and of New School and Old School parties in the 1800s, are good illustrations of this pattern.[9]

Three trends within theological education were in place within the colonies by the time of the Revolutionary War. First, there was the continued reliance on the established European churches to supply ministers for the emerging congregations, which was especially true of Anglicans, Dutch Reformed, and Lutherans — as well as of the Catholic Church. Second, early schools were established in the colonies to train ministers for the growing congregations within the various faith traditions, which was especially true of the Congregationalists. Third, there was the development of what today would be called "nonformal" approaches to training ministers. This was especially true among those groups that were shaped by the revivalist side of Christianity, which by the end of the eighteenth century included the growing number of Baptists and Methodists, along with groups that had splintered off from the Presbyterians.[10]

Transition Period: Revolutionary War

Several things were becoming clearer by the mid-1700s. First of all, the larger established churches in the colonies, Anglicans in the South and Congregationalists in the North, found it impossible to keep other Christian faith traditions from invading their territories. The democratic spirit emerging in the colonies, along with the increasing influence of free-church ecclesiology (introduced by the formerly persecuted sects of Europe), spelled the death of any serious ability to establish only one church in any colony based on geography.

The adoption of the Act of Toleration in England in 1689 was the beginning of the end for the exclusive, formal establishment of the church in that country. It also deeply influenced eighteenth-century developments in

8. See Barry Johnson, *Polarity Management: Identifying and Managing Unsolvable Problems* (Amherst, MA: HRD Press, 1996).

9. Ahlstrom, *A Religious History,* 287-90, 464-66.

10. Miller, *Piety and Intellect,* 23.

the colonies, where religious diversity was becoming the norm, especially in the middle colonies. Locke had argued in his 1685 *Letter Concerning Toleration* that the church should be founded on a voluntary basis as a social contract of consenting participants.[11] This followed the same logic of his proposals for civil polity, ideas that became foundational for the development of the U.S. Constitution. Ideas such as Locke's blended with the realities of the day and led by the time of the Revolutionary War to calls for the official separation of church and state. The adoption of the first amendment to the Constitution of the newly formed United States in 1789 made this a reality. This new political framework helped stimulate the development of denominations, and it was not long before these newly forming denominations in the newly formed United States had to reckon with significant challenges within theological education.

Period Two — Expansion, Late 1700s to Mid-1800s: Developing Denominational Systems and the Minister as Gentleman Pastor

The outlines of emerging denominations had begun to come into focus by the mid-1700s. The call for independence and the Revolutionary War furthered their formation, and the separation of church and state institutionalized their necessity: no church would be established as the state (or national) church, and every church would be protected to practice religious freedom. This decision affirmed the organizing principle of denominationalism, and that, in turn, gave impetus to the further development of the denominational, organizational church.[12] The last two decades of the eighteenth century saw representatives of numerous church bodies meeting to form national organizations: for example, the Methodists in 1784, the Episcopalians in 1785, and the Presbyterians in 1789.[13]

The newly emerging denominations and their expanding systems of congregations had to adapt as the original colonies became the newly

---

11. Locke, an English exile in Holland, wrote this letter to his Dutch friend Philip von Limborch in 1685: in it he called for an end to the oppression of people who held unorthodox religious beliefs. The letter was published without Locke's permission after he returned to England following the "Glorious Revolution" of 1688.

12. Van Gelder, "An Ecclesiastical Geno-Project," 11-24.

13. Corrigan and Hudson, *Religion in America*, 136-43.

formed United States. The churches on the left gave up the practice built into their European-shaped polities that relied on the magistrate to privilege the church within civil society. Correspondingly, the churches on the right created new forms to give the church shape within the emerging democratic social order. All of these new denominations had to recontextualize themselves within the dynamic setting of the changed context.

The number of congregations within a few decades dramatically increased as the expanding immigrant population spilled across the Allegheny Mountains. Thousands of new congregations were started on the expanding frontier, and that process lasted well into the latter half of the nineteenth century. Interestingly, it was the newer "made-in-America" — or at least "modified-in-America" — denominations that led this effort.[14] This included the Methodists, who blended their Anglican heritage of bishops with a modified version of free-church congregationalism, employing circuit riders to extend the church into new territories. It also included the Baptists, who readily adapted themselves to the democratic spirit of the United States, which they incorporated within their congregational polity. They used the farmer-preacher to extend their congregations into the new territories. Related to these two groups was the formation of the Christian Church Disciples and the Churches of Christ, which were the product of several impulses: the restoration of the New Testament church, American democratic ideals based on Lockean philosophy, and the methodology of revivals. Revivals reemerged on the frontier after the turn of the nineteenth century in what became known as the Second Great Awakening. The socioreligious gatherings of this awakening helped to start many congregations.

All the newly formed denominations grew during this period; yet the growth of the "upstart" denominations dramatically outpaced the growth of the Presbyterian, Congregationalist, and Episcopalian denominations. These three groups had represented approximately 75 percent of all church membership at the time of the Declaration of Independence.[15] However, their growth rate on the frontier was significantly less than that of the upstart denominations such as the Methodists, Baptists, and Disciples because they continued to rely primarily on an educated clergy for serving

14. Roger Finke and Rodney Stark, *The Churching of America 1776-1990: Winners and Losers in Our Religious Economy* (New Brunswick, NJ: Rutgers University Press, 1992), 54-108.

15. Finke and Stark, *The Churching of America*, 55.

their expanding system of congregations. By mid-century, these upstart groups had become the largest denominations.

This expanding system of congregations required the training of hundreds of new pastors. Denominations approached this need in different ways, but all of them continued to rely on building a system of church-related colleges to support the development of leadership. The Methodists and Baptists relied almost exclusively on church colleges to augment their leadership formation processes, which had less formal educational requirements. The Congregationalists, Presbyterians, and Episcopalians also built church colleges, but they soon added another educational layer to the preparation of persons for ministry by developing a new kind of institution: the theological seminary.

The development of the theological seminary was based on the same European school model that had already been copied by schools such as William and Mary, Harvard, and Yale. What now emerged was the use of the school model that focused exclusively on the preparation of persons for ministry. The formation of denominations at this time was driven primarily by trying to establish a clear confessional or theological identity.[16] Seminaries emerged within the intense furnace of these confessional debates and represented distinct sectarian perspectives.

The first theological seminary founded was Andover: it was organized in 1807 by a group of Congregationalists who were concerned (once again) about the rising tide of Unitarian views within their church. Andover marked a new course for graduate theological education in the United States: the development of a freestanding seminary. What made this school identifiable as the first true theological seminary were the following characteristics, which Yale's President Timothy Dwight identified in his 1808 address at Andover's opening: it had "(1) adequate funding; (2) a program sufficient in length to allow mastery of the subject (. . . three year course of studies); (3) a scholarly understanding of Christian theology . . . ; (4) a professional [and specialized] faculty; (5) a large, committed student body; (6) sound principles of Trustee management; and (7) an extensive library collection" (*Piety and Intellect,* pp. 68-69). These characteristics became the normative framework for the numerous theological seminaries that soon joined Andover's ranks.

The Presbyterians founded Princeton in 1812: it was a school with

16. Miller, *Piety and Intellect,* 21-22.

roots going back to the log college days of Tennent (*Piety and Intellect*, pp. 99-113). Other newly formed seminaries included Bangor (1816), General (1817), Pittsburg (1818), Union Virginia (1823), Mercerburg (1825), Gettysburg (1826), Newton (1826), Southern (1832), Union New York (1836), Oberlin (1838), and Lane (1839), to name a few. In all, at least thirty-two seminaries started up between 1808 and 1840 (*Piety and Intellect*, pp. 201-2).

There were also developments in the formation of divinity schools, or what we have come to know as "schools of theology." Harvard developed its first graduate program for ministerial candidates in 1811. By 1816 it had formed a separate divinity school as the first nonsectarian theological school in the country, with the purpose of ensuring that "every encouragement be given to the serious, impartial, and unbiased investigation of Christian truth."[17] As early as 1746, Yale had recognized the need for establishing a specific professorship of divinity. This shift in focus eventually led to the founding of a separate department by 1822 in what became the Yale University Divinity School.[18] These early schools of theology proved to be quite influential in shaping the establishment of multiple schools of divinity when the modern graduate research institution came into existence in the latter half of the nineteenth century.

Most of the seminaries and schools of theology that were started prior to the Civil War were quite small. A typical school had between two and five faculty members and somewhere between fifteen and seventy-five students; only Andover and Princeton had more than a hundred students in 1840 (*Piety and Intellect*, pp. 201-2). Many of these early seminaries did not survive the nineteenth century, and none of them offered a formal educational degree. Compounding this situation was the gradual standoff between the Northern and Southern states over slavery, which led denominations such as the Presbyterians, Methodists, and Baptists to split into two separate church bodies — one for the North and one for the South — between the late 1830s and early 1850s.[19]

The curricular framework used by these newly formed seminaries followed the European pattern of the theological encyclopedia with its fourfold curriculum: Bible, history, systematic theology, and practical theology.[20] The

17. http://www.hds.harvard.edu/history.html (accessed Sept. 12, 2007).
18. http://www.yale.edu/divinity/abt/Abt.HistMish.shtml (accessed Sept. 12, 2007).
19. Corrigan and Hudson, *Religion in America*, 217-20.
20. Miller, *Piety and Intellect*, 51-53; Miller, *Piety and Profession*, 48-49.

basic approach to the educational process focused on the development of the mind and the character of the pastor who was being prepared for ministerial leadership in a congregation. The goal was the formation of what might be called the *gentleman pastor,* a man who had a prepared mind. However, some church groups, especially Baptists and Methodists, emphasized moral formation as the more important of the two emphases. Little attention was paid in any of the schools to providing educational training in the actual practices of ministry.[21]

Pastors also continued to be formed for congregational leadership in nonformal ways as these early seminaries developed. The normal practice was to associate with a mentor who could provide exposure to ministry and guidance in how to read the Bible and how to prepare sermons. This continued to be especially common among the upstart denominations such as the Methodists, Baptists, and Disciples.

During this time the Catholic experience paralleled that of the Protestant churches to some extent. From the time of the Middle Ages, the Roman Catholic Church developed and relied on a system of schools to educate its people, while it also prepared leadership for the church, and this included the development of seminaries. Formal theological education for Catholics in the United States had its origin in 1791, "when French Sulpicians established at Baltimore the first seminary in the United States."[22] Additional Catholic seminaries were founded as the Catholic population increased and scores of new parishes were established.

Transition Period: Civil War

By the time of the Civil War, the various denominations had developed clear identities and practices for ministry, which included approaches to theological education. The emphasis on supporting moral agendas, such as the abolition of slavery during the Civil War, continued into the latter half of the nineteenth century with issues such as temperance and women's suffrage. However, the Civil War marked a transition in a number of ways for both denominations and theological education. Denominations that had earlier divided along Northern and Southern lines regarding the issue of slavery now

---

21. Miller, *Piety and Intellect,* 26-28.

22. Earl C. Muller, S.J., *Theological Education in the Catholic Tradition: Contemporary Challenges* (New York: Crossroad, 1997), 1.

had to consider how they would relate to one another; furthermore, those training for ministry had to decide where to go to secure that training.

The frontier continued to expand to the west. As new congregations were formed, new seminaries were founded to prepare leaders for these congregations, with Chicago becoming the center of much of this activity, according to Glenn T. Miller in his book *Piety and Profession* (p. 40). In addition, the thousands of freed blacks, many of whom had adopted the Christian faith, created their own denominational structures and then schools for the preparation of ministers. Work in this area had been started by the African Methodist Episcopal denomination, formed in 1816 (p. 347), which established its first college, Wilberforce, in the 1850s (p. 341). The initial establishment of literacy initiatives, along with the later building of colleges, continued apace for the first several decades following the Civil War. Many colleges were founded by Northern denominations and mission societies working in the states of the South (p. 367).[23] As soon as the newly formed African-American denominations gained some financial stability, they also started up a number of colleges, mostly between 1880 and 1900 (p. 367).[24]

The Civil War marked a transition in immigration and migration patterns. The population continued to diversify and increasingly migrated toward the growing cities. This shifted the focus of many seminaries and schools of theology to a more urban perspective. Perhaps most important for theological education, though, the period of that war marked a transition in both the method and spirit with which theologians approached the reading and interpretation of the Bible. This part of the story moves us into the next period of time.

Period Three — Maturing, Late 1800s to 1920s: Denominational Institutional Systems and the Minister as Churchly Pastor

The expansion of the system of congregations continued into this next period: the number of congregations in the United States dramatically in-

23. Examples include Talladega, Tougaloo, Bennett, Clark, Clafin, Meharry Medical, Morgan, Philander Smith, Rust, Wiley, Benedict, Bishop, Morehouse, Shaw, Spelman, Virginia Union, Biddle, Knoxville, and Slip-on Seminary.

24. Examples include Morris Brown, Paul Quinn, Allen, Shorter, Kettle, Edward Waters, Payne, Campbell, Turner, and Lampton.

creased between 1870 and 1920. This growth resulted from a number of influences, but the two most important were the increase in immigration from overseas and the migration within the country from the rural areas to the urban centers. Immigration had remained strong throughout the nineteenth century, but several changes took place toward the end of that century. First, there was a significant increase in the number of immigrants arriving each year: the numbers went from an average of about 500,000 per year at mid-century to over a million a year in the 1890s and early 1900s. Second, a change took place in where the immigrants were coming from, shifting from northern European countries to countries in southern and central Europe. This resulted in a substantial increase in the number of Roman Catholics and Jews joining the masses of immigrants.[25]

Much of this expanding immigration settled into the urban centers, especially in the Northeast and along the upper Ohio Valley, where the railroads, steel mills, factory systems, and agricultural centers were creating new economic opportunities. These growing urban centers expanded geographically by means of the technology of streetcars, and new city neighborhoods were created to house the growing population. Thousands of neighborhood congregations were started along streetcar lines to accommodate this growth, including hundreds of parish churches built to serve the rapidly growing Roman Catholic population.

Other segments of this immigrant population settled into the farmlands that were continuing to open up in what became the central and upper Midwest states. These groups brought with them strong confessional identities and established denominations, and they founded schools to reinforce their theological and confessional traditions. This followed the earlier nineteenth-century pattern of building seminaries that were confessionally oriented. Two examples of such denominations and their schools include the German Lutherans, who formed the Lutheran Church — Missouri Synod in 1847, but who had already started Concordia Seminary in St. Louis in 1839; and the Dutch Calvinists (the Gerevormeerde Kerk in the Netherlands), who formed the Christian Reformed Church in 1857 and Calvin Theological Seminary in 1876.

Several other changes at this time had an impact on denominations and theological education. First, many seminaries and schools of theology

25. http://en.wikipedia.org/wiki/Immigration_to_the_United_States#Immigration _1850_to_1930 (accessed Sept. 12, 2007).

gradually adopted the methodology of higher criticism that had been pioneered in Germany. This new approach to biblical studies sent "shock waves" through the theological educational system and "redrew the theological landscape."[26] The traditional view of reading Scripture as divine revelation was being deeply challenged. That approach, coupled with the increasing influence of evolution after Darwin's publication of *On the Origin of the Species* in 1859, signaled that significant changes were underway in reconceiving the Christian faith.

Toward the end of the nineteenth century, some professorships were being challenged, and several teachers were dismissed, for example, Professor Crawford Toy at Southern Seminary in the late 1870s and Professor Charles Briggs at Union Seminary in 1893 (*Piety and Intellect*, pp. 92-97, 104-8). By the first decades of the twentieth century, these developments had contributed to the modernist-fundamentalist split, which had an impact especially on the Presbyterians, who saw the Orthodox Presbyterian Church split off from its main body, and on the Northern Baptists, who saw the formation of the General Association of Regular Baptists. A reaction to the "social gospel" (pp. 168-74) and the rising influence of dispensational theology among many of the more conservative Christians led to the founding of numerous bible schools, and many of those later developed their own seminaries, such as the current Biola University (1908) in southern California, with Talbot School of Theology starting in 1952; the current Colombia International University (1921), with CIU Seminary and School of Missions starting in 1936; and Evangelical Theological College (1924), which became Dallas Theological Seminary in 1936 (pp. 184-93).

Second, there was a significant expansion in the number and size of colleges and universities from the Civil War all the way into the first decades of the twentieth century. Led by the land-grant universities that came out of the 1862 Morrell Act, states founded colleges and universities for public education. These were complemented by an expansion of private colleges and universities, for example, Vanderbilt (1873), Johns Hopkins (1876), Stanford (1876), Clark (1889), and the University of Chicago (1892). Joining these were many previously established church colleges and universities, which later became increasingly nonsectarian. With this huge increase in the number of schools and their expanded enroll-

26. Miller, *Piety and Profession*, xxii.

ments, seminaries and schools of theology began to be pushed to the margins within the larger educational arena.[27]

Third, organizational changes were also taking place within the system of seminaries and schools of theology. The growth of denominations by the late 1800s led to an expansion of national church agencies and departments, and the management of these expanded systems drew readily on the principles of scientific management that were then in vogue.[28] The increased emphasis on the corporate denomination also influenced developments leading to the increased professionalization of ministry and the emergence of what might be called the *churchly pastor.* New standards were being developed for what constituted *professional* ordained ministry, and accompanying these new standards were new educational requirements that directly impacted both the number of persons seeking theological education and the educational process they encountered in doing so. Furthermore, accompanying this organizational revolution in theological education, says Miller in *Piety and Profession,* was the rise of "a new type of president" as "the executive officer of the management of the business of the seminary"; academic deans would join this new organizational complexity by mid-century.[29]

Fourth, there was the rise of the research graduate school and its influence on theological education. This approach was patterned after a University of Berlin model that was formed in the early 1800s. The emphasis there was on preparing professionals in the fields of medicine, law, and theology, and the approach was one of generating research. The first such school in the United States was Johns Hopkins University, founded in 1876. Several seminaries and schools of theology either came into existence for this purpose or began to adopt this approach by the latter part of the 1800s into the early 1900s, including Harvard, Yale, Union (New York), Chicago, Drew, Perkins, Duke, Brite, Candler, Vanderbilt, and Iliff. This helped foster the development of specialized disciplines within the theological curriculum and furthered the formation of theological guilds along the lines of these disciplines. The theological curriculum increasingly came to re-

27. http://en.wikipedia.org/wiki/Land-grant_university (accessed October 8, 2007).

28. The influence of Frederick Taylor, *The Principles of Scientific Management* (New York, NY: Harper & Brothers, 1911), is clearly evident on Shailer Matthews, *Scientific Management in the Churches* (Chicago: University of Chicago Press, 1912).

29. Miller, *Piety and Profession,* 271.

flect the values of research and scholarship as a driving force, as opposed to the earlier emphasis on confessional and doctrinal approaches.

Fifth, there were significant changes taking place within the curriculum, and there were increased pressures toward creating standards and the need to achieve some consolidation within the system of seminaries. An extensive survey of seminaries, sponsored by the Interchurch World Movement in 1920, noted that the curriculum in most seminaries had shifted to include more social-science perspectives, and also to have a more direct engagement with the world, including increased fieldwork requirements (*Piety and Profession,* p. 341).[30] But one of the biggest challenges facing most seminaries was the lack of any agreed-upon standards or criteria for what constituted professional theological education. Thus there began to be a push for establishing such standards, and they followed the pattern of other professional graduate schools of the time (p. 339). Accompanying the absence of standards was the unwieldy character of a system of seminaries that had grown up piecemeal, resulting in too many schools that were underresourced. The dual challenges of addressing standards and achieving some level of integration and consolidation became the primary agenda for the next several decades.

Roman Catholic theological education during this period also underwent changes and developments along some of these same lines. Catholic seminaries had continued to expand in number during the nineteenth century, especially after the increased immigration from southern European countries in the 1880s. There was a need to bring some normative structure to their standards and curriculum. This was accomplished at the Third Plenary Council of Baltimore in 1884, when the Roman Catholic Church developed a "thorough systematic structure and course of studies that lasted into the early 1960s" (*Piety and Profession,* p. 1). One important development for Catholics that paralleled Protestant practices was the founding of the Catholic University of America in 1889 to help promote graduate theological education. Other Catholic universities had followed suit by the 1920s (p. 29).

Transition Period: Great Depression and World War II

Several significant shifts took place in the early decades of the twentieth century, and the implications of those shifts were becoming clearer by the

---

30. This survey was conducted by Robert Kelly and O. D. Foster.

1930s and 1940s. One was the second disestablishment of the church in the United States.[31] This involved the loss of place and prestige by the Protestant evangelical alliance in shaping the broader culture. The reform efforts of the Progressive Era at the turn of the century, along with the adoption of the Eighteenth Amendment (Prohibition) in 1917, had marked the apex of the Protestant influence in America. Correspondingly, the adoption of New Deal politics and the repeal of the Prohibition in the early 1930s marked its nadir: significant transitions took place within U.S. society, and religious life would now come to be conceived of in terms of Protestant, Catholic, and Jew — with relationship to the Judeo-Christian heritage.[32]

The loss of many of the Protestant churches' prestige and influence was compounded by the economic challenges they faced during the Great Depression. Church construction came to a screeching halt, and the rapid expansion of the number of new congregations was put on hold for over a decade — until the end of World War II. The Depression influenced the church in other ways as well: secularization patterns had become more evident by the 1920s in the aftermath of World War I with (a) the increased vitality of other faiths in the world, (b) the decline of the modern missions movement, and (c) the loss of confidence in the gospel of liberal theology.

This erosion of confidence in at least this segment of Christianity was compounded during the Depression and war years by the inability of the churches to respond to the overwhelming needs of society. The government stepped into this vacuum and displaced the role of the church as the primary means of responding to basic human needs, civilizing new immigrants, and shaping cultural values. Seminaries and schools of theology reflected all of these shifts, and they needed to find ways to respond to these changes and challenges. Coming out of World War II and the aftermath of the Depression, how would denominations and theological educational institutions respond?

An association of seminaries and schools of theology known as the Conference of Theological Seminaries had come into existence in 1918; by the late 1920s this association was calling for a survey of theological educa-

---

31. Robert Handy, *A Christian America: Protestant Hopes and Historical Realities* (New York: Oxford University Press, 1971).

32. Will Herberg, *Protestant, Catholic, Jew* (New York: Doubleday, 1955).

tion, which was eventually completed in 1934.[33] This important survey focused on the need for creating standards, and it recommended the founding of an association to accomplish that: the American Association of Theological Schools (AATS) was formed in 1936, it adopted standards for judging quality of theological education, and it published its first list of accredited schools in 1938. The association was incorporated and secured a full-time staff in 1956, and it is now known as the Association of Theological Schools (ATS).[34]

Period Four — Expansion, Mid-1940s to 1970s: Professional Ministry in a Growing Church and the Minister as Pastoral Director

This period saw a remarkable development in the expansion of both the number and types of congregations. The phenomenal rise of the suburban church following World War II is certainly a matter of record. It was a migration of residents from both the city centers and rural areas that fed the growth of these suburbs. Continued high levels of denominational loyalty during this period allowed for the rapid growth of suburban congregations by almost all denominations.[35]

Thousands of congregations were begun as local franchises of their particular denomination. The logic of the denominational church, with its organizational self-understanding concerning a purposive intent, was now coming to full expression as the good life of the American dream was packaged and commodified into the suburban ideal.[36] This movement had

---

33. Mark Arthur May, William Adams Brown, and Frank K. Shuttleworth, *The Education of American Ministers* (New York: Institute of Social and Religious Research, 1934).

34. http://www.ats.edu/about/overview.asp (accessed Sept. 16, 2007).

35. A Gallup poll in 1955 found that only 1 in 25 persons switched from their childhood faith as an adult; by 1985, in constrat, 1 in 3 persons were found to have switched (reported by Robert Wuthnow, *The Restructuring of American Religion* [Princeton: Princeton University Press, 1988], 88).

36. David Halberstam captures the dynamics of this new suburban growth well in *The Fifties* (New York: Villard Books, 1993), 131-43. This expansion was fueled by numerous influences, including high birth rates for over two decades (the baby-boom generation from 1946-64), an expanding middle class, increasing levels of education, the mass-produced automobile, oil at $3 a barrel, a newly expanding interstate highway system, and the creation of the thirty-year fixed-rate mortgage. All these factors contributed to suburbs becoming the new destination of choice.

profound success during the two and a half decades between 1945 and 1970 and was an ideal to which millions aspired; but it was mainly realized by the emerging white middle class. The darker side of this suburban success was what Gibson Winter labeled in 1962 the *suburban captivity*.[37]

This growth of the suburban church ran parallel to several other trends. One was the decline of the rural and small-town church: scores of congregations were being closed in these areas while the suburban churches were growing. Another was the decline of membership in most congregations of the older city neighborhoods: the children who had been raised there moved out to the newly forming suburbs to raise their own children. A third was the emergence of a new form of civil religion: this was a development fed by the political ideals of democracy standing strong against the totalitarian enemy of communism, which contributed to a strong coalescing of God and country. This last development was symbolized most clearly by the addition of the words "under God" to the Pledge of Allegiance in 1954 (which, interestingly, was a result of a campaign by the Knights of Columbus). The pledge was now both a "patriotic oath and a public prayer," thus epitomizing the ethos of civil religion.[38]

Several significant changes took place in the delivery of theological education during this postwar period. There were 144 seminaries and schools of theology that had by this time become members of the AATS, but Princeton and Southern were the only two moderately conservative schools among them.[39] Evangelicalism had a significant resurgence during and after World War II: the National Association of Evangelicals was formed in 1943, and fifty Bible schools had formed their own accrediting association by 1949; in addition, the crusade work of Billy Graham, as well as the general revival that was taking place in the 1950s, furthered evangelical growth. Many new seminaries were now being founded by evangelicals: the most significant was Fuller Theological Seminary (1947), but others included schools such as George Fox Evangelical Seminary (1947), Conservative Baptist Theological Seminary (1950), Gordon-Conwell Theological Seminary (merger 1969), and Biblical Seminary (1971). There were also increasing fractures within some denominations that led to the formation of

37. Gibson Winter, *The Suburban Captivity of the Churches: An Analysis of Protestant Responsibility in the Expanding Metropolis* (New York, NY: The MacMillan Company, 1962).

38. Baer, John, *The Pledge of Allegiance, A Revised History and Analysis, 2007* (Annapolis, MD: Free State Press, Inc., 2007).

39. Miller, *Piety and Profession*, 620.

alternative seminaries that were more conservative than the main church body's seminaries. A representative example is Reformed Theological Seminary in Jackson, Mississippi (1966), which positioned itself as a conservative alternative within the Presbyterian Church USA.

Leadership formation within the larger church also saw the rapid expansion of parachurch societies and their alternative leadership formation processes. Significant college campus organizations such as Campus Crusade were begun, and others such as InterVarsity and the Navigators expanded operations. Hundreds of men and women entered active ministry through the informal leadership formation processes begun by such organizations. These movements coalesced with the expanding youth culture of the time and became for many a vehicle for effecting change in the church and the world. Increasing numbers of these leaders entered seminary as young adults; they tended to enroll in the more evangelical and conservative seminaries, such as Dallas Theological Seminary or Fuller Theological Seminary.

Seminaries and schools of theology experienced increased enrollments following World War II as many GIs took advantage of the educational opportunities afforded by the GI Bill. The expanding suburban system of congregations readily absorbed this increased supply of ministerial personnel. From the mid-1960s until the early 1970s, enrollments in seminaries continued to expand again; however, this time it was driven in part by students seeking to avoid the military draft by receiving a ministerial deferment.

The delivery of theological education underwent significant change during this period. The AATS engaged in an important study of its member schools in the mid-1950s, funded by Carnegie and headed by H. Richard Niebuhr, Daniel Day Williams, and James Gustafson.[40] The first phase of this study was published in 1956 and entitled *The Purpose of the Church and Its Ministry;* the second phase was published in 1957 and entitled *The Advancement of Theological Education.*[41] These studies focused on what was theological about theological education, which was identified as "extending the love of God and love of neighbor in the world." Seminaries

---

40. Miller, *Piety and Profession,* 671.

41. H. Richard Niebuhr, Daniel Day Williams, and James Gustafson, *The Purpose of the Church and Its Ministry* (New York: Harper & Row, 1956); *The Advancement of Theological Education* (New York: Harper & Row, 1957).

were to serve as the intellectual centers for each denomination and to prepare professional *pastoral directors* who could lead the expanding system of suburban congregations. Graduate theological education was now becoming the norm, and the study showed that seminaries needed to attend to matters of governance, funding, and faculty development.[42]

The curriculum of theological education underwent significant development at this time. New courses were added that placed increased emphasis on using the social sciences for developing ministry skills. Educational theory began to reshape the pedagogy of how courses were being taught. An increased emphasis was being placed on students gaining some field experience during their course of training. Finally, CPE was also introduced into the curriculum of many schools, its genesis being the T-Group and sensitivity training models of the 1960s.[43]

Changes in Catholic theological education, paralleling those of the Protestant churches, were significant in the aftermath of Vatican II in the early 1960s. The Catholic theological education system reached is peak at that time, with "169 theologates enrolling 8,916 students," though "more than two-thirds of these institutions had fewer than fifty students." Vatican II envisioned the renewal of theological education, and in 1969 a *Basic Plan for Priestly Formation* was published, attempting to standardize the work of the schools.[44] Two important new schools also came into existence as a result of the consolidation of smaller schools: Catholic Theological Union in Chicago in 1968 and Washington Theological Union in 1969. Another development came in Berkeley, where several Catholic seminaries joined other denominational schools to form the Graduate Theological Union.

The biggest change to note among Catholic schools during this time was that "[s]ince 1965 enrollment figures for seminarians in theological studies have dropped more than 60 percent."[45] By 1995 there were only 2,781 students enrolled in the remaining Catholic schools, which led to the closure of many schools and the consolidation of others, leaving twenty-five freestanding schools, ten university-related schools, and another ten collaborative schools as of the mid-1990s. Another major change has been

---

42. Miller, *Piety and Profession*, 669-99.

43. http://www.edbatista.com/2007/02/tgroups_trust_a.html (accessed Oct. 9, 2007).

44. Robert J. Wister, "Theological Education in Seminaries," in *Theological Education in the Catholic Tradition*, ed. Patrick W. Carey and Earl C. Muller, S.J. (New York: Crossroad, 1997), 155.

45. Wister, "Theological Education in Seminaries," 161.

the increase in the number of women and laypeople teaching in Catholic theological programs, including graduate theological education. A further change was the increase of programs, especially an expansion of the master of arts degrees.

The Recent Transition and the Theological Education Conversation

Transition Period: Social Upheavals, 1960s-1970s, and the Minister as Therapeutic Pastor

The 1960s and early 1970s were marked by significant societal upheavals that greatly interrupted all of society, including denominations and their congregations. The early civil rights movement of the 1950s became a powerful force for political change in the 1960s, leading especially to the Voter Rights Act of 1964 and Open Housing Act of 1968. The social consciousness of the dominant culture was deeply challenged and forever changed. The youth and counterculture movements of the 1960s and 1970s paralleled the civil rights movement in reshaping society, but did so primarily in the area of challenging prevailing cultural values. Related to these events were a whole series of other movements that redefined almost every dimension of life, including the feminist, antiwar, and ecology movements.

Some refer to this period of time as the third disestablishment of the church in the United States.[46] Mainline denominations simply quit growing in the midst of all these changes. After decades of continued numerical growth, this came as quite a shock — though church membership growth in proportion to the expanding population had been declining for many years. Various reasons account for this shift, not the least of which was the end of the baby-boom cycle that had fed the expansion of the church. That generation of youth left the church in greater numbers than had any previous generation, and they came back in smaller numbers when they began to have their own children.[47]

---

46. Wade Clark Roof and William McKinney, *American Mainline Religion: Its Changing Shape and Future* (New Brunswick, NJ: Rutgers University Press, 1987), 11-39.

47. Dean R. Hoge, Benton Johnson, and Donald A. Luidens, *Vanishing Boundaries: The Religion of Mainline Protestant Baby Boomers* (Louisville: Westminster John Knox Press, 1994).

Other shifts were also taking place, including the initial rise of television evangelists and the creation of media followings. This took place against the backdrop of the increasing influence of the more conservative and evangelical denominations, which began to show significant growth in membership. Dean Kelley's book *Why Conservative Churches Are Growing* aptly anticipated the controversy surrounding this phenomenon.[48]

Some churches responded to these changes by attempting to form a different identity for pastors. A key adaptation to the earlier model of the pastoral director was developed, mostly by mainline churches, as they turned to the *therapeutic pastor* as an alternative approach. This concept of a pastor relied heavily on psychological models, especially the work of Carl Rogers, but it was not particularly theological in its approach, and it experienced an uneasy welcome within theological education.[49] The time had come for theological educators to engage in some significant soul-searching regarding the very character of theological education.

An Interlude: The Theological Education Conversation

The changes taking place in the system of congregations in the 1960s and 1970s had a profound impact on theological education. By the early 1980s a flurry of publications had begun to appear calling for a deep reexamination of the very nature of theological education, a discussion launched by Edward Farley in his book *Theologia: The Fragmentation and Unity of Theological Education* (1983).[50] He profoundly critiqued the classic four-fold division of theological education, noting its inadequacy to address the substance of theology. He also challenged its tendency to support the clergy paradigm of ministry with its focus on instrumental skills, which was conceptualized by H. Richard Niebuhr as the professional "pastoral director."[51] Farley's work gave birth to a lively debate.[52]

---

48. Dean M. Kelley, *Why Conservative Churches Are Growing: A Study in Sociology of Religion* (New York: HarperCollins, 1972).

49. Carl Rogers, *Carl Rogers on Personal Power: Inner Strength and Its Revolutionary Impact* (Philadelphia: Trans-Atlantic Publications, 1978).

50. Edward Farley, *Theologia: The Fragmentation and Unity of Theological Education* (Philadelphia: Fortress, 1983). See also his later work, *The Fragility of Knowledge: Theological Education in the Church and the University* (Philadelphia: Fortress, 1988).

51. Niebuhr et al., *The Purpose of the Church*, 80-82.

52. Robert Banks provides a helpful summary of this discussion in his book

While the details of this discussion are too extensive to include in this essay, it is worth noting some of the key authors and their contributions, including Charles Wood, who emphasized theology as a process of critical inquiry; Joseph C. Hough, Jr., and John B. Cobb, Jr., who tried to give more content to Farley's proposal by focusing on Christian identity; the Mud Flower Collective, who brought a feminist critique to the conversation with an emphasis on story and the voice of the marginalized; Hough and Barbara G. Wheeler, who placed the conversation into the context of the congregation in order to break free from the clerical paradigm; Rebecca Chopp, who constructed an approach to theological education around feminist practices; Max Stackhouse, who brought theological education into conversation with globalization, contextualization, and mission; and David H. Kelsey, who reframed the "Christian thing" in theological education as an effort to understand God truly.[53]

All of these authors were trying to frame an approach for keeping God, whether directly or indirectly, in the conversation about theological education. To do this, there was general agreement regarding the importance of collapsing the Enlightenment divide between theory and practice and undoing the unfortunate marginalization of practical theology. The proposed reconstruction was toward finding some way to reintegrate theological knowledge *(theoria)* with practical wisdom *(phronesis)*, and for these to be shaped by personal *(paideia)* and communal *(habitus)* formation.

This literature functions on a couple of levels: first of all, it works as a kind of barometer of the flux that is now present within the system of seminaries and schools of theology; second, it provides a framework for defin-

---

Reenvisioning Theological Education: Exploring a Missional Alternative to Current Models (Grand Rapids: Eerdmans, 1999).

53. Charles M. Wood, *Vision and Discernment: An Orientation in Theological Study* (Atlanta, GA: Scholars Press, 1985); Joseph C. Hough, Jr., and John B. Cobb, Jr., *Christian Identity and Theological Education* (Atlanta: Scholars Press, 1985); The Mud Flower Collective, *God's Fierce Whimsy: Christian Feminism and Theological Education* (New York: Pilgrim Press, 1985); Joseph C. Hough, Jr., and Barbara G. Wheeler, *Beyond Clericalism: The Congregation as a Focus for Theological Education* (Atlanta: Scholars Press, 1988); Rebecca S. Chopp, *Saving Work: Feminist Practices of Theological Education* (Louisville: Westminster John Knox, 1995); Max L. Stackhouse, *Apologia: Contextualization, Globalization, and Mission in Theological Education* (Grand Rapids: Eerdmans, 1988); David H. Kelsey, *To Understand God Truly: What's Theological About A Theological School* (Louisville: Westminster John Knox, 1992) and *Between Athens and Berlin: The Theological Education Debate* (Grand Rapids: Eerdmans, 1993).

ing the issues that need to be addressed with regard to theological education at the beginning of the twenty-first century.

Framing the Issues Associated with Theological Education: The Recent Conversation

There are at least eight issues that recent writings on theological education have identified. This section provides a summary of these issues and outlines some of the challenges confronting theological education that need to be addressed as we try to navigate the future of theological education in the United States as it moves into what appears to be a fifth period of development.

Issue 1: Use of the School Model

The school, as noted earlier in this chapter, became the model of choice for most denominations in providing theological education. This approach had its roots in the rise of the university in late-medieval Europe, when theological education began to be relocated from the monasteries and dioceses to these new institutions. The school model for theological education brings with it a whole array of associated practices and values. First, it introduces a specialized environment for the delivery of the content it hopes to convey. This construction includes: (a) persons who serve as teachers — the qualifications they should have; (b) the identity of teachers — their relationship to their guilds by disciplines; (c) the gathering of students — the kind of community that should be formed; (d) the development of a curriculum — the kind of course work that should be required; (e) the use of a pedagogy — how the instruction should take place; and (f) the intended educational outcome — the kind of degree that should be granted.

The question needs to be raised whether this construction inherently limits or unhelpfully influences the formation of those who will serve as congregational leaders. Is there anything about the use of the school for delivering theological education that creates difficulties in preparing church leaders? Efforts by seminaries and schools of theology to address these issues tend to divide along the lines of those focusing primarily on creating an expanding body of knowledge *(Wissenschaft)* and those seeking to help students engage in a certain kind of formative experience *(paideia)*.

Issue 2: The Fourfold Curriculum

What became known as the fourfold curriculum was developed by Protestants in the European context following the Reformation. It breaks theological education into these disciplines: Bible, church history, systematic/dogmatic theology, and practical theology. Schleiermacher attempted to redefine this curriculum in the professional theological school of the newly formed University of Berlin in the early 1800s by proposing a threefold curriculum, but it did not catch on. However, some aspects of his concept of theological curriculum did come to have a profound influence. The assumptions of the Enlightenment were clearly evident in his proposal for making practical theology the critical application of the theology developed by the other disciplines in the academy. This reflected the theory/practice split that is still largely with us in theological education today.

The rise of specialized disciplines and academic guilds are also of importance with respect to the development of the fourfold curriculum, especially in light of the formation of the modern research university. The theological education conversation has clearly documented the continued fragmentation of the curriculum. The challenge of trying to foster integration and develop coherence in theological education now confronts every seminary and school of theology.

Issue 3: The Theory/Practice Split

Noted above is Schleiermacher's influence in helping to foster the theory/practice split. The Enlightenment was searching to establish foundations for human knowledge, and it sought to do so through the use of the studied discipline of experience and the exercise of reason. Objectifying ideas out of their historical circumstances became the common method. Understanding ideas as the basis for shaping human action was the operating assumption. The development of theory in this context became the focus, and its critical application came to be seen as a separate and sequential action. This split between theory and practice has profoundly shaped modern thought, including theological understanding.

The challenge to theological education is how to incorporate practice into the theological. Schleiermacher's proposal for a practical theology department continues to be followed by most seminaries. However, the hermeneutical turn in the twentieth century and the recognition that all human thought is located and influenced by both preunderstanding and social location has challenged the viability of the theory/practice split. The introduction of praxis, where it is understood that all actions have embedded within them theoretical assumptions, now permeates the conversation.[54] How does this reshape theological education?

Issue 4: The Focus of Theological Education

There has been an increased diffusion of goals within theological education during the past century, and the recent conversation on theological education has spent much time debating its purpose. Alternatives include the following: (a) theological education as being primarily about character formation — *paideia;* (b) theological education as being primarily about the creation of theological knowledge through engaging in research — *Wissenschaft;* and (c) theological education as being primarily about preparing professional clergy for the church — *vocatio.*

Which of these should it be? This is the key question facing seminaries and schools of theology today. Many schools find that they have over time come to adopt some combination of these purposes. They also find that these multiple purposes are not always compatible, or at least are not integrated into a cohesive whole from both theological and student perspectives.

Issue 5: Cultural Plurality and Diverse Contexts

Globalization is now the common milieu within which the church lives and ministers, but an awareness of its impact on theological education is fairly recent, dating basically from the 1980s. Globalization makes us aware of cultural plurality, ethnic diversity, and religious pluralism, and as a phenomenon it is related in many ways to the hermeneutical turn.[55] The

54. Gerben Heitink, *Practical Theology: History, Theory, Action Domains* (Grand Rapids: Eerdmans, 1999), 149-54.

55. Jean Grondin, *Introduction to Philosophical Hermeneutics* (New Haven: Yale University Press, 1994).

church has become increasingly aware of the situated, perspectival, and interpreted character of all human thought and experience. We must pay attention theologically to such a reality, and that requires a theological approach that is able to attend to a multiperspectival reality.

This continues to challenge the delivery of theological education on all fronts, including: (a) appointing a more diverse faculty and administration for gender, ethnic, and culture inclusivity; (b) recruiting a student population that reflects the same diversity; (c) developing varied theological perspectives that can speak to and from this diversity; and (d) designing curriculum, pedagogy, and educational experiences that incorporate this diversity. These are huge challenges for many seminaries and schools of theology, especially those related to ethnic traditions that are quite homogeneous or those having confessional stances that are quite strict. Challenges in these areas are also quite substantial for smaller schools that may lack the critical mass to accommodate such diversity.

Issue 6: The Telos of Theological Education

There are now a number of different ways to understand how a school conceives of the intended result of theological education. Are leaders being prepared to serve primarily the church? Or are leaders being prepared to help the church engage the world? This is largely a missiological question, one that has profound implications for ecclesiology.[56]

It is clear today that the emerging postmodern condition is challenging theological education to rethink the church — but to do so in the midst of a changed world. Many newly emerging congregations today are focusing on engaging the changed context as their primary concern. Seminaries and schools of theology are also being challenged to think more carefully about their own identity and purpose in light of this changed context; but many seem hesitant to do so. This represents one of the greatest challenges and opportunities now confronting the formal system of schools that is providing theological education.

---

56. Craig Van Gelder, *The Essence of the Church: A Community Created by the Spirit* (Grand Rapids: Baker, 2000).

Issue 7: The Content of Theological Education

The hermeneutical turn in the twentieth century, as well as the increased ethnic and cultural diversity, have raised questions about the content of theological education. There have been regular calls for adding courses to the curriculum as new emphases have emerged. But seminaries and schools of theology are now facing a more systemic issue regarding content. David Kelsey frames the question well when he asks, "What is theological about a theological school?"[57] Another way of framing this issue from a missional perspective is to ask: How does one keep God in the theological education conversation? Numerous answers to Kelsey's question have been proposed: (a) engaging in theological reflection; (b) doing theology in context; (c) focusing on Christian practices; and (d) reimagining practical theology.

This content issue is related to how the relationship of the church to the world is conceived. To the extent that theological education tends to focus on preparing leaders for the church, it tends to reinforce the status quo of ecclesiastical practices in many ways. To the extent that theological education tends to focus on preparing leaders to engage the world through helping the church participate in God's mission, it tends to call the church to live beyond its own limits. This is a challenge that needs to be considered: To what extent should the *missio Dei* in relation to the kingdom of God as announced by Jesus be at the center of the content of theological education?

Issue 8: Key External Forces

The system of seminaries and schools of theology that provide for the delivery of theological education is deeply embedded within complex sociocultural, economic, and political realities. One constraint facing most schools is the attempt to stay in touch with a changing culture and an emerging generation that is always changing. Another constraint concerns finances and how to appeal to constituencies that may be at odds with — or less than favorably inclined to support — the direction the school feels it is called to pursue.

A third constraint deals with issues of standards and accreditation.

57. Kelsey, *To Understand God Truly*, 13-14.

To what extent are seminaries and schools of theology served by adopting accreditation standards, such as those of the ATS, and to what extent does this begin to constrain their approach to the purpose they feel God is calling them to pursue?[58] A fourth constraint deals with governmental standards related to providing funding to students as well as controlling visa processes for international students. A further constraint today concerns the grant funding that has become available to seminaries and schools of theology from entities such as the Lilly Endowment.

Period Five: Searching for New Directions
at the Beginning of the Twenty-first Century

A Changing System of Congregations:
Yet Once More, and the Pastor as Entrepreneurial Leader

Important shifts are continuing to take place in the system of congregations in the United States. One change of critical importance is the dramatic decline in the mainline denominations. The vast majority of these congregations are on a membership plateau or are in decline, with significant numbers of congregations either merging or closing. Loyalty to mainline denominations has dramatically declined among constituents, and funding is continuing to erode, especially to governing structures at the regional and national levels. Efforts to start up new congregations or to redevelop existing ones are continuing; but many of these mainline denominational efforts seem to be driven more by pragmatic techniques and practices borrowed from Evangelicals (e.g., Purpose-Driven, Alpha, and Natural Church Development) than by those being shaped in relationship to their own theological traditions. In the midst of these shifts, many seminaries and schools of theology associated with these mainline denominations are experiencing difficulties in attracting new students into the ministry, as well as in funding their operations. This is taking place at the same time that they are being challenged to focus more attention on new church development and congregational revitalization.

---

58. Interestingly, a marked change in the constituency of ATS is now taking place, with increased numbers of conservative and evangelical schools becoming accredited and assuming leadership roles within the larger arena of seminaries and schools of theology.

In contrast to declining mainline denominations, the church overall appears to be in a fifth period of the rapid expansion of congregations. This expansion is somewhat different from previous ones and has four diverse streams feeding it. One stream is coming from those denominations that are more conservative and evangelical. Here congregations are increasingly coming into existence through strategies that do not require the primary leadership of national and regional administrative structures. The primary emphasis is on congregations starting congregations. Interestingly, alongside this expansion of congregations, seminaries and schools of theology associated with these more conservative and evangelical denominations are beginning to move to the front in theological education as increasing numbers of them seek and secure accreditation from ATS.[59]

A second stream in the expansion of congregations today is coming from independent congregations that exist outside of any formal denominational structure. These independent congregations are known by different names, such as community churches, fellowship churches, Bible churches, and so forth. A significant number of these parenting congregations are part of what are now known as megachurches, those congregations that have over 2,000 people worshiping in them on a weekly basis. Extensive networks for forming leaders and providing them with the necessary resources now exist, for example, the Willow Creek Association, which has over 12,000 churches in thirty-five countries[60]; and the Purpose Driven Network of Saddleback Church, which has trained over 400,000 pastors from 162 countries under Rick Warren's model of church.[61]

These expansive approaches to starting new congregations have led many out of the more evangelical churches to reshape pastoral identity in yet another new direction: the *entrepreneurial leader*. This approach draws heavily on secular business models that place an emphasis on visionary leadership. Many seminaries and schools of theology have had a difficult time warming up to this emphasis, noting that it lacks theological integrity in its approach. But in the midst of this general discomfort, there appears to be a growing recognition among the more formally structured, denomi-

59. In February 2007, the executive director of ATS reported in a conversation that the makeup of member schools and leadership in the association was continuing to shift to those schools that are more conservative and evangelical in their emphasis.

60. https://www.willowcreek.com//membership/index.asp (accessed Sept. 13, 2007).

61. http://en.wikipedia.org/wiki/Purpose_Driven#Purpose_Driven_Network_and _the_P.E.A.C.E._Plan (accessed Oct. 12, 2007).

national churches that they need to pay more attention theologically to the issue of leadership.

Additional streams that are contributing to changes in the system of congregations are being introduced by the emerging church[62] and the immigrant church.[63] Most constituents in the former movement are from the younger generation, and many of those congregations being formed are independent or only loosely associated with any formal denomination. The latter movement shows many immigrant congregations coming into existence, some with relationships to existing denominations, some alongside those denominations, and others as independent groups. Most of those serving as ministerial leaders in these two movements are not seminary trained, and they appear to have limited interest in (the emerging church) or access to (the immigrant church) formal theological education.

Leadership for many of the newer congregations now being formed is being raised up within their own local communities, and some are taking on primary roles of leading without pursuing any formal theological education. Distance-learning programs and online courses offered by seminaries are now increasingly used to try to incorporate some kind of formal theological education for many of these people. Other in-ministry approaches and alternative routes to providing theological education are also being used, often developed to serve communities of color where the requisite requirements for graduate theological education cannot be met, or where there are people who are unable to relocate to a residential campus for three years.

Locating Theological Education with Regard to the Growing Missional Conversation: The Pastor as Missional Leader

This essay has identified several different ways for conceiving of congregational leadership in this review of the historical development of theological education in the United States, and each has been defined in relationship to the systems of congregations that continued to grow and morph. These include:

62. A helpful introduction to the emerging church movement is Eddie Gibbs and Ryan K. Bolger, *Emerging Churches: Creating Christian Community in Postmodern Cultures* (Grand Rapids: Baker, 2005).

63. Michael W. Foley and Dean R. Hoge, *Religion and the New Immigrants: How Faith Communities Form Our Newest Citizens* (Oxford: Oxford University Press, 2007).

- Resident theologian — colonial period
- Gentleman pastor — early 1800s
- Churchly pastor — late 1800s to mid-1900s
- Pastoral Director — post-World War II period
- Therapeutic Pastor — transition period, 1970s-1980s
- Entrepreneurial Leader — transition period, 1980s-2000

In something of a contrast to these conceptions, a number of which are still very much with us, we are beginning to see the emergence of a different understanding of congregational leadership emerging at the beginning of the twenty-first century: the *missional leader,* one who is being shaped to some extent by the rapid expansion of new types of congregations. A primary commitment to being missional is seen by many as an increased emphasis on congregations engaging their changing contexts. But more importantly, it is the development of missional theology in light of recent moves to integrate missiology and ecclesiology within a missional church understanding that is more deeply shaping an understanding of missional leadership-formation.[64]

The Development of a Missional Theology

A missional theology has been introduced into the discussion via the missional church conversation, and this has introduced a new dimension into the discussion of the identity of the church. At the center of this conversation is the relationship of the church to its context in light of a different understanding of the nature — or essence — of the church. Mission is no longer understood in this conversation primarily in functional terms as something the church *does;* rather, it is understood in terms of something the church *is,* something that is related to its nature. This understanding is what undergirds the conception of congregational leadership that I have referred to above as a *missional leader.*[65]

64. See Darrell L. Guder, *Missional Church: A Vision for the Sending of the Church in North America* (Grand Rapids: Eerdmans, 1998); see also Van Gelder, *The Essence of the Church.*

65. A recent publication using this description is Alan J. Roxburgh and Fred Romanuk, *The Missional Leader: Equipping Your Church to Reach a Changing World* (San Francisco: Jossey-Bass, 2006).

Such a leader is deeply formed by living into and out of the fullness of who God is, what God has done, and what God is doing with respect to both the church and the world. Understanding the formation of missional leadership, then, must be rooted deeply in Trinitarian understandings. There are two primary streams for understanding the Trinity. One stream stems from the Western church through Augustine and was reintroduced into the twentieth-century conversation by way of Karl Barth and Karl Rahner. It focuses on the sending character of God: God is a missionary God who sent Jesus into the world, and through the sending of the Spirit by the Father and the Son, the church is sent into the world to participate in God's mission. The second stream stems from the Eastern church through the Cappadocian fathers and comes into the twenty-first-century conversation primarily via John Zizioulas. It focuses on the social reality of God and the in-relation aspect of the three persons of the Godhead.[66]

Implications for Theological Education

The subtitle of this chapter is, "Can Seminaries Prepare Missional Leaders for Congregations?" This is a critically important question, and in light of the developments that are presently unfolding, the answer to this question is best stated as "possibly." The combination of the changing system of congregations today along with an emerging missional theology now being developed out of the missional church conversation offers real potential for redefining theological education in terms of its purpose, method, and to some extent its location. These developments are also creating capacity for seminaries and schools of theology to address many aspects of the eight issues regarding theological education that were identified in the previous section. The following possibilities are viable for bringing missional theology to the front and center of theological education:

1. *Missional Hermeneutic:* Missional theology calls for utilizing a missional hermeneutic that cuts across the various disciplines within theological education

66. Craig Van Gelder, "How Missiology Can Help Inform the Conversation about the Missional Church in Context," in *The Missional Church in Context: Helping Congregations Develop Contextual Ministry,* ed. Craig Van Gelder (Grand Rapids: Eerdmans, 2007), 27-30.

2. *Missional Theology:* A missional hermeneutic requires an interdisciplinary approach to theological education and helps to develop more perforated boundaries within the classic fourfold curriculum.

3. *World as Horizon:* Missional theology calls for keeping the world as the larger horizon of God's work, thus keeping leadership development focused on leading congregations into mission within the world.

4. *Focus on Congregations:* Missional theology requires that a deep connection be made between theological education and congregations in context as students engage in the process of understanding how to lead congregations into participating in God's mission in the world.

5. *Integration of Purposes:* Missional theology helps foster an integration of the various foci within theological education by incorporating formation, education, and vocation within a larger framework of God's mission in the world and the church's participation in it.

6. *Attending to Contexts:* Missional theology recognizes the contextual character of all theology and cultivates an imagination for relating to the "other."

7. *Practical Theology:* Missional theology, in focusing on doing theology in context, privileges the development of practical theology as a larger framework within which all the disciplines converse and work: biblical studies, history, systematics, and church practices.

Conclusion

Will seminaries and schools of theology rise to the opportunity that is now before them? This remains to be seen, but clearly there is an opportunity for seminaries and schools of theology to explore common ground for coming together around missional theology to engage in this process of redefining theological education for the purpose of missional leadership formation.[67] The days ahead of us are full of possibilities.

---

67. There was recently a project sponsored by Allelon in partnership with Church Innovations Institute that brought together more than twenty quite diverse seminaries and schools of theology into a multiyear project for this purpose.

CHAPTER 2

Missional Theology for Schools of Theology: Re-engaging the Question "What is Theological about a Theological School?"

Kyle J. A. Small

Theological education in the United States has historically been caught between the crossroads of Christian formation *(paideia)* and academic acumen *(Wissenschaft)*, or, as David Kelsey illustrates, caught between Athens and Berlin.[1] "Berlin," in its focus on academic acumen, currently seems to be dominating with its fourfold curricular structure, academic guilds, and professional training. It continues to mark U.S. theological education in such a way that, for all practical purposes, it appears that "theological education can be done without God."[2]

In 1992, Kelsey introduced the question of whether theological schools are actually able to be theological.[3] Several authors picked up on his recommendation for reconceiving theological education in the concrete, yet little work has been done on framing the actual theology or theologies of specific schools. In this chapter I wish to pick up on the challenge that Craig Van Gelder presented in the preceding chapter, and I will seek to create a constructive conversation between the theological-education debate of the past several decades with the emerging missional-theology conversation. My approach follows the intent of Kelsey's pro-

1. David H. Kelsey, *Between Athens and Berlin: The Theological Education Debate* (Grand Rapids: Eerdmans, 1993); Kelsey, *To Understand God Truly: What's Theological About a Theological School* (Louisville: Westminster John Knox, 1992).

2. Noted by Patrick Keifert at the Allelon Missional Theological Schools Project, Feb. 22, 2007, Dallas.

3. Kelsey, *To Understand God Truly,* 34.

posal, though it brings several additional things into the argument. First, the intended outcome of my proposal, similar to Kelsey's, is that we may "understand God truly."[4] Yet, divergently, I also seek more fully to define "the Christian thing" in concrete ways through the theological framework of a missional theology,[5] one that is related to the ancient Christian tradition of *paideia* and to a revised understanding of *Wissenschaft*.[6]

Second, this chapter extends Kelsey's focus on leadership formation as constituting the central work of theological schools. Though I am in full agreement with Kelsey, I argue that theological education should not attempt to function primarily as professional education; rather, it should orient itself toward Athens while carrying a passport from Berlin. We are beginning to discover that the true reform of theological education today is less and less reliant on revisions of the curriculum, mission statements, and administrative realignments. The reformation that is actually required is clarifying an identity issue. This necessitates a *theological* engagement within theological education that should be asking these questions: Who is God amidst theological education? What does God intend?

In the final section of this chapter, I briefly argue that seminaries and schools of theology might best find themselves in this space of theological and organizational awareness through the use of a theologically informed discovery process. Such a process allows us to encounter theological and identity questions through a sociotheological assessment of a school's internal and external culture, its structures, and its curriculum.

---

4. Kelsey, *To Understand God Truly,* 34.

5. Craig Van Gelder has articulated six aspects of theology that guide a missional hermeneutic. These theological frames have significant implications for the cultures, persons, and organization of theological schools: (1) the perichoretic, sending, triune God is creator of all things; (2) God is at work in all of creation; (3) God redeems and seeks reconciliation with all things; (4) the kingdom of God is at the center of reconciliation; (5) the church exists *now* as a sign, foretaste, and instrument of the kingdom of God — "unmasking principalities and powers"; and (6) the church longs for the *not yet* of the kingdom. Van Gelder, *The Ministry of the Missional Church: A Community Led by the Spirit* (Grand Rapids: Baker, 2007), 110-11.

6. Werner Wilhelm Jaeger, *Early Christianity and Greek Paideia* (Cambridge, MA: Harvard University Press, 1985).

An Entry Point: Participating in a Larger Conversation

The current theological education debate began in the early 1980s with Edward Farley's *Theologia: The Fragmentation and Unity of Theological Education.*[7] From that time until the early 1990s, various theologians picked up on Farley's work in attempts to answer the question about fragmentation: "How do we put theological education back together following Schleiermacher's Berlin construction?"[8] The response to this question in several subsequent books emerged along three lines: character or moral formation,[9] vocational identity,[10] or liberation and perspectival theologies.[11] At the same time, scholars reengaged practical theology in an effort to integrate several of these dimensions.[12]

7. Edward Farley, *Theologia: The Fragmentation and Unity of Theological Education* (Philadelphia: Fortress, 1983).

8. A brief history of the theological education debate and a list of important works can be found in Craig Van Gelder's preceding chapter, p. 33.

9. Richard John Neuhaus, *Theological Education and Moral Formation* (Grand Rapids: Eerdmans, 1992); Barbara G. Wheeler and Edward Farley, *Shifting Boundaries: Contextual Approaches to the Structure of Theological Education* (Louisville: Westminster John Knox, 1991).

10. Joseph C. Hough and John B. Cobb, *The Education of Practical Theologians* (Chico, CA: Scholars Press, 1986); Joseph C. Hough and John B. Cobb, *Christian Identity and Theological Education,* Scholars Press Studies in Religious and Theological Scholarship (Chico, CA: Scholars Press, 1985); Max L. Stackhouse, *Apologia: Contextualization, Globalization, and Mission in Theological Education* (Grand Rapids: Eerdmans, 1988); Richard A. Muller, *The Study of Theology: From Biblical Interpretation to Contemporary Formulation, Foundations of Contemporary Interpretation* (Grand Rapids: Zondervan, 1991).

11. Katie G. Cannon and Mud Flower Collective, *God's Fierce Whimsy: Christian Feminism and Theological Education* (New York: Pilgrim Press, 1985); Cornwall Collective, *Your Daughters Shall Prophesy: Feminist Alternatives in Theological Education* (New York: Pilgrim Press, 1980); Rebecca S. Chopp, *Saving Work: Feminist Practices of Theological Education* (Louisville: Westminster John Knox, 1995).

12. Don S. Browning, *Practical Theology* (San Francisco: Harper & Row, 1983); Don S. Browning and David Patrick Polk, *The Education of the Practical Theologian: Responses to Joseph Hough and John Cobb's* Christian Identity and Theological Education, Studies in Theological Education (Atlanta: Scholars Press, 1989); Gerben Heitink, *Practical Theology: History, Theory, Action Domains,* Studies in Practical Theology (Grand Rapids: Eerdmans, 1999); Hough and Cobb, *The Education of Practical Theologians;* Richard Robert Osmer, ed., *Developing a Public Faith: New Directions in Practical Theology* (St. Louis: Chalice Press, 2003). The practical theology conversation developed within a fragmented system and thus left behind two-thirds of seminary faculties. The reconceiving of practical theol-

Each volume in the early period of the debate (1981-1990) usually presented a critique of theological education and then made a proposal that most often revolved around curriculum revision. Near the end of this time, the conversation had wrestled with most of Farley's questions; yet the conversation ignored the central issue requested by Farley: "to uncover and assess the deep presuppositions and dominant paradigms which determine how the unity and aims of theological education are understood."[13] If anything, by 1991 this growing literature was actually beginning to demonstrate Farley's initial concern about continued fragmentation.

A Turning Point in the Debate: David Kelsey

In 1992, David Kelsey contributed new directions to the conversation. His two books and his work on the "Basic Issues in Theological Education" project for the Association of Theological Schools initiated the second phase of the theological education debate. Kelsey did not leave previous work behind; rather, he began more substantively to engage Farley's concern on the "deep assumptions."[14]

Kelsey's key contribution to the debate was his commitment to the

---

ogy from skills training to theological identity is essential to the entire enterprise of theological education; yet the conversation continues to be an internal discourse for practical theology departments.

13. Browning, *Practical Theology,* 201.

14. The Basic Issues conversation was largely contained in *Theological Education,* the journal of the Association of Theological Schools. Articles associated with "Basic Issues" include: "Issues, Setting, and Process in Education for Ministry," vol. 5, no. 4, Supplement I, Summer 1969; "Critical Issues — 1972," vol. 9, no. 1, Autumn 1972; "Issues in Theological Education — 1977," vol. 8, no. 2, Winter 1977; "Basic Issues in Theological Education," vol. 17, no. 2, Spring 1981; "Issues in Theological Education," vol. 20, no. 2, Spring 1984; David H. Kelsey and Barbara G. Wheeler, "Mind Reading: Notes on the Basic Issues Program," vol. 20, no. 2, Spring 1984; "Defining Issues in Theological Education," vol. 21, no. 2, Spring 1985; W. Clark Gilpin, "Basic Issues in Theological Education: A Selected Bibliography, 1980-1988," vol. 25, no. 2, Spring 1989; Garth M. Rosell and George P. Schner, "Responses to Issues Research Seminar," vol. 26, no. 2, Spring 1990; David H. Kelsey, "Thinking About Theological Education: The Implications of 'Issues Research' for Criteria of Faculty Excellence", vol. 28, no. 1, Autumn 1991; David H. Kelsey and Barbara G. Wheeler, "The ATS Basic Issues Research Project: Thinking about Theological Education," vol. 30, no. 2, Spring 1994; Joseph C. Hough, Jr., Richard J. Mouw, and Robert M. Franklin, "Issues and Challenges in Theological Education: Three Reflections," vol. 37, no. 2, 2001.

cultures of specific schools. Prior to Kelsey, the conversation tended to be framed in universal terms, and few of the writers considered how to think of unity amid locality. Kelsey opened this opportunity, and Rebecca Chopp and Robert Banks built on this in their attempts to construct local theologies for theological education.[15]

However, the specific questions Kelsey raised have yet to see significant engagement in the cultures of most theological schools. He asked:

- What are the purposes and priorities that really govern and structure this school?
- What is realistic to expect of theological education, whether done in this school or some other?
- If institutional reality could be remade to one's heart's desire, what would the ideal theological school be like?
- Since it is theological schools and theological education we are questioning, what is theological about them?
- Theologically speaking, what ought to be the purposes and nature of theological education?
- What theological commitment ought to be decisive criteria for assessing and reshaping the ethos and polity of a theological school?[16]

Kelsey's move toward the concrete was a necessary turn that built on Farley's earlier work. He argued that the *ideal* proposal needs to be rooted in the *concrete*, the theological nature of theological education, thus raising the important issue of theological identity.

Kelsey contributed four things to the debate. First, he introduced a more explicit theological relationship between congregations and a theological school, noting that each needs to discover for itself who it is and why it seeks to "understand God truly."[17] Second, his ideal proposal was helpful in giving direction to a conversation that had become severely fragmented.[18] Third, his lack of normative statements opened the possibility

15. Chopp, *Saving Work;* see also Robert J. Banks, *Reenvisioning Theological Education: Exploring a Missional Alternative to Current Models* (Grand Rapids: Eerdmans, 1999).

16. Kelsey, *To Understand God Truly,* 14.

17. Kelsey, *To Understand God Truly,* 14.

18. The theological-education debate between 1981 and 1992 did not resolve the fragmentation but proved it. Proposals ranged from political theological education to feminist theological education, character-based or moral theological education, contextual theologi-

to think about theological education in relationship to local congregations without having to adopt a certain ideology (political, feminist, or otherwise). Fourth, Kelsey raised concrete questions about theology in context by asking about how boards, finances, facilities, faculties, and policy structures are related to the theological commitments of theological schooling.[19] These contributions helped move the theological conversation from the abstract to the concrete, which also opened up the opportunity for framing the missional question with respect to theological education: "What is God up to here?"[20]

The World of Excellent Education: Is a Critical *Paideia* Possible?

Most theological institutions live somewhere between the Athens and Berlin divide. Schools of theology usually consider themselves to be either places of student formation (Athens/*paideia*) or of theological research (Berlin/*Wissenschaft*).[21] Yet, even when Athens is considered to be the primary form of education, it is largely nestled within Berlin's assumptions of individualism and expertise. Interestingly, free-church educational institutions (many of which are more conservative) tend to stress the formation of individuals for ministry, while more mainline institutions (many of which are more liberal) see themselves as centers for research and critique. However, both of these cultures are embedded within the *Wissenschaft* tradition, while both also miss important aspects of schooling that *paideia*

---

cal education, as well as others. (Muller proposes a North American evangelicalism as the basis for all of theological education.) The wide range of possibilities fought for "one-way" or a universal approach to theological education.

19. Kelsey, *To Understand God Truly*, 22-27.

20. The conversation extended beyond Kelsey with Chopp, *Saving Work;* Banks, *Reenvisioning Theological Education;* Jackson W. Carroll, *Being There: Culture and Formation in Two Theological Schools* (New York: Oxford University Press, 1997).

21. See Kelsey, *To Understand God Truly;* Ellen T. Charry, *By the Renewing of Your Minds: The Pastoral Function of Christian Doctrine* (New York: Oxford University Press, 1997); Jürgen Moltmann, Nicholas Wolterstorff, and Ellen T. Charry, *A Passion for God's Reign: Theology, Christian Learning and the Christian Self* (Grand Rapids: Eerdmans, 1998), 1-64. David Kelsey offers us that helpful phrase "between Athens and Berlin" (and its various turnpikes), and in turn introduces a lost Christian practice, *paideia*. See Jaeger, *Early Christianity and Greek Paideia;* see also Jaeger, *Paideia: The Ideals of Greek Culture,* 3 vols., 2nd ed. (New York: Oxford University Press, 1986).

emphasizes: the students (plural), the community of learners consisting of students and teachers, and public truth, including "self-conscious cultural transactions with its host culture, and conversion."[22]

Wissenschaft *Revised: Cultivating a Critical Paideia*

Friedrich Schleiermacher accepted the position of chair of theology at the University of Berlin in 1810, and he argued for the establishment of a school of theology in the university. While he did what was necessary to continue the life of theology in a new, modern, and secular university, he did not recognize that his proposal would eventually relegate theology to a soft, second-class science. Nor did he recognize that his clerical proposal within the modern university would result in a professionalized, fragmented, objective, competitive, and skeptical clergy class. His immediate goal was to preserve a high place for theology, which as a discipline was no longer the "queen of the sciences" by his time.

Schleiermacher adapted the key purpose of the nineteenth-century German university for the teaching of theology, which was *Wissenschaft*: "critical research that is orderly and disciplined" (*To Understand God Truly*, pp. 90-93). *Wissenschaft* has four significant characteristics that cultivate a suspicion and critical hermeneutic to Christian theology: (1) professionalism, which bears itself as clericalism; (2) objective reasoning, which attempts to elevate critical distance; (3) unequal student-teacher relationships, in which the teacher is the Grand Knower and the student a vessel for dumping in knowledge; and (4) a public-ness that engages the broader world as a critic (pp. 90-93). The *Wissenschaft* model, utilized by modern theological education, requires neither a conversion to nor an acceptance of the Christian faith (p. 91). *Wissenschaft* brings a spirit of skepticism and distance that considers the academic exercise to be complete within itself. Thus virtue and formation are too often acceptably absent in the *Wissenschaft* model.

Wissenschaft has served as a primary framework for most, if not all, of graduate education in the Western world.[23] It is elevated as an honest critical engagement with the world, and it offers a sense of sophistication

22. Kelsey, *To Understand God Truly*, 22.
23. Kelsey, *Between Athens and Berlin*, 12-18.

and rationalism that is deeply prized within the tradition. From this perspective, *paideia* often appears less than scholarly, something that deals only with secondary issues. I believe that the relationship between *paideia* and *Wissenschaft* needs to be reframed to focus on the formation of persons in a way that does not completely leave critical perspectives behind.

Paideia *for Theological Education*

Paideia is an ancient practice that relies on texts for the culturing and formation of a person.[24] It is a form of education that is centered in virtue and cultural engagement through the continual practices of learning *(mathesis)*, teaching *(didaskalia)*, and practice *(askesis)* — with the goal of creating a *habitus*, or "second nature."[25] This second nature is a disposition of redemption; it is a baptismal identity. Redeemed identity, or *habitus*, "abandons the aristocratic idea that character and morality can be inherited by blood, but not acquired."[26] *Habitus* is a return to the *imago Dei* within a Christian understanding of *paideia*, which throughout Scripture calls forth participation with God and one another through the power of the Holy Spirit.[27] In this way, the *missio Dei* is enacted through a collective living toward the *imago Dei* amidst a broken and fallen world.[28]

24. Paul Ricoeur's work on action and text and the naiveté/critical moment construction conceives of *paideia* as a cultural engagement with written, visual, and living texts that lead toward responsible action in the world. "Reading" becomes an enlivened activity where both the text and the reader become more alive through one another. A Ricoeurian understanding of texts is helpful for reclaiming *paideia*. Modern notions of reading have unfortunately become a static practice of "mastering" an object versus an invitation for constructive engagement and formation.

25. *Paideia* predates the theory/practice split and conceives of learning as ongoing action. When action occurs, it is recorded, studied, and re-acted through the generations of learners.

26. Jaeger, *Paideia: The Ideals of Greek Culture*, 303.

27. Jaeger, *Early Christianity and Greek Paideia*.

28. *Missio Dei* reconceived mission through the nature of the triune God with respect to the world. Inspired by Karl Barth and developed by the Willingen Mission Conference in 1952, *missio Dei* became a central feature of mission rooted in Western Trinitarian theology, now operationalized by the missional church. *Missio Dei* redefines mission as the very nature of the triune God — in agreement with Vatican II — and denies that functional activities and programs of the church constitute mission. *Missio Dei* argues that mission is theocentric, not ecclesiocentric. See David Jacobus Bosch, *Transforming Mission: Paradigm*

In ancient Greece, *paideia* was a process of culturing the soul. Christians adapted *paideia* into an educational process with the intention of knowing the good and the divine and achieving the Christian transformation of the person.[29] Greek *paideia* saw the divine in nature *(physis)*; but Christianity reconceived *paideia* toward life with the triune God.[30] The goal of Christian *paideia* is formation, including virtue, knowledge of the divine, wisdom, and conversion. The basis for *paideia* was an engagement with texts, and the movement went from text to a personal appropriation of the source, and from revealed wisdom to an appropriation of revealed wisdom in a way that was identity-forming and personally transforming. This is less linear and less fragmented than *Wissenschaft's* movement from theory to practice.

Paideia is an excellent model for theological schools and congregations to use in discerning God's mission. It is a community endeavor: "teachers and learners together constitute a community that shares the common goal of personally appropriating revealed wisdom. It is, then, a community ordered to the same end, a community under orders" — a community seeking to understand God truly.[31]

Living a Critical Paideia

Accepting *paideia* as primary and *Wissenschaft* as secondary results in a criticial *paideia* that offers promise as a way forward. First, such an approach welcomes us as co-learners into the pursuit of the good through tradition, where we use critical rationality for the critique of ideology. Christian "good" is defined according to the reconciling reign of God (shalom and befriending), and not according to the critical rationality rooted

---

Shifts in Theology of Mission, vol. 16, American Society of Missiology Series (Maryknoll, NY: Orbis, 1991), 390; and Darrell L. Guder, *Missional Church: A Vision for the Sending of the Church in North America,* The Gospel and Our Culture Series (Grand Rapids: Eerdmans, 1998), 4-7. See also Craig Van Gelder's first chapter in this volume, pp. 11-44.

29. Kelsey, *Between Athens and Berlin,* 6-9; see also Jaeger, *Paideia: The Ideals of Greek Culture,* and Jaeger, *Early Christianity and Greek Paideia.*

30. Jaeger, *Early Christianity and Greek Paideia,* 18.

31. Kelsey, *Between Athens and Berlin,* 9. Christian teachers would gather students to study texts, and "all the teacher [could] provide a student [was] indirect assistance, intellectual and moral disciplines that will capacitate the student for the student's own moment of insight," or moment of understanding.

in the suspicion of Kant, Nietzsche, and Marx. Second, a critical *paideia* does not pursue virtue as professionalism; rather, it allows — even invites — all to participate in the learning process. Third, a critical *paideia* uses and produces texts for the cultivation of character formation.[32] Fourth, a critical *paideia* acknowledges the public nature of knowledge in contributing to society's virtuous possibilities, thus tempering the destructive tendencies of critique while cultivating good will and trust.

Finally, the theologian, whether pastor, scholar, or lay disciple, understands that by embracing *paideia,* she can understand her Christian life as a process of ongoing conversion. Christian conversion is embodied in discipleship practices, such as corporate worship, solitude (especially for scholars in the practice of writing), and "artegenic" reading.[33] Upholding practices with regard to vocation opens the possibility of being "self-reflective" toward doing theology. Practices cultivate "a settled disposition to act in a characteristic way."[34] These practices are invitations to *habitus.* Active and continual conversion is central to *paideia.* No longer can theological education adopt *Wissenschaft's* assumption that conversion is unnecessary for teaching in a theological school. However, true conversion occurs only through critical confrontation with God, self, and the world.

David Kelsey developed a helpful typology about Athens and Berlin. However, he argued that most schools are located somewhere in between these extremes, somewhere in a crossroads hamlet where there is a diversity of subject matters, understandings, and communities.[35] Yet the culture of theological education, as he argues in *Between Athens and Berlin,* tends to move all of theological education toward Berlin in areas such as assess-

32. Kelsey, *To Understand God Truly,* 71. Thomas à Kempis does a brilliant job explicating how being learned is for humility, not for critical violation of another.

33. Ellen Charry borrows from Aristotle and defines *artegenic* as "conducive to virtue," denoting moral excellence, and she argues that artegenic reading is a virtue-shaping function. See Charry, *By the Renewing of Your Minds,* 19.

34. Kelsey, *To Understand God Truly,* 202, 126. "Insofar as people who make up a congregation are serious enough to be critically self-reflective about their own lives as acts of discipleship, they are doing theology, at least in an ad hoc and piecemeal way. The more clearly it is understood that ministry or . . . that worship is the work of all people the more explicit will their doing theology be. Moreover, the more theologically educated (intentionally self-reflective on God) the people are, the more self-critical will their doing theology be. . . . It is critically important for the well-being of congregations that the persons who do their theology be capacitated to do it as well as possible."

35. Kelsey, *To Understand God Truly,* 30-60.

ment and accreditation processes, research expectations for faculty, library holdings, and pedagogical styles.[36] It is not beneficial in this framework to eliminate the practice of *Wissenschaft*, but it is possible to give it a more useful place in the vocation of a theologian.

Missional Theology: A Conversation Partner in the Debate

Six years after the publication of Kelsey's book *To Understand God Truly*, a seemingly unrelated volume was published, *The Missional Church: A Vision for Sending the Church in North America*.[37] This book asked a similar question: "What is theological about a congregation?" The missional church conversation emerged alongside the one being stimulated by Kelsey, and it was fundamentally asking the same theological, cultural/contextual, and organizational questions — except that it did so concerning the status of Christian congregations in the United States. Kelsey had refrained from making normative statements, instead adopting ambiguous phrases such as "the Christian thing" and "in Jesus' name" to talk about God. By contrast, the missional church conversation made a number of normative theological claims about the *reign of God* in relationship to the *missio Dei*.

The missional church conversation seeks to wed two theological disciplines — missiology and ecclesiology — in order to understand God truly. Missiology is more than a discipline of strategies and methods for evangelizing the world; missiology is a *theological* discipline that discerns how the triune God is at work in the world and how the church might participate. Historically, Protestant missiology developed out of German Pietism during the seventeenth century, and it found growing appreciation within the modern missions movement of the nineteenth century. Since it began outside of the systematic theology encyclopedia, it has unfortunately usually been assigned a position within practical ministry departments.[38] Today, however, its theological center is being reclaimed.[39]

36. Kelsey, *Between Athens and Berlin*, 19.

37. Guder, *Missional Church: A Vision for the Sending of the Church in North America*.

38. This is not always the case. In a few schools, all departments have a missiology appointment. In other schools, thinking of a Roman Catholic school and a Lutheran Seminary in particular, missiology is located within the systematic theology department.

39. See esp. David Bosch, *Transforming Mission*, and Stephen B. Bevans and Roger P. Schroeder, *Constants in Context: A Theology of Mission for Today* (Maryknoll, NY: Orbis, 2004).

Ecclesiology seeks to understand how God gathers people for doxology and service. This discipline engages questions concerning the nature of the church, worship, ministry, organization, ordination, and leadership.[40] Ecclesiology took root as a separate discipline during the Reformation, when the church was recovering its sense of New Testament identity in opposition to the Roman Catholic Church. However, the bent toward "right belief" often left ecclesiology "over-intellectualized," leaving room for only an invisible church that omitted the years between the early church and the sixteenth century.[41] Current developments in ecclesiology have wrestled with questions about post-Christendom, the global Christian movement, and contextualization, issues that most denominational systems have yet to confront.

Missional ecclesiology, which is beginning to be referred to as "missional church theology," seeks to integrate these two disciplines, where the work of God in the world calls forth the church as a sign, instrument, and foretaste to participate more fully in the redemptive reign of God. The genius of this conversation has its roots to some extent in Lesslie Newbigin's question, "What would be involved in a missionary encounter between the gospel and this whole way of perceiving, thinking, and living that we call 'modern Western culture'?"[42] It is also rooted in the developments surrounding the *missio Dei* from the late 1950s. Unlike in the 1960s, when Johannes Hoekendijk argued that the mission of God is in the world outside of the church, missional theology believes that, though the church is not the reign of God, it is a central participant in it.[43]

Missional Theology for Theological Education

Missional theology assumes that God is the acting subject. In God's creativity, God has created the church through the Spirit in the way of Jesus. Perspective on God's creative purposes can be gained by examining the

40. Craig Van Gelder, *The Essence of the Church: A Community Created by the Spirit* (Grand Rapids: Baker, 2000), 34-26, 46-48.

41. Veli-Matti Kärkkäinen, *Introduction to Ecclesiology: Ecumenical, Historical and Global Perspectives* (Downers Grove, IL: InterVarsity, 2002), 9-11, 154.

42. Lesslie Newbigin, *Foolishness to the Greeks* (Grand Rapids: Eerdmans, 1986), 1.

43. Johannes Christiaan Hoekendijk, *The Church Inside Out* (Philadelphia: Westminster, 1966).

following: the Trinity, cruciform pneumatology, Scripture, and eschatology. Other theological categories could be considered, but due to the length of the essay, these four are being considered.

Beginning with God: The Doctrine of the Trinity

In teaching confirmation in our local congregation, the pastoral team initially asks, "What does it mean to say that God is triune?" A few moments of silence ruffle the students, and the pastoral team breaks in to ask, "Does it matter to your daily life that God is triune?" The team invites the students, in the profound silence, to think about the triune God through the practice of the Lord's Supper, focusing on relationship through hospitality and welcoming the stranger.[44] The students and teachers begin to recognize that the sacraments are rooted in the reconciling relationships both with God and one another. Students are told to test the ontological reality of relationships by touching their own belly buttons. Connected they came into the world, and connected they will inherit and participate in the reign of God.

In a world where junior-high students are socialized to be autonomous individuals, the understanding of one's belly button — one's essential connection to others — becomes a critical moment. This critical moment is also necessary within the theological-education debate. The doctrine of the Trinity is essential for the reformation of theological education. First, the doctrine of the Trinity begins with God and not us; second, the doctrine of the Trinity eclipses individualism and recognizes God in the other (the neighbor, the stranger, and even the enemy); finally, the life of the Trinity is evidenced in God's sending nature, which encompasses the world. In the end, as disciples of the triune God, we are all invited, concretely, into the divine life of the Trinity. The following is an expression of what this invitation might look like within a theological school.

---

44. We read Luke 24 and Genesis 18:1-11 at the beginning of the conversation to set the stage for a conversation on recognizing God in the stranger. See Patrick R. Keifert, *Welcoming the Stranger: A Public Theology of Worship and Evangelism* (Minneapolis: Fortress, 1992), Epilogue.

Developing Personhood for Theological School
Faculty and Administration

The conversation regarding the Trinity experienced an initial resurgence in the twentieth century via the works of Karl Barth and Karl Rahner, and it continues to gain energy today by way of the contributions of political, liberation, and feminist theologies.[45] Writers across the spectrum of Roman Catholic, Orthodox, mainline Protestant, and Evangelical Protestant have picked up the doctrine, especially concerning issues of ecclesiology.

The doctrine of the Trinity is vital for understanding the divine, our personhood, the church, and the world. Historically, this doctrine emerged from the Eastern and Western church with two divergent understandings. In the East, images such as Rublev's icon depict the interrelationship within the plurality of the triune God.[46] In the West, the Latin understanding of *tres personae, una substantia* focused on the one substance of the triune God, emphasizing their oneness in their action, not their plurality in threeness. Whether one begins with the Eastern or Western conceptions of God, each has significant implications for understanding community, ministry, and organization. Missional theology argues that the church must recover the *relational* theology from the Eastern tradition as well as continuing the *sent-ness* emphasis of the Western tradition in order to express a more faithful understanding of God.

Most practically — and most importantly for this proposal — is how the doctrine influences a definition of personhood. The Western concept of the Trinity formed a personhood in one's self, through Augustine's psychological Trinity. *Imago Dei* moved out of economy and into the imma-

---

45. The contemporary resurgence of the doctrine of the Trinity includes Orthodox, Roman Catholic, Mainline and Evangelical Protestants. See Leonardo Boff, *Trinity and Society,* Theology and Liberation Series (Maryknoll, NY: Orbis, 1988); Catherine Mowry LaCugna, *God for Us: The Trinity and Christian Life* (San Francisco: HarperSanFrancisco, 1991); Jürgen Moltmann, *The Trinity and the Kingdom: The Doctrine of God* (Minneapolis: Fortress, 1993); Moltmann, Wolterstorff, and Charry, *A Passion for God's Reign;* Stanley J. Grenz, *The Social God and the Relational Self: A Trinitarian Theology of the Imago Dei* (Louisville: Westminster John Knox, 2001); Miroslav Volf and Michael Welker, eds., *God's Life in Trinity* (Minneapolis: Fortress, 2006). A helpful summary of this conversation is found in Stanley J. Grenz, *Rediscovering the Triune God: The Trinity in Contemporary Theology* (Minneapolis: Fortress, 2004).

46. See http://www.wellsprings.org.uk/rublevs_icon/rublev.htm (accessed Dec. 10, 2008).

nent Trinity, and personhood was understood through the analogy of the divine in the human psyche, not necessarily in the saving work of Christ. This substantialist understanding of personhood — that is, as consciousness — continues to plague current definitions of personhood in that it is rampant with notions of autonomy and individualism.[47]

In the East, the Cappadocians developed personhood from the Trinity as an interrelated personhood, which is known in, with, and by relationship. The focus on the plurality of the Trinity celebrates threeness while accepting unitary action, redeeming the world. The Eastern concentration on the Trinity is an ontology of relationship that functions as a polarity with respect to the Western ontology of substance. Eastern Trinitarian theology is best known for the concept of *perichoresis,* a mutual indwelling, a companionship, and a neighborliness whereby the Father, Son, and Holy Spirit work in perfect harmony with one another.[48] This teaching on the Trinity is a significant gift to the conversation on personhood and presents a possible cure to the problematic of the individualism and distant deity of Western rationalist philosophy that is so deeply embedded in graduate education in the West.

Academic Freedom Revised: An Example in Trinitarian Identity

Academic freedom is one of the blessed rights for tenured professors in academic institutions throughout the West. For good reasons, this freedom has been developed to create the free exchange of ideas without the persecution from governments or interference from ecclesiastical institutions. Its tradition is to go wherever truth leads without repression. The necessity of academic freedom is to pursue truth in those places where others have too often feared entering. However, in most academic institutions, including theological schools, academic freedom tends to be a status that cultivates competition, infighting, isolation, and arrogance. This is the dark side of the gift. It has too often been interpreted as freedom *from* accountability, collaboration, and interdisciplinary conversation.

Within schools of Christian theology, what might it mean to define

47. John D. Zizioulas, *Communion and Otherness: Further Studies in Personhood and the Church,* ed. Paul McPartland (London/New York: T&T Clark, 2006), 208-12.

48. For a discussion of *perichoresis,* see Miroslav Volf, *After Our Likeness: The Church as the Image of the Trinity* (Grand Rapids: Eerdmans, 1998), 208-13.

freedom within a Trinitarian identity versus a liberal democratic identity? In Western culture, where freedom has been attached to individual rights and to choice, *theological* academic freedom comes with an additional set of questions: Is it "freedom from" or "freedom for" that marks academic work in a theological school? Jürgen Moltmann has offered a helpful definition of Christian freedom through the lens of Trinitarian personhood, noting that freedom as the ability to choose in whatever way one wills is by no means freedom at all. According to Moltmann, true freedom is not the "torment of choice" with its doubts and threats; instead, it is "simple, undivided joy in the good."

Issues of intellectual property and academic promotion are rescued by a Trinitarian cultural ethos. Trinitarian freedom that sent the crucified Son to love and reconcile the world was not a torment of choice for the Father and Son, or a possession of the Son by the Father, but a mutual indwelling of living toward the good. The life that the triune God lives is marked by an unleashing of the power of the good throughout creation. The vulnerable love and the radical kindness that God has shown in the world through the Son and the Spirit was not a choice, but it was a gift for all and a life lived toward "undivided joy in the good." Theologically, then, freedom is a grammar of fellowship and community.[49] "In their reciprocal participation in life, people become free beyond the limitation of their own individuality."[50]

The Holy Spirit: Liberating Power in Reforming Theological Education

The indication that we can participate in the divine life is not intended to mean that a community can simply do this kind of work on its own. Participating with the triune God is only possible through a life engaged with the Holy Spirit. The Spirit creates the church, enlivens the Word, enriches persons, and participates in the world. As is often said today, without the Spirit, *communitas* is an empty humanitarianism; Scripture becomes an

49. Moltmann, *The Trinity and the Kingdom: The Doctrine of God*, 55-56.

50. Moltmann, *The Trinity and the Kingdom*, 56. For an additional critique of servant-hood as problematic to pastoral identity, see Jacquelyn Grant, "The Sin of Servanthood, and the Deliverance of Discipleship," in *A Troubling in My Soul: Womanist Perspectives on Evil and Suffering*, ed. Emilie Maureen Townes (Maryknoll, NY: Orbis, 1993).

empty *paideia,* or a bullet to kill; ministry becomes the empty execution of skills; and the world becomes a dark place of suspicion.[51] God appears distant from the world without a life in the Spirit, and Christian communities retreat from the world for security and survival. Yet, through the power of the Spirit, the church and theological education are empowered to live within the calling of Pentecost — or within the reign of God for the sake of the world.

Pneumatology: A Modern Problem

The history of modern theological education has been a history that has increasingly diminished the power of the Spirit. As an institution embedded in modernity and rationalism, any talk of a nonrational, unpredictable, nonempirical being that guides and enlivens our beings has been less than acceptable within the curriculum. Universalism, dialectic categories, and social moralism (better/worse categories) are categories that dismiss the power and dynamism of Pentecost as foolishness.[52] The absence of the Holy Spirit throughout the public/private and fact/value splits within modernity has left the Western church hyperrational and unable to attest to movements of God that are outside the bounds of repeatable, predictable claims.[53] Theological education is amiss if it continues to adopt the rationalism of modernity over against the work of the Holy Spirit.

Pneumatology: A Biblical Reality and a Postmodern Possibility

The postmodern turn, as abused as the term has been for church marketing, church planting, pragmatic ministry development, and validating poor theology, is an opening for understanding the Spirit.[54] Postmodernity is seeking to open the world to plurality and diversity. The postmodern turn has recognized that there is no center, and that groups on the margins can quickly disturb what appears to be a power center.[55] Against the backdrop of postmodernity and the recognition of liminality, the Holy Spirit

---

51. Patrick R. Keifert, *We Are Here Now* (Eagle, ID: Allelon Publishing, 2006).

52. Michael Welker, *God the Spirit* (Minneapolis: Fortress, 1994), 39.

53. Newbigin, *Foolishness to the Greeks.*

54. Welker, *God the Spirit,* 39-40.

55. Steven Best and Douglas Kellner, *The Postmodern Turn* (New York: Guilford Press, 1997).

arrives in force "in the very situations where human beings and societies are rent completely asunder, in their dispersion and in the act of their being brought together."[56]

A missional theology argues that God's Spirit is at work in actual cultures, organizations, and persons. The Spirit is not merely an emotive presence in worship; rather, the Spirit is the dynamic, liberating, transforming presence of God in the world, both inside and outside Christian communities. A belief in the Holy Spirit rejects narcissism and denies the modern conception that *controlling* domains is possible. The open and dynamic power of God's Spirit calls forth faithfulness that God engages the world. Our actions, faithful or otherwise, encounter God's activity. Yet, even if one's actions are unfaithful, God is the victor, and what "we intend for evil, God intends for good" (Gen. 50:20).

It is somewhat understandable if the reader is skeptical that adopting a pneumatology is a key answer for reforming theological education. Theological schools, like other academic institutions, are "under the power of self-endangerment, self-destruction, and sin, under the power of demonic forces and powers, under the illusion of being distant from God and abandoned by God."[57] Can pneumatology really be an answer to such problems? My response to that question is rooted in accepting that *force fields* exist in organizations, and they have concrete implications. Force-field theory argues that internalizing stimuli actually account for change within an organization or person. Theologically speaking, internalizing the work and power of the Holy Spirit — what Michael Welker defines as faith, hope, and love — actually changes the way organizations and people function.

Back to the Bible: Engaging Scripture with Imagination

I was recently speaking with a friend who had just entered doctoral studies in a school of theology, and her first assignment was to read a book on

56. Welker, *God the Spirit,* 40. "A theology of the Holy Spirit can more clearly call attention to the power that the 'primary witnesses' see at work in the very situations where human beings and societies are rent completely asunder, in their dispersion and in the act of their being brought together. . . . Postmodern ecological sensibility is less of an obstacle to the recognition of the Spirit's action than are the forms of theological reflection that continue to dominate."

57. Welker, *God the Spirit,* 239.

theological education as an introduction to her potential vocational location. After she read that book, she said, "I did not appreciate how little regard [the author] paid to Scripture, but I've started to discover that's not an uncommon theme among some of what I've been reading in my graduate theological education." In order to make the theological argument that God is an acting subject, one must begin at a place where God has been recorded as moving — within Scripture.

No Imagination: Another Modern Problem?

Modernity has not only been a thief of pneumatology, but also of Scripture. Modernity has captured Scripture and relegated it to being yet another text to be analyzed and mastered. Fortunately, the movement from epistemology to hermeneutics has raised the questions that help uncover what is going on in the absence of Scripture in the theological-education debate.[58] The hermeneutical focus on how preunderstanding informs notions of truth and method, to use Gadamer's phrase, alerts us to some possibilities on what has limited the use and authority of Scripture in theological schools.

Protestant theological education is a creation of modernity, and it has been captured by modernity. It recognizes authority within the individual, not in external sources. Competition, linearity in curriculum, individualism, and political correctness locate authority in the autonomous individual, and all of them diminish any sense of moral authority in external or traditional sources. The power of the individual to *know* limits all claims on moral authority, which discounts a possibility for Scripture to gain ground. Science as *Wissenschaft* has little to no room for divine conversations or inspired texts. The modern university has exorcised the spirit of Scripture to the point of obsolescence and relies on reason and empirical evidence to articulate all truth.[59]

As a result, Scripture is often absent from the daily conversations, issues, and problems of congregational life. This "strange silence of the Bible" appears to be increasing, as many pastors leave Scripture behind when they are engaged in serious church conflict. This omission is deeply con-

58. Banks, *Reenvisioning Theological Education,* 73.
59. Glenn T. Miller, *Piety and Intellect: The Aims and Purposes of Ante-Bellum Theological Education,* Scholars Press Studies in Theological Education (Atlanta: Scholars Press, 1990); see also Miller, *Piety and Profession: American Protestant Theological Education, 1870-1970* (Grand Rapids: Eerdmans, 2007).

nected with the historical-critical methods that remove imagination and discernment from the reading of texts and instead focus on knowing the answers or mastering the text. The power of the Spirit to speak through the Word will be limited or altogether missing in theological education as long as reading Scripture is an intellectual enterprise relegated to the scientific method, knowledge of trained experts, and the fragmented curriculum of seminaries.[60]

Recovering Imagination: Reading Scripture

There has been substantial work outside of the theological-education debate concerning reading Scripture for the sake of the church. Richard Hays, Kevin Van Hoozer, and others have contributed substantive volumes for the church on reading Scripture as imagination as well as performance.[61] Reading Scripture in this way is an invitation to move beyond Scripture as a static message to master, toward understanding Scripture as the enactment of God's life in and through the church and world. It is a movement from Scripture "as a reference volume about God" to Scripture as enacting a drama between God and us "that we are even now living."[62]

The church and theological schools are living *in* the story. This changes the very way Scripture is taught, engaged, and used.[63] Ellen Davis has articulated the modern dilemma of teaching Scripture in seminaries

60. Glenn T. Miller, "The Virtuous Leader: Teaching Leadership in Theological Schools," *Faith and Mission* 9, no. 1 (1991).

61. Richard B. Hays, *The Moral Vision of the New Testament: Community, Cross, New Creation: A Contemporary Introduction to New Testament Ethics* (San Francisco: HarperSanFrancisco, 1996); Kevin J. Vanhoozer, *The Drama of Doctrine: A Canonical-Linguistic Approach to Christian Theology* (Louisville: Westminster John Knox, 2005); Richard B. Hays, *The Conversion of the Imagination: Paul as Interpreter of Israel's Scripture* (Grand Rapids: Eerdmans, 2005).

62. Robert W. Jenson, "Scripture's Authority in the Church," in *The Art of Reading Scripture,* ed. Ellen F. Davis and Richard B. Hays (Grand Rapids: Eerdmans, 2003), 28. For an example of the ongoing theological enactment of Scripture in the church, see D. Brent Laytham, "Interpretation on the Way to Emmaus: Jesus Performs His Story," *Journal of Theological Interpretation* 1, no. 1 (2007).

63. I recognize that "use" is a rather unhelpful term that carries with it baggage from Bible-as-object. This is the very thing that is transformed within an enactment/performance understanding of Scripture. Scripture ultimately becomes a formational text that acts: it guides, transforms, and even, as Robert Jenson notes, "constrains our lives and thinking." Jenson, "Scripture's Authority in the Church," 32.

(and the church): she argues that seminarians are taught to read too fast, to "mark mileage," and to write with a rigid certainty. She proposes that teachers of theology reframe their approach to teaching Scripture beginning with reading toward "repentance."[64]

The culture of theological education, indeed the entire academy, has lost (and is attempting to recover) the ability to read a text constructively. The historical-critical method and additional methods in literary criticism have secured sacred texts for the work of destructive critique. The academy has become the master of all sacred texts, and it, in turn, has lost its sense of teaching for the culturing formation. A Trinitarian identity would require a return to Scripture, indeed, to all texts, with an openness to learn from and embrace "the Other" before violating its formative possibilities.

Recovering the Faith: Trusting Scripture

Richard Hays offers a substantial proposal for theological engagement with Scripture in the academy. He critically rehearses the academy's appreciation for an ideological critique of Scripture, and he names what seems to be a constant sense of oppression in Scripture. Hays proposes a "hermeneutic of trust" within the academy toward Scripture. He is concerned with the formation of the imagination and the life of the church; the distrust and suspicion that the academy has toward Scripture limits cultivation of the church as an instrument of the gospel.[65]

Hays assists in the creation of a critical *paideia* by his reflection on faith *(pistis)* and not-faith *(apistis)* as trust and suspicion, respectively. His theology of reading seeks a return to Scripture through a hermeneutic of trust, whereby complexity, suspicion, and critique are not lost but become subservient to the act of trust. This pursuit parallels the reclaiming of *paideia* as primary and *Wissenschaft* as secondary within theological education. The modern academy has embraced Freud, Nietzsche, Marx, and Foucault to the point that ideological critique has eclipsed the very character of literature (Hays, p. 199). Hays declares that this distrust *(apistis)* of

---

64. Ellen F. Davis, "Teaching the Bible Confessionally in the Church," in Davis and Hays, *The Art of Reading Scripture.*

65. Hays, *The Conversion of the Imagination: Paul as Interpreter of Israel's Scripture,* 190-201.

humanity, the "capacity of infinite self-deception, confusion and evil," cannot negate the faithfulness *(pistis)* of God through Jesus Christ (p. 191).

A hermeneutic of trust transfers the reading of Scripture from the place of experience and human suspicion to the cross — the faithfulness of Jesus Christ (p. 194). This invites an end to adopting common sense and experience as authority in favor of receiving Scripture as the interpreter of our experience. A hermeneutic of trust discounts one's own experience, rejects skepticism, and clings instead to God, who, as Paul says in Romans, "gives life to the dead and calls into existence the things that do not exist" (p. 194).[66]

Recovering the Church: Living Scripture

The power of Scripture to understand God truly requires a level of authority and appropriation that appreciates literary criticism yet transcends the historical-critical methods in favor of a polyrational, more postmodern understanding of revelation. *Paideia* has connections to this postmodern inkling in that the subjectivity and autonomy of the reader is displaced by a dramatic intersubjectivity among the text, the reader, and the surrounding realities. The modern Christian relationship morphs, and now the text does not *master* the reader but *befriends* the reader in a deeply imaginative and formational way.

It is ironic that *paideia,* or Athens, has been a central image within the theological-education debate, yet the locus of Scripture is still up for negotiation within the conversation. *Paideia* requires texts to form and shape the "culturing of a human being."[67] But Scripture rarely receives mention amid the talk of *paideia.*[68] Perhaps the competing disciplines in the seminary have acquiesced to the fact that Scripture belongs primarily to the Bible department.

All faculty, including those who teach in the Bible department, are

---

66. Hays tells a story of an English professor, who has "repented" from his love affair with literary criticism and returned to his first love, literature.

67. *Paideia* is not about "character" but about formation. Formation is a holistic understanding that cannot differentiate between "inner" and "outer" being as the conception of character would have. To this end, *paideia* is about ontology (a second nature), not simply behavior. Jaeger, *Paideia: The Ideals of Greek Culture.*

68. Edward Farley, *The Fragility of Knowledge: Theological Education in the Church and the University* (Philadelphia: Fortress, 1988), 153.

responsible as scholars and as Christians to engage Scripture through daily life. It is true that expertise in hermeneutics, canonical history, and literary theory is helpful; but the Reformation view that all are invited to engage Scripture through their own social locations enriches the work of "understanding God truly," and it enlivens a doctrine of vocation and the priesthood of believers. The corporate and imaginative engagement with Scripture develops a "canonical community" for discovering, discerning, and deciding "what is God up to and who is God calling us to be?" As schools of theology develop a hermeneutic of trust located in community, pastoral leadership formation should be transformed.

Eschatology: A Missiological Vision for Theological Education

The movement toward deep adaptive change, or reform, in theological education needs as much focus on the theological ends as on the social location of a school. The divine life and the consummation of the reign of God is the in-breaking to which theological education submits. Theological-education institutions, along with other organizational expressions of the church, live between the inauguration of Jesus and the consummation of the kingdom as a partner of God. Just as congregations serve as local signs, foretastes, and instruments of the reign of God, so also are schools of theology called to be *mobile* companions in this same work.[69] Theirs is an apostolic call, one that carries forth the tradition of the church, as well as one that pushes the edges of understanding God's participation in the world. A missional theology expects nothing less.

Missional schools of theology are not initiators or creators of the work of God for the church and the world; rather, they are participants with local congregations in discerning and acting into and out of God's reconciling mission in the world. This is the expectation of the *missio Dei*, and this is the crux of atonement: all creation being reconciled to God. Instead of finding the one best way to do mission, mission becomes one of the unifying identities in a polycentric vocation of theological education. Mission is participation in the reign of God, and it is an operative *habitus*, as Farley sought, for which leadership is *cultured*.

---

69. See S. Steve Kang, "The Church, Spiritual Formation, and the Kingdom of God: A Case for Canonical-Communion Reading," *Ex Auditu* 18 (2002).

Toward Leadership Formation

Later in this volume, both Cormode and Callahan define this work of forming leadership for congregations as cultivating an ecology of vocation.[70] The participants in this ecology need to be cooperative — whether they are congregations, parachurch organizations, or possibly institutions in civil society. The reign of God is the eschatological vision of theological education, and this identity is rooted in the personhood of God, which is always toward generosity and trust *(pistis)*. Schools of theology do not exist to receive students from congregations, prepare them, and then send them back to "fix" the church. God continually gathers and sends leaders to and from seminaries to participate in congregations that have historically sought to participate more fully in the *missio Dei*. Congregations and schools of theology become broken pilgrims, together discerning God's mission. As partners, schools and congregations discern local actions as they hope to more fully participate in the action of God.

This is a grand vision that cannot be instituted quickly; nor is its exact image conceivable at this time. Yet it is possible for us to reveal glimpses of this image by making theological assessments with a view toward reforming a local school's traditions, structures, and curriculum. The following is a methodological proposal for uncovering images of a missional theology for theological education. The methodology pays attention to suspicion, yet it initiates trust that God's presence is, in fact, operative within cultures of theological education.

Engaging Schools of Theology: Archetypal Discernment

There is no one answer to reform. Most current change in theological education focuses on curriculum reform (for good reason); yet the deeper assumptions of theological education have been left largely unexplored. If we are to adopt a model of schooling, critical *paideia* or otherwise, reform will require a deep understanding of what kind of schooling is currently operating. Hopes for reform will require an exploration — a discovery assessment — of an organization's internal and external cultures, an explo-

---

70. See the chapters in this volume by Scott Cormode, pp. 99-119 and Sharon Callahan, pp. 120-46.

ration that needs to include the administrative, faculty, and ecclesiastical cultures as well as American educational, accreditation, and other external cultures.

Welker argues that what theologians need in order to engage the work of the Spirit is "realistic, honest, self-critical, penitent renewal, not idealistic and moral skimming over the surface"[71] Intense engagement with one's location, both personal and organizational, is the baseline for transforming theological education. But the culture of assessment within theological schools is largely driven by the accreditation process. Schools do not normally take responsibility for theologically engaging the external context, the relational climate, and the theological integrity of a school's system. A thorough theological engagement with the school and its wider world and culture(s) is needed in order to accord with the action of the Spirit.

Neo-Institutional Theory: A Way Forward?

Neo-institutional theory may be one way to engage cultural awareness and adaptive change. Neo-institutional theory assumes that organizations are measurable, and that archetypes, which are the structures that provide meaning and motivation for our lives, can be found and studied empirically.[72] Neo-institutional theory is interested in multiple organizational pressures, including an organization's capacity to engage in change.[73] Neo-institutional theory assumes that organizations function as archetypes that are empirically categorical. When organizations experience deep change, they develop and move toward new archetypes — in the case of the church, *missional prototypes.*[74]

71. Welker, *God the Spirit,* 25.

72. Archetypes are stories and structures that are reflected in symbols, images, and themes common to all cultures and all times. Familiar archetypes can be recognized in popular culture and recur in art, literature, and religion. From http://www.capt.org/training-workshops/Archetype-Training-otci.htm (accessed Apr. 1, 2007).

73. Royston Greenwood and C. R. Hinings, "Understanding Radical Organizational Change: Bringing Together the Old and the New Institutionalism," *Academy of Management Review* 21, no. 4 (1996). The major forces within neo-institutional theory include internal/external, coercive, normative, and mimetic.

74. Greenwood and Hinings, "Understanding Radical Organizational Change," 1046. Prototypes and archetypes have similarities: primarily, they are both patterns or ways to un-

Neo-institutional theory also assumes that, in order for adaptive/radical change to occur, organizations such as theological schools need to be aware of the "new conceptual destination," or missional prototypes, that are both less oppressive and more advantageous to the people within the organization than current operating archetypes. In order to satisfy this assumption, then, we need to clearly articulate the anticipated direction for the institution (theological education).[75]

Central to any kind of honest, Spirit-led action is the recognition that collaboration, listening, and patience are required. This kind of process expects organizations to partner with similar theological-education organizations. The cross-talk available in this methodology is novel, yet it is even more necessary in a complex, open-systems world. It is common for presidents and deans to communicate at ATS events about organizational identity, yet faculty members and staff rarely discuss the theological identity and organizational capacity of their own schools. In moving toward a reform of theological education, we will absolutely need the interaction between diverse schools; our calling to live in the divine life cannot imagine another way.

---

derstand life. However, the differences are theologically significant to a missional imagination. First, "prototype" conveys a *preliminary* sense, or an ongoing reflexive nature for understanding one's relationship to the world. "Archetype" conveys a sense of rigidity and timelessness that, for example, once an archetype is found, the work is completed. An archetype is an ideal form that establishes an unchanging, timeless pattern, whereas a prototype is not a binding timeless pattern or principle. A prototype, therefore, is critically open to the possibility of its own transformation. A missional imagination favors an iterative disposition that welcomes ongoing action/reflection on how one's local community engages with God's world, which is best measured through prototype. For more on a theological explanation of the difference between *prototype* and *archetype,* see Elisabeth Schüssler Fiorenza, *Bread Not Stone* (1984), 10-15; see also Fiorenza, *In Memory of Her* (10th anniversary edition) (1994), 31-36.

75. My doctoral dissertation completed at Luther Seminary in 2009, *Missional Imaginations for Theological Education: Mixed Model, Exploratory, Action Research Mapping the Theological Identity and Organizational Readiness for Change of Five Theological School Systems in the United States Originating after 1945,* explores the challenges faced by seminaries that are seeking to change their identity archetype to become more missional.

Conclusion: An Invitation to Seminaries and Schools of Theology

The question I have addressed throughout this chapter is this: How does a theological institution sociologically embody its primary theological identity? I have argued that the way forward is to recover *paideia* and to relocate *Wissenschaft* via an awareness of current operational identity. The theological-education debate has offered helpful frameworks for asking questions; the missional church conversation has contributed a critical theological framework; and now it is time to merge these perspectives concretely within seminaries and schools of theology.

Theological schools are treasures in earthen vessels.[76] These schools are sociologically and theologically oriented, and it is necessary to engage in their reform with both of these realities in mind. This will only happen through a rigorous conversation between theology and the social sciences, a conversation in which theology is the framework for sociological questions. A missional theology can serve as a hermeneutic to invite schools to measure their current realities, as well as their ability to engage in systemic change.

The hope is that, by engaging in such an assessment, schools will be able to respond more fully to both Farley's question about the "deep assumptions" and to Kelsey's question, "What is theological about a theological school?" This points to the possibility of a day when it will be inconceivable to say that "theological education can be done without God."

---

76. James M. Gustafson, *Treasure in Earthen Vessels: The Church as a Human Community* (New York: Harper, 1961).

CHAPTER 3

Developing Evangelical Public Leadership for Apostolic Witness: A Missional Alternative to Traditional Pastoral Formation

Richard H. Bliese

Introduction

We are encountering an important fork in the road today in the unfolding story of congregational ministry in the United Sates. Which way will we go in order to truly be the salt, light, and leavening in the world? Different notions of how to do church are vying for the hearts of our congregations. Change is rocking the foundation of every ministry. Choices abound. The corpses of failed congregations litter many neighborhoods. The marketplace of religious life isn't tame. It's scary out there! The environment in which ministry is done today has become more difficult in some significant ways. Within this volatile environment, how do we form our future leaders to lead in mission?

Congregations and individual Christians — mainline, Catholic, and evangelical — struggle with a host of leadership issues within a rapidly changing church and world. In the present circumstances, working toward *forming leadership* can seem like shooting at a moving target. Can we remain faithful and true to the gospel while we heed the multifarious calls for risk-taking, congregational growth, and alternative forms of ministry that are likewise contextually relevant?

In response, some have grown skeptical about whether seminaries can be places from which real answers to future leadership needs will emerge. Consequently, numerous larger churches have developed their own systems of leadership formation. "Who has time," some ask, "for arcane theological debates from the sixteenth century when most congregations need practical skills for ministry and management? They are fighting just to survive as congregations and pay their bills in an increasingly competitive church environment."[1] Are congregations better seedbeds of pastoral formation than seminaries?

Aside from those who are skeptical about the established systems of pastoral formation, a majority of church leaders still look to seminaries as places for *answers* and *formation.* They argue that seminaries must serve as beacons for renewal and must become seedbeds of missional leadership if the church has a future. Consequently, the seminary is perennially placed in the strategic crosshairs of various attempts at renewing the church.

Congregations are in need of both renewal and renewed leadership. There seems to be at least some broad agreement on that point. In my own church body, the Evangelical Lutheran Church in America, a simple perusal of the numbers reveals Lutherans are losing ground in both Minnesota — the heart of U.S. Lutheranism — and across the nation.[2] Studies that are probing into the question "why the losses?" turn rapidly into cries that "we've got to do something at our seminaries to fix this!" For many in the ELCA, the AAL's 1993 study, entitled "Church Membership Initiative" (CMI), provided a clear snapshot of the present state of congregational life and ministry. It revealed that, while a portion of ELCA congregations are healthy, growing, and vibrant, an astonishingly high percentage of ELCA congregations (70 to 80 percent) are struggling just to maintain the status quo or even survive. While some of those dynamics have shifted or even intensified over the past fifteen years, the proportion of healthy congregations to unhealthy congregations appears to be constant since 1993, and thus the calls for renewal continue.[3] Naturally, we cannot encourage re-

1. This quote came from a "listening session" hosted by Luther Seminary in preparation for its strategic plan. The lay leader from California was frustrated with his own pastor's inability to manage their congregation.

2. At the end of 2005, there were 831,251 baptized members of the Evangelical Lutheran Church in America in Minnesota. That is 7,295 fewer people than at the same time in 2004. This slide is the same nationwide. In 2005, national ELCA membership was just 4.85 million members, down 79,663 (1.62 percent) from the year before, the largest such drop in 15 years of slippage (reported in the *Star Tribune,* August 12th, 2006, in an article by Pamela Miller).

3. The *Church Membership Initiative Report* was completed in 1994. See the Evangelical Lutheran Church's Department for Research and Evaluation (ELCA, 8765 W. Higgins Road, Chicago, IL 60631) for the report and the research results.

newal merely by reciting disquieting statistics; on the other hand, leaders need to know the "brutal facts" if they are going to truly lead.[4]

This raises the role of the seminary once again. Can a seminary be the place to lead renewal? What is the role of seminaries vis-à-vis the leadership needs of struggling congregations and denominations? In this chapter I argue that seminaries must serve as the leading edge of renewal via their special call of leadership formation. Seminaries must become, in a word, *apostolic.* However, they must accomplish this by promoting missional alternatives to what has been traditional pastoral formation.

Key Environmental Factors for Leadership Formation at Seminaries

We must directly address questions about pastoral formation; but before proceeding with that aspect of the argument, we need to review seven broad contextual issues, each of which is increasingly influencing the way the conversation about renewal is being framed with respect to the formation of leaders by seminaries.

Issue 1: Christendom

Christendom is dead in the United States, or at least it has been significantly wounded. This is most certainly true even in a churched culture such as Minnesota's. Reality is always the atlas of renewal movements. So this question must be asked: To what degree does this "reality" of Christendom's fading influence, an influence out of which our school was born, still shape (i.e., misshape) and form (i.e., deform) the curriculum, mission, and culture of the seminary?

Issue 2: Curriculum

Schools are increasingly asked to defend their curricula to donors, constituents, and their denominational headquarters. The seminary's mission, espe-

4. Jim Collins, *Good to Great* (New York: Harper Business, 2001), 65-87.

cially as it is embodied within its curriculum and faculty, is increasingly becoming the school's identity and its stated raison d'être. *Contextuality* (i.e., relevance) and *catholicity* (i.e., faithfulness to the tradition) are two aspects of the curriculum's identity that must be clear and internally consistent.

Issue 3: Local Churches

Local congregations have become the chief venue of theological reflection, both globally and in the local communities. Contextual theology especially increases in importance when it is seen through the lens of the local church. Theology is not formed in an ivory-tower library where theory and practice are divorced. Theology is formed within communities of faith as they engage their *glocal* (local and global) contexts. Therefore, the internal strength of theological formation depends on an intense connection between local churches, seminaries, and contexts.

Issue 4: Competition

Competition has always been an entrepreneurial mark of ministry in the United States. Such competition now applies to theological schools as well. In addition, an ecumenical openness has been a driver in extending schools' *markets* into other church traditions. Certain denominational schools are now increasingly playing a larger role in forming the pastoral leadership of other denominations.

Issue 5: Change

While change has always been a constant, it now appears to be increasing in speed and intensity. Some seminaries were formed as mission movements; others were designed as guardians and servants of the tradition. The polarity between *movement* and *identity* has become a real dynamic to manage.[5] Issues of programmatic flexibility and adaptability (contextual

5. For an introduction to polarity management, see Barry Johnson, *Polarity Management: Identifying and Managing Unsolvable Problems* (Amherst, MA: HRD Press, Inc., 1992).

relevance) surrounding a mission statement are becoming as important in theological education as is faithfulness to the tradition (catholicity).

Issue 6: Constituency

A seminary's immediate constituency shapes the institution today as much as its denominational headquarters does. Most seminaries are no longer "denominationally kept institutions," as they have been referred to in the past. Seminaries increasingly shape and adapt their missions to their constituencies' needs and demands. This development is now increasing the diversity of the theological schools, even within the same tradition.

Issue 7: Cash

Each seminary must find an internal financial equation that works to provide the best quality education for future leaders — without burdening these future leaders with unreasonable amounts of debt. The relationship between a theological school's donors and its mission must be clear and honest.

All of these contextual dynamics have led to significant changes in the way seminaries form leadership. These changes to theological education, in turn, suggest that any missional alternative to traditional leadership formation must be systemic and not just programmatic in nature. Both technical *and* adaptive changes are required.[6] Within this challenging environment (points 1 through 7 above), how do seminaries approach leadership formation in ways that lead past the status quo toward genuine renewal of ministry within our U.S. context?

In this chapter I argue that the traditional approach to theological leadership formation understands its task to be making an encyclopedic presentation to students of all the theological options for — in this case — renewal. In this model, church history becomes a smorgasbord of renewal movements. Future leaders pick through these options, past and present, choosing for themselves what seems to be the best model for their future

---

6. Ronald Heifitz, *Leadership Without Any Easy Answers* (Cambridge, MA: Harvard University Press, 1994), 14-15.

ministry. However, this can also present a problem. Students are asked to drink from a stream of theological options that are, like the proverbial water hose, neither totally accessible nor spiritually refreshing; that flow, like a river flooding its terrain, can also become destructive. This encyclopedic approach to pastoral formation is impossible for most students to navigate in ways that lead to effective leaders for mission. The result for pastoral formation too often results in fragmentation.

The traditional encyclopedic approach to pastoral formation does not, in the end, serve our churches well, especially those churches that are in need of renewal. An alternative is needed — a missional approach to leadership formation — and I will discuss that alternative below. I will use Luther Seminary's history as a case study of the shift from the traditional to a missional alternative.

The Quest for a Missional Alternative:
The Specific Case of Luther Seminary

The impulse for renewal belongs to the DNA of most Protestant churches. Renewal follows a logic that was affirmed during the Protestant Reformation: namely, a church is by nature always reforming *(ecclesia semper reformanda)*. Luther Seminary now finds itself on a fascinating path of such reforming that goes back to at least 1987. Maintaining a consistent missional conversation during that time, though it has been an uneven conversation at times, has proven to be critical. The first concrete result of many years of internal churning and dialogue was the development of a new curriculum in 1991, a curriculum based on a rhetorical approach to theological education.[7] In an article describing the need for curricular change at that time, one faculty member wrote:

> Widespread restiveness with the existing curriculum, and with the strategy for training clergy that it implied, had led to preliminary conversations among faculty groups during the previous year and a half. . . . We became convinced that the difficulties encountered in

7. Donald Juel and Patrick Keifert, "A Rhetorical Approach to Theological Education: Assessing an Attempt to Re-Vision a Curriculum" in *To Teach, To Delight, and to Move: Theological Education in the Post Christian World,* ed. David S. Cunningham (Eugene, OR: Wipf & Stock, 2004), 281-303.

training pastors for contemporary congregations that we had experienced in our own setting were not simply local; these difficulties arise from major cultural shifts and deep intellectual traditions. Reimagining theological education requires attention to the changes. Proposals must be faithful to normative traditions but appropriate to the new setting.[8]

One primary strategy for implementing change is to engage the history and traditions of a theological school in order to rediscover and recover the genius of the tradition, and then to reapply this genius within a changed context. Unfortunately, this renewal strategy is inherently internally focused, and often it can end up focusing more on recovering the seminary's tradition than applying it to a new context. Craig Van Gelder points to a way beyond the prison of the past:

> The church is always forming (changing) — *ecclesia semper formanda*
> The church is always reforming (seeking continuity) — *ecclesia semper reformanda*[9]

"The issue is really one of finding the right balance between the two logics of outside in and inside out."[10] A polarity exists between change and continuity: the former deals with forming, the latter with reforming.

The turn to mission at Luther Seminary brought about both programmatic and systemic change, as the faculty and seminary community entertained various conversations concerning mission for more than twenty years. As a result of these conversations, the forming and reforming structures of Luther Seminary have evolved in fundamental ways. Changes have come gradually and somewhat painfully, but this influence has been consistent and deep.[11] The markers of this forming and reforming evolution were:

8. Juel and Keifert, "A Rhetorical Approach," 281-82.

9. Craig Van Gelder, *Missional Church in Context: Helping Congregations Develop Contextual Ministry* (Grand Rapids: Eerdmans, 2007), 28.

10. Thomas Schattauer, ed., *Inside Out: Worship in an Age of Mission* (Minneapolis: Fortress, 1999).

11. Significant developments in the life of Luther Seminary over the past fifteen years include:

> 1988: David Tiede: "Quit preparing your graduates for a church that no longer exists."
>
> 1992: Evangelical Public Leaders in Mission in a World of Many Cultures.

- The affirmation of unified curricular strategy to form missional leaders (1991)
- The doctrine of the triune God as central to a missional theology (1991)
- The emphasis on the local church as the locus of theological formation (1993)
- Approval of an institutional mission statement (1995)
- The emphasis on contextual theology through classes such as "Reading the Audiences" (1999) and the Contextual Leadership Initiative (1998)
- The defined polarity between *mission* and *confession* (2000)
- The connection of mission to the priesthood of all believers in the form of another polarity between *vocation* and *justification* (2000)
- The turn from emphasizing "pastoral education" to "educating leaders" (2000)
- The creation of Centered Life as an assessment tool for evaluating the role of vocation in local congregations (2001)
- Four programmatic initiatives express the school's missional commitments: (1) biblical preaching and worship; (2) congregation, mission, and leadership; (3) children, youth, and family; and (4) lifelong learning (2001)
- The further definition of "leadership" in terms of Evangelical Public Leaders for Apostolic Witness (2007)
- The affirmation of building a process of assessment and a culture of assessment (i.e., Learning Organization) as a way to secure quality in forming leaders (2007)

1994: Curricular Revision: Learning the Story, Interpreting and Confessing, Leading in Mission (Discipleship)

1995: Mission Statement: Luther Seminary educates leaders for Christian communities called and sent by the Holy Spirit, to witness to salvation through Jesus Christ and to serve in God's world.

1997: Luther Seminary initiates a process toward a renewed statement of a strategic plan.

1999: The Seminary is described as an abby, academy, apostolate.

2000: Vision (Strategic Plan): We believe God is calling and sending the church of Jesus Christ into apostolic mission in a world of many cultures and religions.

2001-2002: Lilly Grant (failed): grant to study the seminary as apostolate

2003: Wabash Grant: the seminary as teaching apostolate

2007: Vision (Strategic Plan): evangelical public leaders for apostolic witness

Thus the ongoing focus on mission since 1991 has engendered fundamental conversations that have shaped the school's theological imagination and its programmatic emphases. However, this conclusion needs further substantiation, which I provide below by way of a brief look back at the school's history.

Historical Overview — Taking a Step Back: The Path of Mergers

Luther Seminary is a theological school of the Evangelical Lutheran Church in America (ELCA), which has been shaped from 1869 to today through five institutional mergers, each of which worked significantly to form and re-form the school.[12] One way to study the theological commitments that have formed and reformed Luther Seminary, therefore, is to study those mergers that most shaped the school's history. History, as theological archaeology, is instructive in unearthing a baseline of Luther's theological inheritance before the missiological conversations began in about 1991 and, just as importantly, describing what has changed and evolved since then.

The oldest of Luther Seminary's antecedent institutions was Augsburg Theological Seminary, founded in 1869 in Marshall, Wisconsin. Augsburg Seminary's early history can best be seen primarily in the context of the experience of Norwegian immigrants in America. Augsburg moved to Minneapolis in 1872, and it finally merged with Luther Seminary in 1962, at the founding of the American Lutheran Church (ALC). Augsburg College structured its precollege, college, and seminary life to form an organic whole in which to train pastors to serve Norwegian immigrants with a spirit of orthodox pietism for American life and culture.[13] The theological commitments of this school were strongly connected with the Lutheran Free Church, where independent congregations and pastoral authority were key components of their understanding of the Lutheran confessional and pietistic traditions. Mission involved service to immigrant communities that were struggling to adapt, thrive, and contribute to life in America.

12. Frederick H. Gonnerman, ed., *Thanksgiving and Hope: A Collection of Essays Chronicling 125 Years of the People, Events and Movements in the Antecedent Schools that have formed Luther Seminary* (St. Paul: Luther Seminary, 1998).

13. James S. Hamre, "Augsburg Theological Seminary, 1869-1963," in Gonnerman, *Thanksgiving and Hope*, 26.

A second antecedent seminary, Luther Seminary, was located on Hamline Avenue in St. Paul in 1876. It was actually located in several places before finding its home there: Madison, Wisconsin (1876-1888), Robbinsdale, Minnesota (1889-1899), and finally Hamline Avenue in St. Paul (1899-1917). The present Luther Seminary got its name from that school, whose president was the influential G. H. Stub from 1900 to 1917. Seminary students from that tradition had strong ties to Luther College, a Norwegian school in Decorah, Iowa, and their theological commitments tended toward confessional orthodoxy. This tradition enjoyed close theological ties with the Missouri Synod Lutheran Church and its understanding of Lutheran orthodoxy. The key to its graduates' mission was to stay faithful to the gospel in rightly proclaiming God's Word and administering the sacraments.

United Church Seminary was founded in St. Anthony Park, St. Paul, in 1892, only two years after the United Norwegian Lutheran Church (United Church) was founded. Marcus Olaus Bøchman was the seminary's first president, though he also participated in the founding of Northfield Seminary at St. Olaf College in 1886, a seminary of the Anti-Missourian brethren. As the name suggests, these Northfield Lutherans opposed the orthodoxy of the German Lutherans of the Missouri Synod in St. Louis: they found the latter's orthodox position to be too narrow — more Calvinist than Lutheran.[14] The United Church Seminary was an attempt to unite many of the Norwegian pieties into one evangelical Lutheran church for Norwegians, and three colleges that supported the United Church fed into that seminary: St. Olaf (Minnesota), Augustana (South Dakota), and Concordia (Minnesota).

Finally, the story of Northwestern Lutheran Theological Seminary belongs to the saga of the Synod of the Northwest and the subsequent synods of Minnesota and Red River Valley. The life of the seminary sprang first from a largely German constituency, which was then joined and strengthened by the warm piety of the Swedes, Finns, and Danes. A rift at Chicago Seminary in 1920 led one faction to move first to Fargo, North Dakota, in 1921, and then to Minneapolis the following year. Scripture and a spirit of freedom in the gospel gave this tradition an openness to respond to the changing milieu of the twentieth century as it unfolded. Of this tradition, Robert Roth says:

14. For a description of this controversy over election, see Joseph M. Shaw, *Th. N. Mohn: The First President of St. Olaf College* (Northfield, MN: St. Olaf College, 2006), 166f.

So intertwined were the lives of the seminary and church that for years the office of the synod was located in the building of the seminary where the bishop (president at that time) had daily conversation with the students and faculty. . . . The influence of the church on the seminary and the seminary on the church was monumental.[15]

The original four faculty members of the Northwestern Lutheran Seminary set foundational principles that remained with the seminary during its whole life: (1) confessional and biblical loyalty in context; (2) benevolent giving on the basis of gratitude for God's gifts; and (3) missionary propagation of the gospel and extension of the church.[16]

Three Mergers Shape Luther Seminary's Ethos

As Lutheran theological experiments waxed and waned on the prairie, three great mergers brought the aforementioned Lutheran seminaries — and their theological traditions — together in unique ways that formed and reformed the present seminary.

The Great Merger of 1917

Lutheran Theological Seminary was formed from three Norwegian seminaries: United Church Seminary, Luther Seminary,[17] and Red Wing[18] merged in 1917, after the Madison Settlement of 1912 had solved the issue of biblical authority and the predestination controversy of the late 1800s. Many streams of Norwegian orthodox Pietism joined together after that merger and the resolution of those issues.[19]

---

15. Robert Paul Roth, "Northwestern Lutheran Theological Seminary," in Gonnerman, *Thanksgiving and Hope*, 59.

16. Roth, "Northwestern Lutheran Theological Seminary," 60.

17. The pre-1917 name for the school, Luther Seminary, was reclaimed in 1994.

18. The Red Wing Synod School (Hauge Synod) didn't actually "merge" with the Lutheran Theological Seminary in 1917, but students came to this seminary after the 1917 merger. Haugean piety strongly influenced the school from the beginning.

19. Todd W. Nichol, *All These Lutherans: Three Paths toward a New Lutheran Church* (Minneapolis: Augsburg, 1986), 84f.

The Second Great Merger, 1963

Augsburg Seminary merged with Lutheran Theological Seminary in 1963 as the Lutheran Free Church joined the newly formed American Lutheran Church. Augsburg's unique approach to congregational authority, piety, and mission — that is, the Lutheran Free Church tradition — which had held steady since the early 1890s, was the gift that Augsburg brought to this merger with Lutheran Theological Seminary.

The Third Great Merger, 1982

Northwestern Lutheran Theological Seminary merged with Lutheran Theological Seminary in 1982 to create Luther-Northwestern Theological Seminary after six years of functioning under what was referred to as "Maximum Functional Unity." Northwestern was ethnically German and Swedish and was connected to the Lutheran Church of America. This merger resulted in greater ethnic diversity at Luther-Northwestern, along with a different sense of ecclesiology, stewardship, and mission development *(ecclesia plantanda)*.

The history of Luther Seminary's antecedent schools and their mergers is instructive for us as we try to grasp not only its present theological DNA but also its approach to pastoral formation. The mergers brought out three theological issues that were to *form* all future leaders; these categories have occupied the heart of the seminary's theological culture for over one hundred years. When controversial issues have arisen, Luther Seminary's faculty members have translated such issues automatically into questions pertaining to one or more of these three *formational* categories.

Biblical Authority

Even during the earliest days of Luther's predecessor seminaries, issues of biblical authority dominated pastoral formation. The earliest debates involved what is known as "inerrancy." These debates evolved over the years to include issues concerning the historical-critical method (the 1950s to the 1980s) and biblical hermeneutics (the 1970s to the 1990s). In order to be good pastors, seminarians needed to be clear about biblical authority.

Grace and Faith

The relationship between God's grace and faith has been a hallmark of Luther Seminary's history since the predestination controversy broke out among Midwestern Lutherans in the 1870s. Confessional teachers tended to emphasize the nature of "God coming down" to the world through Christ. The gospel is about God's action, not ours. In response, many Pietists, though they affirmed the power of God's justifying grace in Christ, wanted to underscore the additional role of a Christian's faithful response to God's call. This tension between grace and faith evolved over many years and has taken numerous forms. In the 1940s the grace/faith split was transformed into First and Second Form Lutheranism through the teachings of Hermann Preus (1936-1967) and George Aus (1939-1973). Although the tone on campus would have leaned more heavily toward the Pietism of Aus until the 1960s, the dynamics of the 1960s and the arrival of Gerhard Forde (1964-1998) shifted the balance toward the side of confessional orthodoxy. Thus were good pastors formed by a proper relationship to grace.

Pastoral and Ecclesial Authority

The American experience of freedom in the eighteenth and nineteenth centuries allowed Lutherans the room to experiment widely with church structures of every size, shape, and color. The Twin Cities (and by extension both Minnesota and Wisconsin) represent to this day a rich smorgasbord of Lutheran denominations, pieties, mission agencies, theological schools, and congregational commitments. Luther Seminary represents a merger of many different traditions surrounding the role of the pastor and the authority of the congregation. These debates involve the understanding of the pastoral office, for example, vis-à-vis the authority of bishops and the laity. In addition, the debates have been about the right form of congregational life over against a synod or the national church body. Good pastors were thus formed to be committed to certain pastoral roles and ecclesiastical structures.

How do these three categories form students today? Controversies in the Evangelical Lutheran Church in America, no matter what their content, have usually been translated into the three categories enumerated above. Examples of this pattern are three recent Lutheran controversies about sexuality, worship, and ecumenical relationships. All three debates have been defined, filtered, and refined through the seminary's theological culture, and they have formed and reformed a generation of pastors.

The current debate over homosexuality, for example, never focused for very long on the topic of sexuality itself at the seminary. Rather, matters of sexuality were immediately translated into issues about the Bible and its authority: a proper attitude toward sexuality was proof of one's relationship to the Bible.

The same was true about worship. The "worship wars" of the 1980s and 1990s became the chief forums for discussing grace and faith (i.e., confession and mission). Congregations that were outreach-oriented were often described as being "theologically compromised" for the benefit of church growth; in response, these congregations often characterized the confessional camp as being "contextually irrelevant" and unresponsive to human need. They charged that it was no surprise that passive righteousness engendered by confessional orthodoxy produced passive leaders. As a result, "mission" and "confession" became warring camps between which students were expected to choose.

Finally, the tensions over the ELCA's ecumenical relationships, especially its relationship with the Episcopal Church, have highlighted conflicting traditions concerning pastoral and ecclesial authority. The role and authority of bishops vis-à-vis ordination became a particular point of conflict.

Encyclopedic Approaches to Pastoral Formation: The Traditional Approach

In responding to all these issues, Luther Seminary has followed a *traditional* path of pastoral formation for many decades leading up to 1991, a path that can best be described as "encyclopedic and fragmentary." The unifying component of the school's ethos until the 1960s had helped the school defend itself against the fragmentary trends of the encyclopedic approach to pastoral formation. Those old unifying components were grounded in (1) a common Lutheran orthodox pietism, (2) a common Norwegian and/or German culture, and (3) strong ecclesial relationships. With the final merger in 1982, it was clear that the insular glue of Norwegian (i.e., Scandinavian) and German cultural heritages was cracking swiftly.

Heterogeneous culture, however, was creating problems rather than solving them. The church bodies had also grown beyond any claim to be what was historically known as a "family," or "a small Norwegian fishing village." Mergers produced bigger seminaries and more corporate churches. The ecclesiastical systems had grown large and impersonal. With the weakening of the orthodox Pietistic tradition from the 1960s forward, there was no primary unifying glue able to substitute for that tradition in holding the theological unity of the seminary together; in fact, the seminary had few defenses against fragmentation. The result was that, beginning in the 1980s, the school woke up and discovered that its common Lutheran story had become a collection of competing Lutheran stories. Key issues could not be resolved. Unfortunately, this fragmentation came just as the Lutheran denominations in the United States were themselves falling more rapidly into decline. Change was needed.

The Turn to Mission

The key to reading the history that I have briefly outlined above is that an encyclopedic curriculum and theological fragmentation became the dominant *explicit* tradition for pastoral formation at exactly the time of the beginning of a Lutheran decline in the United States. The encyclopedic approach to pastoral formation had been in place for many generations at Luther. But the fragmenting power of that *implicit* system now became explicit and dominant.[20] This system of theological education simply could not sustain the necessary changes to pastoral formation demanded by the new cultural and ecclesiastical directions of the late twentieth and early twenty-first centuries. At Luther, the injection of a missional conversation in 1991 was the one unifying balm that has helped stay the fragmentation of the encyclopedic approach to pastoral formation. It has helped to reestablish a unifying conversation within the seminary.

The conversation about mission has also revised the three key theological issues that have shaped the faculty since 1869 and, in doing so, has reshaped these conversations in a different way. This point is important. The three basic theological categories of biblical authority, grace and faith, and pastoral and ecclesial authority were not discarded; rather, they were

20. E. W. Eisner, "The Three Curricula That All Schools Teach," in *The Educational Imagination* (Upper Saddle River, NJ: Pearson Education, 2001), 87-107.

transformed by the missional conversation.[21] In summary, the conversation about mission at Luther has offered an alternative to the encyclopedic and fragmentary model by creating a space to create a common vision, an integrated curriculum, and a challenge to redefine mission from the standpoint of the Reformation.[22]

The Road Most Frequently Traveled in Pastoral Formation: The Traditional Theological Cafeteria

The unifying conversation about mission at Luther since 1991, despite its dramatic achievements, has uncovered a corrosive dynamic that still affects the seminary at every stage of pastoral formation: the fragmenting power of the theological sciences. In *Theologia: The Fragmentation and Unity of Theological Education,* Edward Farley says: "The story of the rise of the modern theological school is a story of the dispersion of theology into independent sciences."[23] He describes this fragmentation as the result of what has become the *traditional* form of pastoral formation that is shared broadly by seminaries and divinity schools throughout the United States. A study of theological education by H. Richard Niebuhr had anticipated these same conclusions already in the 1950s:

> The greatest defect in theological education today is that it is too much an affair of piecemeal transmission of knowledge and skills, and that, in consequence, it offers too little challenge to the student to develop his own resources and to become an independent, lifelong inquirer, growing constantly while he is engaged in the work of ministry.[24]

Farley and Niebuhr are noting a form of pastoral formation that is technically referred to as the "encyclopedic approach" to education. Farley

---

21. Stated more accurately, the three categories sometimes function in their original form (biblical authority, faith and grace, and pastoral and ecclesial authority) and sometimes in their altered *missional form.*

22. Douglas John Hall, *Bound and Free: A Theologian's Journey* (Minneapolis: Fortress, 2005), 106-121.

23. Edward Farley, *Theologia: The Fragmentation and Unity of Theological Education* (Eugene, OR: Wipf and Stock, 2001), 22.

24. H. Richard Niebuhr, D. D. Williams, and J. M. Gustafson, *The Advancement of Theological Education* (New York: Harper & Brothers, 1957), 209.

is quick to point out that most complaints about pastoral formation add up to a student's experience of the seminary as an atomism of subjects without a clear rationale, end, or unity. This dimension of the problem concerns the content education for ministry, the unity and divisions of that content, and their rationale, which are the consequences of the encyclopedic approach to educating leaders for the church.

Where did this cafeteria style of education arise? The theological encyclopedic approach to pastoral formation arose in the modern German university of the eighteenth and nineteenth centuries. The reason for its absence within the United States in the seventeenth and eighteenth centuries is simple: the context of theological education in the early years of the American republic had little resemblance to the German university, whose faculty had its foundation in philosophy.

Farley lays out the history of the foci of theological education in three stages: pious learning (divinity), the period of specialized learning (scholarship), and the period of professional education (profession). The first period stretches from the beginning of the 1600s to 1800. This situation of pious formation was to change rapidly in the latter half of the nineteenth century, when a "Germanization" of theological education was at work almost as soon as the first of the immigrant seminaries was founded in the United States. This was particularly true for Lutheran seminaries in the United States — because they deeply shared German educational values. Through the mediation of the German approach to theological education, and with it the European encyclopedic structure of education in general, the fourfold pattern of the curriculum came to American Protestant seminaries in the form of Bible, church history, dogmatics, and practical theology.

The nature of pastoral formation thus changed first into Farley's stage of scholarship (in one of the theological disciplines) and then to profession. I will not here review the positive effects of this approach and the underlying attempts at creating unity in the German system. Its effects today, however, have led to a serious fragmentation of pastoral education, which students experience directly. Exit interviews show that their experience of seminary is not so much a matter of a unified pastoral formation as a plurality of specific disciplines, each with its own method. These areas of study are offered without any highly visible rationale that clarifies their importance or displays their interconnections.

Seminary graduates love to complain that their seminary did not adequately prepare them for the nitty-gritty, down-to-earth problems and activities that they describe as being "in the trenches" of congregational life. They complain that the academic and practical were never really integrated. This is not to say that unity and synthesis are utterly lacking in theological education; it simply means that synthesis occurs *in spite of* and not because of the pedagogy and curriculum of the theological school. This is true not only in schools with freer curricula, but also in schools such as Luther, with its heavily required curriculum. To require a pattern of courses among departments whose raison d'être and interrelationships are neither clear nor self-evident cannot establish a unified educational experience. This is the dilemma inherent in the encyclopedic approach to theological formation.

Many schools have manufactured various devices in their attempts to bring the dry courses of the academic disciplines to life: field-based education, clinical pastoral counseling, cross-cultural immersions, case-study pedagogies, internship requirements, interdisciplinary courses, and so on. Various cycles of curriculum change, conferences on theological education, and special projects devoted to such themes as "readiness for ministry" or "excellence in ministry" or "first-call education" all bespeak attempts to address this problem. The emphasis is thus more on *practical* courses because of the seminary's divide between theory and practice. All these responses are recognizable attempts to fix the obvious fragmentation that everyone experiences within the formation process.

Evidence for Farley's argument is readily seen in two areas of any theological school. First, neither students nor the faculty can articulate any unifying theological argument behind the curriculum; therefore, each subject matter strains to find its place and rationale within the whole curriculum. Second, the fourfold pattern of the faculty's work — Bible, church history, dogmatics, and practical theology — fragments the whole educational experience. Fragmented divisions produce fragmented teaching. And yet these divisions continue in almost every theological school. Students taking these fragmented courses hope for a miracle within their internship experience or a final capstone course that might integrate everything — where someone puts the puzzle together for them. In a fragmented process, the curriculum is under pressure to integrate at the end, and thus formation suffers.

This displacement of a theological core (in Farley's terms, "divinity" or "*theologia*") with the theological sciences plays a central role in the current problem of pastoral formation. Emerging here is what has been called in recent decades the "minister as professional." The educational paradigm that this requires is new, distinguishable from both the divinity and specialized-sciences approaches. This new paradigm is not simply an affirmation that the ministry bears the sociological marks of a profession. On the basis of that affirmation, it recommends an education whose rationale lies in its power to prepare the student for designated tasks or activities that occur in the parish or in some specialized ministry. To the degree that this is the case, the theological student neither studies divinity nor obtains scholarly expertise in theological sciences; rather, he or she trains for professional activities.

In summary, a cafeteria approach to theological education is a movement from ministry as "office" to ministry as "profession."[25] The effects of the approach are becoming increasingly corrosive to a church that is in need of renewal and renewed leadership. The consequences are evident: no common mission, no integration of the curriculum, and no possibility of a unified approach to formation.

The Threat to the Missiological Conversation: No Common Approach to Mission

These dynamics have directly affected Luther Seminary in several ways. The cafeteria approach to pastoral formation was an inheritance deeply rooted in the lifeblood of the institution. It is the product of Christendom, and it remains a deep structure around which all faculty think and live. Whereas the missional conversation has served the school in a salutary way since 1991 in addressing the consequences of these structural remnants, the fragmentation of the faculty and curriculum still exists.

The key to continued progress today in fighting the effects of the encyclopedic educational system seems to be contained in the unifying character of the missional conversation. This exposes one final threat to Luther Seminary: the missional conversation itself.

Lutherans do not share a common understanding or mission or approach to its implementation.[26] In fact, they wrestle with the whole ap-

25. Farley, *Theologia*, 11.
26. Richard Bliese, "Lutheran Missiology: Struggling to Move from Reactive Reform

proach to mission due to the apparent lack of a missional theology, a theology that, I believe, is spelled out clearly in the Lutheran confessional writings. Given the absence of a clear confessional approach to mission, Lutherans tend to borrow theologies of mission from other traditions — with mixed results. Three traditions have had a strong influence on how mission is taught at Luther Seminary: covenant/law, nature/grace, and sovereignty/discipleship.[27]

Covenant/Law

A powerful approach to mission at Luther comes from the Conciliar Protestant tradition, especially the Reformed tradition. This tradition is well represented by, for example, the Gospel and Our Culture Network (GOCN)[28] and by David Bosch and his classic text, *Transforming Mission.*[29] Mission-thinking and mission-praxis need to be transformed for the twenty-first century because the Enlightenment paradigms that have been in place in the so-called modern mission era no longer hold water. The European Enlightenment set the rubrics for what we once called the "modern world"; but now the Enlightenment no longer reigns. Terms such as "postmodern," "multicultural," and "globalization" signal that the old wineskins have burst. Therefore, Christian mission-thinking and mission-praxis that were once wed to Enlightenment paradigms must change as well — that is, they must be transformed. Bosch's and the GOCN's agenda (as seen in their publications) is to *transform mission* to serve God's desire to be in covenant with God's mission as it reveals itself in relationship to God's creation. The urgency for transforming mission is precisely for the

---

to Innovative Initiative," in *The Gift of Grace: The Future of Lutheran Theology,* ed. Niels Henrick Gregersen, Bo Holm, Ted Peters, and Peter Widmann (Minneapolis: Fortress, 2005), 215-16.

27. The basis for the threefold approach to mission comes from Edward Schroeder. His use of covenant/law, nature/grace, and sovereignty/discipleship forms the outline of this section. This section is taken from his e-mail journal "Thursday Theology #473" (SABBATTHEOLOGY@HOME.EASE.LSOFT.COM).

28. Darrell Guder et al., *Missional Church: A Vision for the Sending of the Church in North America* (Grand Rapids: Eerdmans, 1998).

29. David J. Bosch, *Transforming Mission: Paradigm Shifts in Theology of Mission* (Maryknoll, NY: Orbis, 1991).

purpose of enabling mission to connect with today's covenant-disconnected humans and to transform their lives into covenant-connected, obedient disciples. This represents the reign of God.

Nature/Grace

Aside from official texts and documents, a fascinating Roman Catholic approach to mission is summarized in a book by Steven Bevans and Roger Schroeder, *Constants in Contexts: A Theology of Mission for Today.*[30] In this creative text, Bevans and Schroeder bring the basic Catholic commitment to a theology of nature and grace into sharp focus within mission history and theology: that is, grace fulfills nature rather than supplanting it. Although this approach is solidly Roman Catholic, its influence is widespread through the Protestant world, including Lutheranism. The book reviews various *contexts,* which serve as referents to nature, and the outline of *constants* refers to grace. Mission, therefore, plays itself out in the following way: God's world (i.e., the context) is now damaged and in need of help. The constants are God's elements of grace that act restoratively throughout history — culminating in Christ and, finally, in Christ's *eschaton.* As in every age, grace-constants bring today's world-contexts to their God-intended fulfillment. Grace fulfills nature, and that is mission.

Sovereignty/Discipleship

A third approach to mission at Luther could best be summarized as "evangelical" and/or "Pentecostal" in perspective. Mission is the call to urge people to respond to Christ and to live lives reflecting his kingdom. The sovereignty of God drives mission. What, then, is our foundation for mission? The foundation is the Bible itself. Lutheran evangelicals and Pentecostals focus on concern for the world and human estrangement from God. The core of our responsibility is: (1) to engage in evangelism and church planting; (2) to disciple those who enter the kingdom so as to build up local churches; and (3) to glorify God by living lives that act as salt and light in a

---

30. Stephen B. Bevans and Roger P. Schroeder, *Constants in Context: A Theology of Mission for Today* (Maryknoll, NY: Orbis, 2004).

flavorless and dark world. Discipleship and growth, both individual and corporate, come via obedience to everything Jesus taught and teaching others to do likewise. Christians are to display kingdom ethics (i.e., ethics built on God's sovereignty over our lives) and to form their lives according to God's rules. Mission is thus the call to urge people to respond to Christ and to live lives that reflect his kingdom, wherein God's rules are followed. This constitutes rightful worship and gives God glory.

I map out these three reigning approaches to missiology for one purpose: a Lutheran conversation about mission must capture the ongoing ecumenical conversations while recasting them within a more faithful *Lutheran evangelical* approach to the aforementioned Reformed, Catholic, and Evangelical positions. What I want to suggest is that Lutherans, while welcoming these other missiological streams of thought, must discover their own way to embrace and interpret covenant/law, nature/grace, and sovereignty/discipleship to be true to their own theological heritage. More importantly, we must do this to be more faithful to God's mission in the world through Christ.

Edward Schroeder suggests a fourth option: a promise-centered mission theology.[31] Is it possible that Lutheranism's view of the gospel as "promise," a tradition deeply rooted in the law-promise tradition of Lutherans' understanding of Scripture, is the key component of a fruitful new way to grasp God's activity in the world? *Promissio* may be the key to the ongoing conversation about *missio*.[32]

The Promising Tradition: A New Road

Most people today agree that seminaries are now facing significant challenges as they try to respond to rapidly changing contexts and congregational needs. If one may be so bold as to speak of a "paradigm shift" in pastoral formation in the United States, then it is this: a growing recognition

---

31. See Ed Schroeder's article above in SABBATHEOLOGY@HOME.EASE.LSOFT .COM. See also Gary Simpson, "A Reformation Is A Terrible Thing to Waste: A Promising Theology for an Emerging Missional Church," in *The Missional Church in Context: Helping Congregations Develop Contextual Ministry,* ed. Craig Van Gelder (Grand Rapids: Eerdmans, 2007), 65-66.

32. See Robert Bertram, "Doing Theology in Relation to Mission," in Crossing's webpage: http://www.crossings.org/archive/bob/DoingTheologyinMission.pdf.

by Christian leaders that we are now in need of conceiving of our own context (the United States) as a mission location, an awareness that is generating fresh opportunities for new ministry.[33] But it is also introducing disruption into long-standing practices, including traditional pastoral formation. In any event, business as usual is no longer a possibility for most seminaries in the United States.

Given the many clarion calls from every corner of the church to do something, William Abraham points out that "the Western church is currently awash in a sea of renewal movements — so much so that she is in danger of drowning."[34] This dynamic is not only true for U.S. seminaries as a whole (which might be considered a healthy thing), but for each seminary individually (the result of encyclopedic forms of education). Seminaries have become battlefields of renewal: they play a fascinating role as both *advocates* for various renewal movements and, at the same time, *defenders* against alternative renewal movements that may be harmful.[35] As a battleground for these renewal movements, our seminary, in its formation of future leaders, must choose between what is fragmentary and what is focused.

Luther Seminary has embarked on a fascinating path of renewal as it has centered its identity on the generative question of mission, which has served to inject life into its curriculum since 1991. The results have been significant. The modern questions about biblical authority have shifted within the curriculum: now students affirm and study the power of the biblical story rather than arguing and contesting it. The questions concerning grace and faith have likewise shifted into two polarities: between confession and mission and justification and vocation. Here the theological tension between confession and mission (i.e., grace and faith) has been

33. For a view of North American mission, see Robert Schreiter, "North American Mission Theology," in *Dictionary of Mission*, ed. Karl Müller, Theo Sundermeier, Stephen Bevans, and Richard Bliese (Maryknoll, NY: Orbis, 1999), 332.

34. William Abraham, *The Logic of Renewal* (Grand Rapids: Eerdmans, 2003), 1.

35. One of the most celebrated criticisms of renewal movements can be found in Ronald Knox's massive study of "enthusiasm": R. A. Knox, *Enthusiasm* (Oxford: Clarendon, 1950). Knox really had little time for the renewal movements of the seventeenth and eighteenth centuries, which he saw as doing more harm than good. We must surely acknowledge the possibility of unintended side effects in proposals for renewal. In fact, the two most conspicuous side effects of renewal are judgmentalism and schism. Renewal, then, is often a paradoxical affair. It is a sobering thought that sometimes our best efforts wreak havoc in the body of Christ.

affirmed as a theological polarity to manage rather than warring principles between which to decide. The emphasis on vocation has also helped students reread the Reformation tradition in ways that emphasize a richness of principles and not just justification by grace through faith.

The questions concerning pastoral and ecclesial authority have shifted to missional ecclesiology and evangelical public leadership. This shift is significant. The movement in 2000 was framed as being from "pastoral formation" to "leadership." This emphasis on leadership opened up Luther Seminary to various master's programs and to lay formation. But this initial move still left a question unanswered: What kind of leadership are we promising to the church? An attempt to answer that question emerged in the present strategic plan: we educate "evangelical public leaders." Thus the movement since 1991 has looked like this:

Biblical Authority → Biblical Power (Power of the Word of God)

Grace and Faith → Confession/Mission and Justification/Vocation

Pastoral and Ecclesial Authority → Missional Ecclesiology and
    Evangelical Public Leadership

In short, the school's embrace of the missional conversation has led it back to embrace the power of the Word of God instead of biblical authority; to a both/and rather than an either/or approach to grace and faith; and to identifying the scope and nature of its formation of leaders instead of producing clerical professionals. These shifts are dramatic, and these shifts are as theological as they are programmatic. A sustained conversation about mission has also produced the following special dynamics: (1) the role of contextual theology; (2) the question about how God is deeply active within the world; (3) the role of practical theology; (4) the synergy of theology and practice; (5) the significance of Trinitarian theology for mission; and (6) an appreciation for ecumenical engagement.

Conclusion

Mission has shifted key foundational commitments at Luther Seminary. In this chapter I have argued that the prolonged focus on mission since 1991 has helped to create a mission statement for the school, pushed the seminary into curricular reform, led to fascinating programmatic experiments, and encouraged steps toward a unified curriculum. However, I have also argued that this missiological conversation cannot be maintained if it does not root itself in our own Lutheran identity as an alternative form of being *evangelical.*

Transposing other missiological traditions on our school, whether Reformed, Catholic, or American Evangelical, will prove insufficient to carry on this conversation in a generative fashion. These other missiologies are and will remain important conversation partners at Luther Seminary; they need to be at the table. But it will ultimately be in the discovery of our own evangelical tradition of *promissio* that we will discover a powerful enough understanding of *missio* to carry on the apostolic formation and reformation of leadership that will serve a church seeking to renew as it more fully engages God's world.

MISSIONAL LEADERSHIP FORMATION IN RELATION TO CONGREGATIONS

This second section of three essays provides the reader with perspective on how missional leadership formation can best be cultivated within and through congregations. Congregations have clearly become a primary focus in recent years with regard to the development and formation of leadership. Seemingly endless strategies and methodologies have been promoted toward that end. The chapters in this section pick up this important issue, as the authors helpfully frame their proposals in light of the missional conversation.

Scott Cormode leads off this section by offering the concept of "mental models" as a way to get at the reframing of leadership formation. He proposes that all leaders work out of a variety of mental models that have been picked up along the way from sources such as congregational cultures, mentors, and educational experiences. Using a missional framework as a conceptual backdrop, Cormode argues that we need to shift our focus to viewing the formation of leaders within what he labels an "ecology of vocation." This approach helps us attend more carefully and constructively to the previous experiences persons have had as they come into leadership roles. This approach also provides us with more flexibility and perspective as we help people, if necessary, rethink and reframe their present mental model.

In the next chapter, Sharon Callahan builds on this idea of an ecology of vocation by laying out an extensive vignette of a specific congregation's experience. This congregation serves as a helpful point of reference for Callahan to develop a missional perspective on how congregations shape and form leadership, especially lay leadership. Using both Western and Eastern Trinitarian perspectives to frame her missional understanding of leadership, Callahan grounds her approach to leadership formation in a theology of baptism. She makes a clear proposal about how the vocational call of every believer should be directed toward service both within the church and outward to the world.

In the final chapter in this section, Dave Daubert offers a dramatically different approach to the formation and cultivation of vision within congregations. He notes how much of the current writing on vision and leadership tends to privilege the pastor as the one responsible to set and cast the vision. Daubert disagrees: he says that such an approach is not the intent of Scripture, and he argues instead for the missional practice of the empowerment of all of God's people as active participants in such a process. He grounds his approach in the missional conversation, and he helpfully brings into play theoretical perspectives from Gadamer and Habermas.

CHAPTER 4

Cultivating Missional Leaders:
Mental Models and the Ecology of Vocation

Scott Cormode

John is the pastor of a growing congregation that just purchased land near the interstate. John grew up going to church, attended seminary soon after college, and started his first congregation in his living room. Charlotte is the new pastor of an older congregation. She did not grow up in a church and did not attend seminary until her children were in school. Mike, on the other hand, is an elder who spends his days managing a drugstore that is part of a big chain. He grew up in a large, Presbyterian congregation, but now he makes his home in an intimate Pentecostal church surrounded by his closest friends.

Each of these Christians proclaims the love of Jesus in the work she or he does, and each one is considered an important leader in his or her congregation. However, each one has a very different definition of what leadership means. That's because each one was nurtured by a very different collection of organizations and relationships.

The purpose of this chapter is to examine how leadership formation takes place, and to focus especially on how that formation takes place in such a way that it promotes a missional ecclesiology and practice of leadership. In this chapter I argue that every leader emerges within what I will call an "ecology of vocation." By this I mean that there is an interconnected network of organizations and relationships that nurtures the development of a leader's vocation in the same way that an ecosystem of streams, soil, and sunshine nurtures a fern growing by a lake. But before we get too far into the main argument of this chapter, it is important for me to state up front some of the theological premises on which I base my argument.

Theological Premises about Leadership Development and the Missional Church

All Christian mission begins with God's prior work, work that proceeds from the very nature of God. All that we do as Christians flows from God, who, according to Second Corinthians, was "in the world reconciling the world to Himself in Christ" (2 Cor. 5:19). This prior action, which proceeds from the grace-filled heart of God, is the basis for our calling, our *vocation* as Christians.[1] The full verse reads: "God was in the world reconciling the world to Himself in Christ, not counting [people's] sins against [them]. And He has committed to us the ministry of reconciliation." The God who seeks the lost thus calls us to be "Christ's ambassadors" (v. 20). This ministry that begins with the mission of God is thus utterly dependent on God for completion. The apostle Paul planted the seed with those same Corinthians; Apollos watered it; but "God made it grow" (1 Cor. 3:6). Our vocation from God proceeds from the mission of God, and only God can make that calling bear fruit.

There is what might be called both a "push factor" and a "pull factor" as God extends God's love into the world. The push comes as God sends the people of God out into the world as ambassadors. This is the part of the calling that we Christians tend to emphasize, perhaps because it is easy to delude ourselves into believing that this part of the gospel call makes us the center of God's plan. But there is a pull factor as well. God is also always drawing all people to Godself. Sometimes we have a tendency to overemphasize the push factor (the part where Paul plants and Apollos waters), but we can never forget that mission is always primarily about God drawing people to Godself. In other words, all that planting and watering only matters because "God gives the increase" (1 Cor. 3:6).

Most people who read this chapter are likely familiar with the foundational work on this idea of mission that has been developed in the last

---

1. Throughout this chapter I will be using the terms "calling" and "vocation" interchangeably.

few years. It began with Lesslie Newbigin,[2] and it has continued with the work of scholars such as Darrell Guder and Craig Van Gelder.[3] But my favorite summary of this idea comes from a biblical scholar, C. J. H. Wright: "Mission (if it is biblically informed and validated) means our committed participation as God's people, at God's invitation and command, in God's own mission within the history of God's world for the redemption of God's creation."[4]

There are some important ecclesiological corollaries that come from these insights. First, the mission of God belongs to the whole people of God; it is not the special possession of the clergy. What Mike, the store manager, does on a Thursday in his drugstore is no more or less a calling and an extension of God's invitation to a dying world than is the work that Charlotte, the small-town pastor, does when she preaches on Sunday morning, or the work that John, the church planter, does when he talks after the Sunday service to a new Christian about the love of God. Because each Christian is called to be an ambassador, the mission of God cannot be confined to what happens during a Sunday morning service. The mission of God goes out with the people of God into the world as they leave the church property and as they encounter fellow humans that Jesus died to save.

There is, however, a special role for clergy and for the Sunday morning worship service.[5] The Sunday morning service is the place where the people who worship God become equipped and prepared to do the work of mission that extends that worship into the world.[6] This means that the congregation is the most immediate and crucial part of the ecology that cultivates leaders to do God's work in the world. The special task of the minister is to be the gardener who tills that ecology.

2. See esp. Lesslie Newbigin, *The Open Secret: An Introduction to the Theology of Mission*, rev. ed. (Grand Rapids: Eerdmans, [1978] 1995).

3. See, e.g., Darrell L. Guder, ed., *Missional Church: A Vision for the Sending of the Church in North America* (Grand Rapids: Eerdmans, 1998), and Craig Van Gelder, *The Essence of the Church: A Community Created by the Spirit* (Grand Rapids: Baker, 2000).

4. C. J. H. Wright, *The Mission of God* (Downers Grove, IL: InterVarsity, 2006).

5. When I say Sunday morning service in this setting, I am using it as a placeholder for all the activity of a congregation that takes place primarily among the faithful. This could just as easily be a Saturday evening service, a Wednesday night covenant group for working moms, or a Saturday morning men's breakfast.

6. The worship of God is certainly the centerpiece of what happens on a Sunday morning. Indeed, the mission to which God calls us is a continuation of that worship as we honor God by conforming our actions to God's sinner-loving work.

Contradictions and Tensions within Ministry

There are many contradictions and tensions embedded within ministry. One of them is particularly important as we think about missional leadership. Let's begin with one of the premises just described: it proclaims that we as Christian leaders can do no more, and presume to do no less, than cooperate with God in God's redemptive work.[7] That brings us to embedded tension number one: we are committed to the work of God, but we have to focus our energies on the labors of humans. This leads naturally to embedded tension number two: we know that the vast majority of God's labor in the world happens through the endeavors of laypeople outside the church walls, yet most of our energy is focused on what happens within the church. Put those two tensions together, and we have a daunting mandate for missional leaders. Our ministry is to equip the people of God to engage in the mission of God outside the church, but we are to do it by using the time that we have with those people when they are at church or are engaged in churchly activities.[8]

How Can We Possibly Do This?
What Does It Mean to Lead in This Way?

The first step is to change what we mean by leadership. There is and has for some time been disagreement in Christian circles about what leadership means. Some have argued that leadership happens from the top down: the leaders (i.e., those with authority) teach, equip, and exhort the people of God. This is the perspective that tends to emphasize Jethro's advice to Moses about delegating, or to celebrate Nehemiah's decisive action in rebuilding Jerusalem. I am certain that, if I paused for a moment, you could conjure up images of both healthy and hurtful leadership in this mode. We

---

7. Even the way we state this premise betrays a bit about our theological choices. While I say "cooperate with God," the phrase is usually rendered as "participate in God's mission" in order to keep God as the acting subject.

8. Note that there is a certain simplification even in this statement of embedded tension. A more complicated (and accurate) description would incorporate the role the Holy Spirit plays in prodding and preparing each congregant and in prodding and preparing each minister. But since we have already emphasized that the prior action belongs to God, we will proceed with this simplification for the sake of explaining the argument of this chapter.

might summarize this model by saying that some leaders lead by telling people what to do.

On the other hand, there is a contrasting school of thought that says that leadership happens from the bottom up: leaders listen to and enable the people of God, who are themselves responding to the Holy Spirit. This position tends to emphasize the metaphor of Jesus as the Good Shepherd who laid down his life for his sheep, or that of Barnabas the encourager. We might summarize this model as one where leaders lead by following — that is, by following the people of God, who are themselves following the movement of the Spirit.

Both of these models have strengths, and both have weaknesses. For example, the greatest strength of the top-down model is also its greatest weakness, and the model can be quite clear. Say that I am a banker and I ask my pastor how I should act at work. She might say that I should act with integrity and compassion, that I should embody the love of Jesus. From my pastor's perspective, she has given me instructions that are quite clear. But the problem comes when I face a situation where there are embedded tensions. What do I do when it feels like I have to choose between two goods, or worse, when I have to choose the option that is less bad? What if I am a manager and I have to choose between my responsibilities to my boss and my responsibilities to my employees? How do I have integrity toward my boss and compassion toward my workers at the same time? The top-down model fails at this point because my pastor cannot come to work with me, and she cannot anticipate every circumstance I will face. Eventually I will have to decide for myself. The top-down model does not prepare laypeople to exercise the mission of God in their everyday lives.

The bottom-up model also fails to guide people when they move out of the church and into the world. It is difficult to inspire people to new life from the bottom up; people are too easily tempted to hear what they want to hear. So I, as a layperson, can easily misunderstand the encouragement I receive from my pastor as confirmation that whatever I am doing is the right thing to do. The sociologist Robert Wuthnow found exactly this phenomenon when he studied the effect of small groups on Christians' ability to act out their faith in the world. He found that the ethic in small groups was to confirm a person's decision, no matter what it was.[9] This has the

9. Robert Wuthnow, *Sharing the Journey: Support Groups and America's New Quest for Community* (New York: The Free Press, 1994).

unintended effect of baptizing the person's decision (no matter what it is) and making it seem like God's will.[10] So neither the top-down nor the bottom-up ways of leading will sufficiently prepare God's people to engage in God's mission in the world.

A Third Alternative: Mental Models

I want to suggest a third way to look at how Christian leaders lead, one that specifically helps us deal with the embedded tensions: it focuses on what clergy can do at church that prepares laypeople for what they do far beyond the church walls. Perhaps the best way to describe this third way is to put it this way: Christian leaders can help change the way the people of God see the worlds in which they live.[11] Peter Senge uses the term "mental models" to describe the "ways people see the world." "Mental models," says Senge, "are the images, assumptions, and stories which we carry in our minds of ourselves, other people, institutions, and every aspect of the world. . . . [L]ike a pane of glass framing and subtly distorting our vision, mental models determine what we see." This means that "the term refers to both the semi-permanent tacit 'maps' of the world which people hold in their long-term memory, and the short-term perceptions which people build up as part of their everyday reasoning process."[12] In other words, Christian leaders lead by changing the mental models that the people of God use to make sense of the world.

Mental models are so powerful because people will, without knowing it, distort what they see so that it conforms to their mental models. For example, a college student named Steve noticed that a girl named Jane had

10. Let me be clear: I am not saying that the top-down or the bottom-up methods are wrong per se. Indeed, in other places I have argued that each one of them is necessary and each must complement the other. However, I am saying that neither is particularly effective in preparing Christians to exercise their callings in the world. On the complementary nature of the bottom-up and top-down models, see Scott Cormode, "Multi-layered Leadership: Builder, Shepherd, Gardener," *Journal of Religious Leadership* (Fall 2002): 69-104.

11. Note the assumption embedded in this statement: it assumes that each person lives in her or his own world. There is not just one world that we all live in; instead, we all encounter the outside world in our own ways. As such, each of us creates the world that we individually inhabit.

12. Peter Senge et al., *The Fifth Discipline Fieldbook* (New York: Doubleday, 1994), 235, 237.

a crush on him. This was very good news for Steve, because he was a bit shy around girls in general but was relaxed when he was around Jane. There was only one catch: Jane did not have a crush on Steve. He had come to a faulty conclusion. But that did not really matter. Steve interpreted each of Jane's actions in such a way that it confirmed what he "knew" to be true. The way she smiled at him as they talked; the way she laughed at his jokes; the way she kept turning up when he was around. All of these confirmed her interest in him. No matter what she did, he found a way to make sense of it in light of the one thing he knew to be true: she liked him.

This kind of thing can happen on a national as well as a personal stage. American diplomats and government officials have described what happened at the beginning of the invasion of Iraq. They said to themselves, "We are liberators, so we can safely assume that we will be greeted as liberators." These leaders had created a mental category that made sense of their actions (they genuinely intended to be liberators), and that mental model blinded them to incoming data that might have shown them that their model was not completely accurate. It took many of these leaders years to realize that there were people in Iraq who saw all foreign soldiers as occupiers rather than liberators. But these leaders' mental model prevented them from seeing that others did not share their model.

Before I become too harsh on our national leaders, I must admit that I do this myself. We all do. To judge my actions, I use the meaning I intended to convey rather than looking at how the message was received. For example, not long ago I said something that hurt a friend's feelings. I found myself saying, "But I did not mean to insult her" — a statement that was true. What I was really saying inside my own mind was: "She has no reason to label my actions insulting when I did not mean to insult her." But whether or not I intended to hurt her, the message she received was hurtful. I needed to apologize. My mental image of my actions as well-intentioned prevented me from acknowledging the hurt that I caused. My action (in this case, neglecting to apologize) was determined not by what happened but by what my mental model told me should have happened. Actions proceed from mental models, often bypassing objective facts in the process.

Let me illustrate how this works by looking at how Jesus worked with his disciples. The apex of Mark's Gospel turns on Jesus' reconfiguring of the disciples' mental models and then showing how that reconfigured understanding changed the choices they needed to make. In Mark 8, Jesus asked the disciples about the mental models that the crowds used to interpret Jesus. "Jesus went on with his disciples to the villages of Caesarea Philippi; and on the way he asked his disciples, 'Who do people say that I am?' And they answered him, 'John the Baptist; and others, Elijah; and still others, one of the prophets'" (8:27-28). Then Jesus became more personal and asked what mental models the disciples' themselves used when they interpreted Jesus. "He asked them, 'But who do you say that I am?' Peter answered him, 'You are the Messiah.' And he sternly ordered them not to tell anyone about him" (8:29-30). The disciples had decided that Jesus was the Messiah, and that the concept "Messiah" was the best mental model to use in interpreting Jesus' ministry. But Jesus knew that what they understood by a messiah was not what he intended to be. So he explained to them that, while he was the Messiah, they were going to have to change their mental models of messiah if they were going to understand what he was doing. "Then he began to teach them that the Son of Man must undergo great suffering, and be rejected by the elders, the chief priests, and the scribes, and be killed, and after three days rise again. He said all this quite openly" (8:31-32). Peter found this new mental model so offensive that he tried to correct Jesus. "Peter took him aside and began to rebuke him. But turning and looking at his disciples, he rebuked Peter and said, 'Get behind me, Satan! For you are setting your mind not on divine things but on human things'" (8:33).

Finally, to drive the point home, Jesus summoned the crowds and explained that this new understanding of the Messiah carried with it a new understanding of *disciple.* "He called the crowd with his disciples, and said to them, 'If any want to become my followers, let them deny themselves and take up their cross and follow me. For those who want to save their life will lose it, and those who lose their life for my sake, and for the sake of the gospel, will save it. For what will it profit them to gain the whole world and forfeit their life? Indeed, what can they give in return for their life?'" (8:34-37). The mental model a person adopts dictates the action a person takes — just as the model of the Messiah changed the action of the disciples. So if you want to change how Christians act outside the church, change the mental models they carry with them as they go into the world.

Approaches to Mental Models

The most important mental models we carry in our heads are what are technically referred to as "archetypes."[13] We use various archetypes to frame basic Christian constructs. For example, we might explore a certain question: What is the biblical ideal for a leader?[14] Think back to the models I described earlier. There is the model of the leader as organizer, which calls on Jethro's advice to Moses about dividing the people into orderly groups, or Nehemiah's marshaling the discouraged inhabitants of Jerusalem to rebuild the wall. Then there is the model of the leader as Good Shepherd, which calls on Jesus' caring for the confused disciples; or we can consider Barnabas's mentoring of Paul. Finally, there are those who see the leader as a teacher: their model is Jesus delivering the Sermon on the Mount or the prophet Nathan telling King David a story in order to convict him of sin. The models we carry in our heads usually shape the actions we take.

I could make a similar analysis of archetypes with regard to ecclesiology or power relations. There are those who believe that the church is what happens on Sunday mornings (a mental model I earlier disputed). There are plenty of Christians, especially pastors, who have a mental model of the power relationship between clergy and congregations that implicitly says, "The congregation should always listen to the pastor, but the pastor does not always have to listen to the congregation." When I state it that baldly, most pastors would shy away from the authoritarian implications. But think of how often we clergy are insulted when our congregations do not do as we say. The models we carry in our heads are different from — and far more powerful than — the ones we proclaim aloud.[15]

So we have already been talking about the idea of mental models without calling it that. When I say the word "leader," what do you picture in your mind? Do you picture a top-down organizer? Do you picture a

13. See the discussion of archetypes in Kyle Small's chapter in this volume (chap. 2).

14. Note that behind this question is a mental model shared by many but certainly not all Christians, namely, that the Bible serves as a model for contemporary action, especially contemporary Christian leadership.

15. Chris Argyris's distinction between espoused theory and theory-in-use is particularly important for understanding the mental models that are so implicit that we hide them from ourselves. See Chris Argyris, "Teaching Smart People How to Learn," *Harvard Business Review* (May-June 1991): 5-15.

nurturing comforter who comes alongside someone? What does a congregant picture? Does Mary Sue expect you to be a nurturer or an organizer? Does her husband, Bob, have the same expectation? If we are going to minister to the people God has entrusted to our care, we will have to learn about the mental models they carry in their heads, even if people have taken those models for granted so much that the people themselves cannot explain them to us.

An Ecology of the Formation of Mental Models

Where do mental models come from? The tendency is for people to think that such models come from conscious and clearly constructed thought. But this is not necessarily the case: most people merely assimilate the mental models they regularly use to make sense of their world; those models seep into their minds without a lot of reflection.[16] Think, for example, about what it means to be a high school student. It is fairly easy to picture high school in our minds, but where do those pictures come from? They usually come either from movies or from our own experiences. In fact, when you ask most people to imagine being in high school, the high school they picture in their mind is the one they attended. Without realizing it, people then tend to extrapolate their own experience onto everyone else's. In other words, each of us unconsciously says, "I was in high school. So I know what high school is like." We do the same thing with lots of mental images. Picture what it means to be a mother (you'll likely picture your own family) or what it's like to be sick (seminary students who have not done extensive hospital visitation usually picture their own experiences).

What does all this have to do with leadership formation? Picture what it is like to be a leader. As we have just asked, what does it mean to lead the people of God, and what kinds of characteristics should a leader embody? You likely have a set of strong opinions about that. Where did those opinions come from? Where did you get your mental model of a Christian leader?

16. Ann Swidler, *Talk of Love: How Culture Matters* (Chicago: University of Chicago Press, 2003).

The Formation of a Christian Leader

I believe that mental models about leadership grow from what might be called "an ecology of vocation." Perhaps the best way to begin is with an analogy to show what I mean by ecology. Then I will tell the story of a particular leader's vocational journey in order to show how the concept of an ecology helps us understand the development of vocation. Note that, though I describe an ordained minister's development, a similar story could be told to describe the development of a layperson who leads.

The best metaphor for understanding the development of a minister may be to think of a river flowing from the hills to the sea. Think of the life course of a leader's development as the flow of that river. The river passes through a number of different environments on its way to the sea. A confluence of smaller streams may come together to form the river; the river may pool at some point to create a lake; there may be rapids and there may be deep, still segments. The river may pass through a forest or create a meadow. The point is that the river itself is a larger ecosystem even as it passes through and is shaped by a network of smaller ecosystems. Together, these various ecosystems create the ecology of the river. In the same way, a leader's development over time has a logic of its own. That makes her development like a river: that is, it has its own ecosystem. At the same time, however, a leader's development is influenced by a number of other organizations and entities. These are like the lakes, forests, and hillsides that shape a river. We cannot understand the river or the leader until we look at the entire system as a whole, which is why we need to understand the ecology of vocation.

But what does that look like in the life of a particular leader? Let us focus on one example. Even before John Kramer arrived at seminary, he felt sure he was called to plant new churches. Soon after he graduated from the school in the 1990s, he and his wife began hosting a Bible study in their living room. It eventually grew into a congregation of over 200 members, almost all of whom had no faith commitment before encountering his church. The church recently purchased land near a freeway and is hoping to build a new sanctuary and gymnasium.[17] In short, Rev. Kramer has become the kind of minister that most seminaries want their graduates to be: he is pastoral with his parishioners, preaches solid biblical sermons, and

---

17. I verified the information in this profile of Rev. Kramer in a day-long interview on Aug. 31, 2006.

has a commitment to evangelism. The question is, "How did he become such a minister?"

While it is true that Rev. Kramer learned a great deal about ministry in the seminary classroom, many of the key moments that formed him for ministry came outside the school. He came to faith as a child through an independent Bible church. Then, when he was in high school, his parents moved the family to a Presbyterian congregation, where the youth minister (fresh from seminary) had a profound effect on John. During his time in college, InterVarsity Christian Fellowship gave him valuable experience not only in leading groups but also in starting new ministries. After he graduated from college, he worked as a youth minister under the tutelage of an old and wise Presbyterian pastor. But when that pastor retired, Kramer had a very frustrating experience working with an interim pastor who did not value innovation or evangelism.

The frustration continued when, during seminary, the denominational credentialing body informed him that they believed only older, more experienced pastors should be planting churches. Conversely, after he founded his congregation, he encountered a wise denominational leader who mentored him. All along the way, a network of friends confirmed his gifts and discussed the questions that were closest to his heart. Those experiences shaped his understanding of ministry and his assumptions about his gifts for church planting. It is clear, then, that many of the lessons he learned that made him such a strong graduate came from outside the seminary classroom. Some even came along after he had earned his degree. In other words, much of the success of a theological school's ability to form students for ministry depends at least to some extent on these external entities. It depends on an ecology of vocation.

But how do these entities form an ecology? Each of these entities creates an environment for learning and formation. Learning and formation are not mechanistic processes.[18] They grow in the same way a plant grows

---

18. The current literature on leadership formation has a tendency to proceed with a mechanistic understanding of how leaders develop. They tend to list "four steps to this" and "five steps to that." They treat leaders like ball bearings. One of my students was the president of a ball-bearing manufacturer. He knew for sure that if he put a certain amount of raw material into the machine, and then followed the prescribed steps, he would get ball bearings to a certain specification every single time. The process was unambiguous. But leaders do not develop that way. We all know that we can take all the "right" steps and end up with something we did not intend.

out of an ecology.[19] When we examine the range of leaders being formed for ministry, we find that the organizations and entities that shape them fit together in a system of mutual dependence in just the same way that an upstream ecosystem affects what happens downstream. This interdependence makes the learning environment into an ecology. Anything that affects one part of the system affects everything else in the system.

There is a diversity of organisms and organizations in any ecology. In Rev. Kramer's ecology, we find not only the seminary but also a nondenominational church that provided his initial faith formation, a number of Presbyterian congregations that gave him the opportunity to experiment with his gifts, a couple of judicatories (one that helped and one that hurt his development), an InterVarsity chapter that thrust him into a creative leadership position, and many mentors and friends. The weakness in the wide literature on leadership formation is that it neglects all these other influences because it proceeds as if seminaries stand alone. There has been very little discussion of how theological schools fit into an ecology of vocation.

Keys to the Development of an Ecology of Vocation

There are at least five key parts to the ecology of vocation.[20] Each of these parts is really a cluster of organizations and experiences, in the same way that the rapids of a river or the place where it pools into a lake is both an ecology unto itself and part of the overall ecology of the river.

Formative Faith

The first part of any leader's ecology of vocation is his *formative faith experience,* which often takes place in the congregation that first nurtured him

19. Even God faces this problem. Look at the book of Judges, where God leads the people of Israel most directly. Even under God's careful tutelage, the people constantly wander away from God and call out only when they need help. God creates an environment where the people can thrive and invites them to dwell in relationship with God. But then God gives people a choice — one that they often abuse.

20. There are, of course, a range of relationships that I have not emphasized here but that even a commonsense approach would include in any person's ecology of vocation. I am thinking, for example, of one's parents, spouse, children, and so on.

to faith. If the leader first came to faith at a young age, this first component may include an experience of youth ministry. If so, that experience may have made a lasting impression. In Kramer's case, much of the work he does as a church planter harkens back to his high school experience of youth ministry. The camps and the mission trips, the music and the mentors that went with youth ministry — they all shaped his mental model of Christian ministry. If that formative faith experience happens in adulthood, it influences a leader in a different way. But the important point is that most leaders, throughout the course of their development, engage in an implicit dialogue with their formative faith experiences: the dialogue is about what is the best way to lead.

College/First Career

The second key component of the ecology is one's experience of faith during college (and, if one had it, a first career). Even those ministers who look back on the college years as spiritually barren have nevertheless been shaped by that experience. At this stage, campus ministries or parachurch organizations can be important influences, as can camps, books, and Web sites. These often provide future leaders with a safe training ground in which to nurture their skills. Indeed, it may be that a significant number of future leaders first discover their gifts for ministry in these college contexts. On the other hand, there are those future leaders who graduate from college with no plan to be a minister. They prepare for some other profession and then discover their call to ministry later in life. It would be interesting to compare the college experiences of first-career and second-career ministers to see if there is something distinctive about the college experience of either group.

Work experiences can be as important as college experiences in shaping the mental models of ministry. For those who perceive a call after the age of thirty, there is usually some kind of first career. It is important to investigate the influences that different careers have on their mental models about ministry. For example, when I talked to Rev. Kramer about the influences that formed him, he talked about working in his family's restaurant. Being a part of a small business taught him a sense of responsibility, and it taught him how to deal with the ambiguous boundaries that both small business owners and pastors experience. This pastor's reflection came up as he was describing the difficulty he has had hiring youth ministers. He observed that fledgling ministers who have known only nine-to-five jobs are not prepared for the intrusive nature of youth ministry. He wants a youth minister to know instinctively that it is important to show up at high school basketball games, winter concerts, and Fourth of July parades.[21] So he asks potential youth ministers about their job experience in order to gauge their ability to manage the elastic hours that ministry demands. There is much to learn from tracking the work experience of candidates for ministry.

Congregation of Call

The third key component is the *congregation of call.* At some point, every minister perceives some kind of call. Usually this happens in the context of a community of faith. This congregation of call may be a community that has already been important in a candidate's development (e.g., the congregation that originally formed a candidate or a college ministry), or it may be a community that one encounters after leaving college. But the context in which the potential minister receives the call has a large influence on what the candidate believes she or he is being called to be and do.

Seminary Years

The fourth key component of the ecology of vocation is the nexus of organizations that shape a student during his or her *seminary years.* For the purpose of this chapter, I am especially interested in those influences that take place outside the classroom, which include: (a) the internship or field education context (this may include the ministries students do for academic credit and those they pursue simply to pay the bills or to continue their calling); (b) relationships with a credentialing body such as a presby-

21. Rev. Kramer also reported that the potential youth ministers he interviewed used the language of self-care when rejecting the hours a youth minister usually works. They said to him that they could not take the time to visit teens and hang out with youth because they had to make sure to take care of themselves and their families first. Rev. Kramer was appalled that these would-be ministers had been formed in such a way that they could see ministry as anything but a life of sacrifice.

tery, a Methodist annual conference, or a Lutheran synod; (c) clinical pastoral education (particularly in a hospital setting); and (d) extracurricular student activities within the seminary.[22] Each of these learning environments shapes students during their seminary years, but none is directly related to what happens in the classroom.

Steps Into Ministry

Finally, the fifth key component of this ecology concerns the experiences that a pastor encounters as she *steps into ministry.* Particularly important are the first summer after graduating from seminary and the first five years in ministry. As new ministers make sense of these new experiences, they either internalize or shed lessons they learned in seminary. They also become attuned to questions that they could not ask until they took up the mantle of pastoral leadership. Each of these five key components is a nexus of organizations and influences surrounding a developing minister; each provides an environment for learning; and each is in some way shaped by the others. Together they form the ecology of vocation.

Preparing the Laity for Ministry

We have established that the mental models that shape leaders grow out of the ecology that forms these leaders. But what does this have to do with our original goal of looking at how ministers use the time laypeople have in church to prepare them to participate in the mission of God beyond the church walls? It is important for us, as we try to answer this question, to recognize that laypeople go through the same process that pastors go through. They carry mental models in their heads of what faithful action looks like. They know that God calls them to have integrity and to show compassion. But when you ask someone what integrity or compassion

---

22. Here I am particularly interested in extending the notion of "seminary culture" described in Jackson Carroll et al., *Being There: Culture and Formation in Two Theological Schools* (New York: Oxford University Press, 1997). Experiences such as campus chapel or influences such as on-campus speakers or especially small Bible-study groups composed of other students can provide important environments for students to explore new ways of imagining what it means to be in ministry.

looks like, each person is going to have a different mental picture for each of those terms.

Here is where this chapter's focus loops back to where we started. At the beginning of the chapter I lamented the embedded tensions of ministry. I discussed how the mission of God cannot be confined to the four walls of the church. This is where we figure out how to prepare the people of God to engage in the mission of God. Christian leaders lead by changing the mental models that parishioners carry in their heads so that they enable those parishioners to imagine themselves into more faithful action.

To show how this works, allow me to give one more example, this time of a layperson. Mike is an elder at his church, although elder may be a bit misleading when describing a thirty-five-year-old. Mike is the store manager at a big-chain drugstore. He started working for the company when he was nineteen, sweeping the floors and working the check-out lanes. He worked his way up to department manager, and then assistant store manager, before he was eventually given his own store to manage.

Mike believes that he is called to show integrity and compassion out in the world, that is, beyond the church walls. This is his part in exercising the mission of God, though his denomination's theological formulation would not state it that way. He believes that the work he does with customers truly helps them, especially those elderly people who come in from the retirement community next door. He believes that he also helps his employees, many of whom are still navigating their way to adulthood as they figure out how to show up for work on time and how to be trustworthy employees. In other words, Mike believes that he cannot simply embody integrity and compassion in the way he treats his customers; he also gets to teach these Christian values as he manages his employees.

But Mike has a problem. The character of the company that owns the drugstore is changing. In order to boost the short-term stock price, the company has made some changes. The company has eliminated a layer of management: there are no more department managers, which means that the assistant store manager and the store manager (Mike) now have a lot more work to do. The company has also cut back on hours for most employees: essentially, they are no longer full-time employees. Along the way, the company has also eliminated benefits for those employees who remain. All this has been designed to cut costs and boost the short-term stock price. Not only that, but the company has always expected the store manager to implement the changes and to explain them to the employees. In

115

other words, Mike's company has started to do things that he can see lack integrity and compassion, and the company has asked Mike to defend them as they are being implemented.

This is exactly the kind of moment that those of us who write about the mission of God have in mind when we talk about God's mission extending beyond the church's walls. It is just the moment when a congregation should help Mike see his situation from a spiritual perspective. What is Mike to do in such a situation? The mental models that Mike carried gave him only two options. He was told — and he wholeheartedly believes — that you either have integrity or you don't. Therefore, he could either continue as store manager and help his company exploit people, or he could quit and maintain his integrity. There really was no middle ground.

So what did Mike do? He quit. He took a job reading meters for the gas company, and he began studying to become ordained as a minister in his denomination. According to the theological models his congregation had helped to form, that was the best way for him to maintain his integrity and continue working to participate in God's work. But what if there were a third option? What if there were a way to maintain his integrity and retain his position? This question reaches right to the core of the New Testament, right to the debate we've been having about the mission of God, because it asks this: Can a person like Mike maintain his place in the world without being compromised by it?

This is where it becomes important to think about mental models. Mike chose between the only options available to him — as we all tend to do. I am not Mike's pastor, so I do not want to make a judgment on his choices. But for the sake of this chapter, let us assume that we wanted to help Mike think about staying in his job as a store manager. What would we do?

Alternatives That Might Be Considered

The key to helping Mike see the world differently would be to help him construct a new mental model of integrity and a less clergy-centered model of mission. We have already discussed the biblical precedent for seeing that the mission of God belongs to the whole people of God. We could make that argument with Mike. But it would likely fall on deaf ears because his theological tradition does not talk that way. He would need to consider a more direct biblical precedent.

Let me say this in a different way, one that corresponds to the argument I have been making in this chapter. By understanding the ecology that formed Mike's mental model of mission and his theological understanding of integrity, we can better know how to help him imagine a new way of faithful living. The next step for Mike will need to be along the same path that his ecology has already blazed. Let me be more specific: Mike consciously chose to become part of a small, Pentecostal congregation as a clear alternative to the Presbyterian congregation of his youth. So any theological argument that sounds like something those Presbyterians would say will not have the ring of truth for him.

The Presbyterian congregation in which he was raised often paired scriptural reasoning with theological constructions. Words like "hermeneutics" were not out of the ordinary at that Presbyterian church. But in the Pentecostal congregation where he has put down roots, one either reasons directly from Scripture (complete with exact quotations from the Bible), or one describes the process that led him or her to hear God's leading directly — usually as the result of prayer over a long period of time. That means that talking to Mike about the *missio Dei* would likely have little effect. It would sound too much like the congregation he left and not enough like the congregation where he now lives.[23]

Perhaps the best way to help Mike create a different mental model for his work as a store manager would be to invite him into a study of particular biblical characters. Let me give a few quick examples. Let us start with Joseph, the son of Jacob. When most people study Joseph as kids, they learn about the coat of many colors and perhaps about his dreams. But with Mike we might spend some time looking at the chapters after Pharaoh puts Joseph in charge of Egypt (Gen. 42–48). This is an example of one of the most celebrated patriarchs of the Old Testament working for a person whose values he could not share. But through it all, Joseph maintains his integrity because that is where God planted him.

The goal of discussing Joseph with Mike would be to change Mike's mental model of integrity. Mike seems to think that it involves working for an organization that represents the values he represents — or more importantly, that Christ represents. But Joseph seems to have been able to thrive in a place where God placed him by succeeding in Egypt on Egyptian

---

23. One corollary of this insight is that clergy have a responsibility to engage in *systematic listening* so that they can understand the mental models that have formed their people.

terms. The most important summary of the Joseph narrative may be when he says to his brothers after all is revealed, "You meant evil against me; but God meant it for good" (Gen. 50:20). One way to change Mike's mental model would be to argue that integrity has more to do with doing God's bidding than it does with the people who employ you.

This leads nicely into a discussion of Jesus, who was repeatedly accused of lacking integrity because he spent time with the wrong crowd. Jesus ate with sinners, prostitutes, and tax collectors. When the righteous people of his day asked him about the hypocrisy of a rabbi associating with people who do not honor God, Jesus said, "It is not the healthy that need a doctor, but the sick" (Matt. 9:12). The Pharisees wanted to treat righteousness like Mike treated integrity — as an all-or-nothing state. But Jesus made it clear that loving people and doing the work of God sometimes carries God's people into situations where they would not choose to go.

A final example might be to consider the apostle Paul on Mars Hill (Acts 17). Paul argued philosophy with secular philosophers on secular terms. Paul explained why he did such things in another letter: "I have become all things to all people so that I might by any means save some" (1 Cor. 9:22). The point, no matter which passages one selects, is to help Mike see that God often invites people to proclaim the grace and compassion that Jesus embodied in a setting where that grace and compassion are sorely lacking. This takes us back to the Scripture passage we discussed at the outset. We are called to be "ambassadors" and "ministers of reconciliation" (2 Cor. 5). Like Jesus, who said that physicians go to the sick (Matt. 9:12), we have to understand that ambassadors usually live in foreign lands. So, if we were to try to change Mike's mental model for a Christian's role in the world, we might point to Joseph, to Jesus, or to Paul.

Summary

Mike chose in the end to do what made the most sense to him in light of the model that his congregation imparted to him. His congregation celebrated his choice because he did something difficult and costly in the name of preserving integrity. So please do not think that I am questioning that judgment. Rather, my goal has been to show how that decision grew out of the mental models that his ecology nurtured within him and to illustrate how a leader might have helped Mike make a different decision if that had been necessary.

In sum, the purpose of this chapter has been to show (a) that the actions we take flow from the mental models we carry in our heads; (b) that these models are formed by the ecology of relationships and organizations that have nurtured us; and (c) that the best way to prepare God's people to carry God's message of hope into the world is to change the models that support this perspective.

CHAPTER 5

Forming Lay Missional Leaders for Congregations and the World

Sharon Henderson Callahan

Introduction

Rooted in the insights of the emerging Trinitarian theologies, my theme in this chapter is baptismal vocation as a response to the overwhelming grace of the Trinitarian God. As I considered this subject from a lay — and admittedly mostly Roman Catholic — perspective, I found myself revisiting Scripture texts and theological documents to describe my own deep commitment to missional leadership as I understand it.

I first relate a vignette that suggests a lived example of what I consider to be missional leadership. Next I explore the theological implications of baptism that support such a lived reality, stipulating that baptism necessarily compels the believer toward a creative, generative faith actualized within the tension of the reign of God as both *now* and *not yet*. Finally, using the School of Theology and Ministry (STM) at Seattle University as a case study, I consider the contribution that seminaries and schools of theology can make in the ecology of supporting and forming missional leadership within the Christian church. Throughout this chapter I argue that seminaries must fulfill their role in the ecology of developing missional leaders for the sake of the church and the world.

Part One: Missional Leadership Rooted in Baptism

A Vignette

A Presbyterian church sits on a hillside in a very prestigious neighborhood in the greater Seattle area. It is a large church built to accommodate several services of several hundred every Sabbath. A senior pastor oversees the entire work and life of the congregation that built this church. It supports the local presbytery according to its polity. Associate pastors assist in specific tasks related to the life of the congregation. A large staff of laypeople serves in capacities such as youth ministry, Christian education, publication, administration, and "mission."[1] The people in this congregation tithe appropriately; they mostly represent people in the top 3 percent of income in the nation. They can afford to have a separate building for Christian education, to hire a chef for Sunday brunch after Sunday services, to offer generous hospitality to their members and guests, and to support worship that is full and vibrant.

Situated in the Pacific Northwest, the congregation reflects its context. According to recent research, only 37 percent of all people in this geographic region claim affiliation with a particular religious group,[2] and of

1. Several layers of meaning define this word "mission." Many organizations use the word in a broad sense to indicate their purpose statement. I will use either mission statement or purpose when I mean "mission" in that common usage. Many congregations, such as the one in the vignette, use the word to describe outreach projects, and they hire people or form committees to ensure that the believing body attends to this important aspect, usually related to justice issues. The vignette congregation hired someone to attend to this second definition. Some churches describe this as outreach or social justice. As other literature has documented, mission also can connote a series of activities in which congregations, denominations, and individuals proclaimed the Word of God in such a way that entire peoples were colonized to Christianity as well as Western European and Northern American cultures. Significant reflection on this practice at times equated this understanding of mission with imperialism. Several countries and cultures continue to resist "mission" as they reflect on that previous historical period. At no time does "missional leadership" suggest that the church return to that understanding. Rather, it builds on the work of movements formed to redefine understanding since the early 1900s. Missional leadership is emerging as a result of renewed Trinitarian theology. Throughout this article I use the word in the way it is currently being redefined.

2. Patricia O'Connell Killen and Mark A. Shibley, "Surveying the Religious Landscape: Historical Trends and Current Patterns in Oregon, Washington, and Alaska," in *Religion and Public Life in the Pacific Northwest: The None Zone,* ed. Killen and Shibley (Walnut Creek, CA: AltaMira, 2004), 28.

these, approximately 6 percent are non-Christian affiliations.[3] These people are the inheritors of the missionary activity of the proclamation of the gospel in this area as recently as one hundred years ago. The lived experience of mission that was influenced by the days of its colonizing modality remains palpable. This is especially evident among the Native Americans, who cautiously approach the perceived dominant white interpretation of Christianity.

The many Asian immigrants who came to this area also remember this history: the Chinese, who were persecuted during the building of the railroads; the Japanese, who were interned in camps on our soil; and the Vietnamese, who struggled for independence. Those who moved to this area from the Midwest or the East Coast were looking for new opportunities and to escape from hardship. They often started life here by breaking their ties to tradition, including religious practice. As historian Patricia Killen observes, people "who enter the region must choose whether and how to reconnect. That choice is part of a larger question of community in the Pacific Northwest, a question about how an individual can be fully free, in nature, and part of society."[4]

Within this Presbyterian congregation, the senior pastor has encouraged his somewhat insulated congregation to engage its context. Rooted in both the Western notion of mission as *being sent* and the Eastern concept of deep response to the creative indwelling of the triune God, the congregation has supported his vision. These items form the heart of their outreach:

- Taking three trips a year to Vietnam and Cambodia, to show the Communist governments that Christians can relate in ways different from what the Vietnamese and Cambodians have previously experienced, and to support the efforts of people within those countries toward reconciliation, education, health, and economic development;
- Support in tithing and volunteer work toward sustaining and healing children, mothers, victims of land mines, and victims of physical and sexual abuse;
- Support of homeless in the area;
- Contributions toward housing, programs that care for victims of abuse, and support of United Way in the Seattle area;

3. Killen and Shibley, "Surveying the Religious Landscape," 23.
4. Killen and Shibley, "Surveying the Religious Landscape," 13.

- Initiation of collaboration between one of the richest school districts in the state and one of its poorest and also most racially segregated districts;
- Reparation of presbytery racial discrimination with ongoing attention to eradicating racism in the congregations and the district.

As is so often the case, these remarkable engagements by a predominantly white, upper-class, Western European Protestant group reveal a leader who has been able to galvanize a faith response beyond attendance at Sunday church services. This congregation's mixture of lay and ordained leadership, combined with its unique relationship to STM suggests that this ecology of ministry formation supports identifying, preparing, commissioning, and collaborating with missional leaders.[5] Laypeople from the congregation serve on the STM's advisory boards and fundraising campaign groups. Several ministry candidates have also surfaced in the congregation, and the church has supported their vocations by sending them to STM.

One of the STM's tenured faculty members served as senior minister for a very poor and marginalized congregation in Seattle. During this faculty member's time as pastor, the district superintendent, also an STM supporter, discovered a grave injustice that had been done to that church community. Fifty years prior to her pastorate, the Seattle presbytery had required a white church to combine with a black church. That decision entailed moving the people from the black church to the white church; selling the building that the black church had built; giving the money from that sale to a new church start on Mercer Island; permitting white church members to relocate to neighboring congregations, taking their tithes with them; and attempting to close the small remaining black church community for the remainder of the fifty-year period.

When the superintendent discovered this racially influenced wrong, he and the STM faculty member serving as the senior pastor of the suffering black church, plus the senior pastor at the Mercer Island church — all agreed to work out a way to move toward reconciliation in this matter. The process entailed months of pulpit exchanges, laypeople and elders in dialogue, initiation of a book club, and participation in worship by members

---

5. For a discussion of an ecology of ministry formation, see the chapter by Scott Cormode in this volume (chap. 4).

of both congregations. Finally, after deep dialogue, the members of the Mercer Island congregation committed themselves to a process of reparation toward reconciliation. They allocated thousands of dollars to rebuild and reroof the failing black church building in Seattle. They involved union workers from the greater Seattle area, and over 150 people volunteered their labor and goods toward the renovation of the old building.

As that renovation project evolved, the STM pastor of the poor black church collaborated with the pastoral staff of the Mercer Island congregation to work toward rectifying the larger issues of racism and injustice. Together, they nurtured efforts toward racial reconciliation that reached out beyond the immediate congregation members. They involved the rich school district on the island with the poorer school district of central Seattle. Together they forged ways to bring diverse social classes, as well as races, together toward mutual understanding and reconciliation.

The congregation expanded its horizons: members decided to assist those who did not have adequate medical attention. The pastoral staff, ordained and lay, sponsored immersion trips to Vietnam and Cambodia. Responding to the invitation of Vietnamese dignitaries, the congregational members entered reciprocal relationships with people from Vietnam. The STM pastor met some of the Vietnamese dignitaries while hosting them for an event commemorating Martin Luther King, Jr. Impressed by that, the government officials extended an invitation for the STM to collaborate with universities in Vietnam. The STM pastor's efforts involved others, so that now the STM has a fully translated program of Scripture study in Vietnam piloted in two major areas: these are with students and faculty from the school working with the Mercer Island leadership toward other measures of leadership with the Vietnamese community, both in the Seattle area and in Vietnam. The circles of influence continue to expand, all in response to the daily activity of God in the midst of a forward-looking congregation that is connected with the STM's missional leadership.

This vignette is necessarily short, but it offers insights into what missional leadership looks like. The senior pastor joined with an associate pastor, who burned with a passion for justice that was rooted in the love of God for God's people. Through preaching, worship, prayer, study, and a call to action, a community of believers embraced a new vision. Eventually, lay members assumed leadership in response to their own ongoing conversion. They proposed ways to expand their horizons as followers of the triune God living a Christian life. They struggled with their own privilege, and they sought ways to enter into dialogue. They accepted the call to discipleship, which demanded that they empty themselves in order to be transformed into the body of Christ. Their collective witness called forth others to embrace their baptismal call in ways that stretched them beyond their limited and privileged social location. Essentially, they discovered that their baptismal response involved them in acting for justice in ever-increasing, diverse, and expansive circles of engagement.

Part 2: Baptism: Call and Response

The people depicted in the foregoing vignette rooted their lived faith in a shared scriptural heritage. From Hebrew Scripture they learned how God's people were called to witness to God's reign: both individual stories (Abraham and Sarah, Isaac and Rebecca, Jacob and Rachel and Leah, Moses, Hannah, David, etc.) and the story of a whole people of God demonstrating a response to God's initiative.

The preaching engaged people in appropriating Scripture for their own lives. They entered the pattern of call and response: someone heard or experienced God in a profound way; most often fear or awe accompanied that experience; God's messenger assured the people that God intended only love, mercy, compassion, and justice; and a response to this news was translated into action — care for the oppressed, the marginalized, and the poor. As the pattern continued, God and the people entered into a covenantal relationship in which the covenant required the person to stay connected to God, and God promised to be with the person forever. At times the covenant was sealed with a sign: these people responded to the invitation to increase their service to God through their baptismal vocation.

Mark's Gospel depicts baptism as both an initiation into a community of believers in God's saving action and as a call to discipleship. Throughout Mark's account, those who followed Jesus became a group of companions. They shared meals, conversation, and prayer; they witnessed and performed miraculous acts; they challenged previously held beliefs; they wrestled with the call to radical love that defied their imaginations and expectations.

Their discipling process demonstrated the lifelong process of formation to God that the baptismal event initiates. Each of the disciples learned, first, the good news that God loved them immeasurably and, second, that

God's love generated a response from them. Through Jesus' life story, the community discovered this dual action of love and response. As the first of the Gospel narratives to be written, Mark offers an early insight into the struggles of the first Christian communities as they attempted to live their call to mission. Indeed, Peter's first proclamation of Jesus as Messiah, followed by his rebuke of Jesus' understanding of that role, demonstrated the clash of expectations the disciples encountered in their lives of faith.

Jesus sharply rebuked Peter for insisting on a more grandiose vision of Messiah, and he predicted, first, his own imminent death, and then the deaths of those who would follow him. "If any want to become my followers, let them deny themselves and take up their cross and follow me. For those who want to save their life will lose it, and those who lose their life for my sake and for the sake of the gospel will save it" (Mark 8:34-35). Throughout his gospel, Mark shows that the disciples were struggling with these sayings. Jesus' baptism called disciples to enter not only into baptism, but also into a life that would drink the same cup that Jesus drank, a life that would lead the way to participate in the reign of God through service to God's people and the world.[6]

The believing community celebrates through baptismal rites God's initiating activity of love in God's creation. Flowing out of God's own Trinitarian nature, God remains passionately loving, always creating, restoring, and sustaining. As theologians now describe it, the three-ness of the Trinity unified in their oneness suggests that the essence of God is necessarily relational.[7] The act of baptism marks the moment in which a person enters more fully into relationship with the triune God. As Christians, we understand that this moment demonstrates again the unconditional love God shares with God's creation. We acknowledge this within a community of believers, underscoring our belief that to be with God is to be with each other. Through the love we share for each other, we become the visible expression of the body of Christ, a demonstration of the presence of the reign of God.

6. Mark 10:43-45. "Whoever wishes to become great among you must be your servant, and whoever wishes to be first among you must be the slave of all. For the Son of Man came not to be served but to serve and to give his life as a ransom for many."

7. Edward P. Hahnenberg, *Ministries: A Relational Approach* (New York: Crossroad, 2003), 90. Hahnenberg develops an entire theology of lay ministry rooted in baptism and the Trinitarian nature of God. He develops his thesis by discussing such Catholic theologians as Richard McBrien, Thomas O'Meara, Edward Schillebeeckx, and Yves Congar.

We often name our response as representing the work of "priest, prophet, and king" within God's order. More contemporary understandings might reframe these words as: priest, one who invites to holiness and mediates God's word; prophet, one who listens to God and obeys; and king, one who attunes self and others to God's work in the world. As Paul instructed the first communities, all people — male and female, rich and poor, slave and free, Gentile and Jew — equally participate in a new order in which the triune God creates, sustains, forgives, reconciles, and empowers all creation to live in hope, joy, and unity (Gal. 3:27-28; Col. 3:5-11).

The opening paragraphs of the Second Vatican Council's *Dogmatic Constitution on the Church* eloquently name this process as the action of the Holy Spirit, who eagerly desires to shed on all people "that radiance which brightens the countenance of the Church. This it will do by proclaiming the gospel to every creature."[8] Recognizing a contemporary understanding of people's sense of interconnectedness, the document continued by naming God's plan of creation as an invitation to participate in God's divine life. It further articulated the mission of the church as the manifestation of the outpouring of the Spirit after Jesus inaugurated the reign of God on earth. Calling the people of God a holy people, the document declares that the community shares in "Christ's prophetic office. It spreads abroad a living witness to Him, especially by means of a life of faith and charity and by offering to God a sacrifice of praise, the tribute of lips which give honor to His name" (*Dogmatic Constitution*, n. 12).

This statement of the bishops of the Roman Catholic Church, in the context of an ecumenical council, reminded the whole Christian Church that "the faithful are by baptism made one body with Christ and are established among the People of God. They are in their own way made sharers in the priestly, prophetic, and kingly functions of Christ. They carry out their own part in the mission of the whole Christian people with respect to the Church and the world" (*Dogmatic Constitution*, n. 31).

In 1982, the Faith and Order commission of the World Council of Churches invited Christian ecclesiastical communities to consider a paper on a shared theology of baptism, Eucharist, and ministry. By studying and embracing this "Lima Document," Christian churches recognized baptism as the initiating moment that both launches call and response and equips people for their journey of faith. Declaring their belief that all Christians

---

8. Walter M. Abbott, *The Documents of Vatican II* (New York: Guild Press, 1966), 1.

are called in this way, these ecclesiastical traditions affirmed that baptism is related not only to "momentary experience, but to life-long growth into Christ. Those baptized are called upon to reflect the glory of the Lord as they are transformed by the power of the Holy Spirit into his likeness."[9]

Many stories in Scripture depict instances of God's transformation. Thus, Christian memories of Mary, Elizabeth, Paul, Peter, and Mary Magdalene recounted how God broke into each person's consciousness. These stories often depict the comforting angel or messenger of God saying, "Do not be afraid!" The apparent movement toward fear or awe on the part of the person encountering God seemed to indicate the recognition of his or her unworthiness. Dean Brackley, a Jesuit priest who has worked in El Salvador for the last twenty-five years, speaks of this interaction as an overwhelming experience of the power of God's love for us. He suggests that as one receives God's love in a profound way, one almost immediately moves toward a recognition of one's total unworthiness for such unconditional love. According to Brackley, one sees more clearly the effects of sin and recognizes one's self as the "earthen vessel" so unworthy to hold or receive this pure, vast, gracious love that is the Trinity. Using an Ignatian spirituality lens, Brackley says that this encounter with God is a call to holiness — a call to collaborate with Christ.

The bishops and theologians of the Second Vatican Council claimed that all the baptized are "called . . . by God so that by exercising their proper function and being led by the spirit of the gospel they can work for the sanctification of the world from within, in the manner of leaven. In that way they can make Christ known to others, especially by the testimony of a life resplendent in faith, hope, and charity."[10] Indeed, the baptized are called to a "participation in the saving mission of the Church itself. Through their baptism and confirmation, all are commissioned to that apostolate by the Lord Himself. Moreover through the sacraments, especially the Holy Eucharist, there is communicated and nourished that charity toward God and human which is the soul of the entire apostolate."[11] All baptized persons are invited to recognize their gifts and devote these gifts to the good of the whole (1 Cor. 12). No wonder the first angelic

9. *Baptism, Eucharist and Ministry,* Faith and Order paper no. 11 (Geneva: World Council of Churches, 1982), 9.

10. *Dogmatic Constitution,* n. 31.

11. *Dogmatic Constitution,* n. 33.

assurance is "do not be afraid!" A response of "yes" commits followers to bold action as called for by God. The only response is readiness, willingness to go where led, and continual attention to God's initiating action.

Baptism: Trinitarian Mission and Missional Theology

Currently, many theologians are inviting new reflections on the Trinity, moving from a utilitarian emphasis toward a fundamentally relational understanding of the Trinity rooted in God's abundant love. This theological insight unites both our vocation and our call to God's love. Love operates as a verb that inevitably leads to service within the reign of God, a service that is justice-oriented.

In *The Holy Longing*, Ron Rolheiser, president of the Oblate School of Theology, amplifies these understandings with respect to the Christian church. He proposes that "the mission of the church is not to enlarge its membership, not to bring outsiders to accept its terms, but simply to love the world in every possible way — to love the world as God did and does." For Rolheiser, "the body of Christ is a network of organic connections between people, connections which make one's joy another's joy, one's suffering another's suffering."[12] As the Lima Document confirmed, those "baptized are pardoned, cleansed, and sanctified by Christ, and are given as part of their baptismal experience a new ethical orientation under the guidance of the Holy Spirit."[13]

Paul underscores this dynamic in what we know as his first letter to the Corinthians, where he first speaks of the variety of gifts (1 Cor. 12), which all come from baptism and are rooted in the Holy Spirit. Paul then appropriates the metaphor of the human body to offer an image of the Christian community. This metaphor depicts people using gifts for the good of the whole. It is a deep and substantive metaphor from which to build an ecology of missional leadership. In many ways, this ecology resembles the more contemporary vignette I related at the beginning of this section. For Paul's church and for the vignette church, leaders (lay and ordained) emerged to offer gifts of word, action, listening, interpreting, and

---

12. Ron Rolheiser, *The Holy Longing* (New York: Doubleday, 1999), 134.
13. *Baptism, Eucharist and Ministry*, n. 4.

wisdom, so as to foster a community of love that was patient, kind, and ever-expanding.

Within this basic construct of communal life, then, Paul articulates specific gifts that build up the body of Christ. Christian communities such as the one I depicted in the vignette cultivate gifts as contexts change. As Quaker theologian Parker Palmer has observed, "religion, like the public life, has to do with unity, with the overcoming of brokenness and fragmentation, with the reconciliation of that which has been estranged. The very root of the word religion means to 'rebind' or 'bind together,' so deep does this meaning go. Both 'the kingdom' and 'the public' are visions of human unity, so it would seem natural that they have something to do with one another."[14] The vignette congregation revealed a pastoral leadership that was committed to *rebinding* and reconciling both locally and globally. The pastor preached, led the assembly, and asked donors to put their funds where faith demanded. The lay leaders formed children, youth, and adults within the message of Christ. Lay and ordained together ensured that the group who ministered to others also participated in communal worship, theological reflection, and service.

These acts of binding or yoking are costly. As the gospels depict, love within the triune God cost Christ his earthly life.[15] Indeed, the earliest proclamations of the cross revealed the communities' attempts to reconcile their own expectations of glory with the humiliation and pain of the cross.[16] These texts universally demonstrate Jesus' warning of his disciples to expect similar fates.

One of the leaders in the vignette struggled with hopelessness, pain, and fear of death during his six-year solitary confinement in prison — just after the "liberation" by Ho Chi Minh and his followers. Subjected to torture, abandonment, and every kind of mental and physical cruelty, he survived by holding fast to his faith in Christ. Now he marvels at his release, his escape to the United States, his position as an ordained leader within his presbytery, and his privileged position as liaison and reconciler. His response to his baptism in the power of the Holy Spirit was to consider acts of justice and love that seem counterintuitive.

---

14. Parker Palmer, *The Company of Strangers* (New York: Crossroads, 1992), 87.

15. Mark particularly connects discipleship to the cross and baptism in Mark 8:34-38.

16. See esp. the hymn and the following reflection to the community at Philippi (Phil. 2).

During the June trip to Vietnam made by the vignette church, a room full of vowed religious women in Hue eagerly entered into Scripture study and dialogue. Using the Moses texts as recorded in Exodus, these faithful lay ministers reflected on how the biblical writer portrayed God as one who listened deeply, heard the cry of God's people, and responded out of care and compassion. One sister spoke eloquently of this great God who cared deeply, and she asserted her belief that God extended that kind of care to her and others. She encouraged the other sisters to respond in kind. A second sister, however, dared to differ. This faithful sister named her belief that the Israelites experienced God in this way, but she wondered aloud whether that same God heard the cry of the poor in Vietnam. Together, the group considered how they should carry the commitment to justice that proclaimed God's presence in the areas suffering most. However, like Moses and the pastoral associate in the vignette, they discovered together that God heard the cry of the poor and sent them to serve in God's name (Exod. 3:7-10).

Paul's profound reflection on the cost of discipleship and our response to God is at the heart of missional leadership or baptismal response. Paul challenged the community of believers at Philippi to "in humility regard others as better than yourselves" (Phil. 2:3). He urged them to look "not to [their] own interests, but to the interests of others" (Phil. 2:4). Through their baptism, they were committed to live new lives in Christ. With others in the community of faith, Paul insisted they allow "the same mind [to] be in [them] that was in Jesus Christ" (Phil. 2:5). He further exclaimed that the community ultimately become "obedient to God, even to death, that every tongue confess Jesus" in relation to the triune God (Phil. 2:6-11).

Paul continues that the Philippians' task is to "work out your own salvation with fear and trembling, for it is God who is at work in you, enabling you both to will and to work for God's pleasure" (Phil. 2:12b-13). He offered the community signs to recognize this response as from God: no murmuring or arguing with one another (Phil. 2:14); people poured out as a libation for the others (Phil. 2:17); joy in God (Phil. 4:4); gentleness (Phil. 4:5); God's imminence resulting in freedom from worry (Phil. 4:5); the peace of God surpassing all understanding (Phil. 4:7). He encouraged all to pray in supplication and thanksgiving. Throughout this passage, Paul summarizes my understanding of the theology and the signs of missional leadership.

Part Three: The School of Theology and Ministry Prepares Missional Leaders

The opening vignette depicted a single Christian congregation operating within an ecclesiastical context in a specific location (demonstrating aspects that both Van Gelder and Cormode discussed in preceding chapters). First, led by a senior pastor and a staff of ordained and lay persons, the members of the congregation witnessed faith to each other. Like the community in Philippi, they prayed together in supplication and thanksgiving, and they poured out their action toward working with God for justice in the world. Thus they participated as a whole in what it means to be missional: grounded in their baptism; taking action toward justice; reflecting theologically in specific relationship to reconciliation; redistributing resources, hospitality, worship, and outreach. Their response cost them their time, and it cost them both financial and psychological resources. The gospel, as preached in word and modeled in action, challenged members to rethink entire sets of assumptions about success, Christian baptismal response, and God's activity in their lives and in the lives of others. In other words, they entered into a discipling process that led individuals and the community to reframe their values and change their priorities. They embodied *metanoia,* or the process of turning ever more toward God and living God's desires in their lives.

Craig Van Gelder's introductory chapter documents the emergence of seminaries in the United States and their participation in responding to the needs of the church and world, as well as their impact on forming and educating the minister leaders. He offers six images of leadership that we have inherited from our traditions over the last three hundred years: resident theologian, gentleman pastor, churchly pastor, pastoral director, therapeutic pastor, and entrepreneurial leader.[17] Scott Cormode considers how the call and formation of ministerial leaders involves an entire process, which he calls an "ecology of leadership formation."[18] The opening vignette in this article reflects on a particular ecology and identifies a congregation within a social location that interacted with the newly emerging STM.

17. Van Gelder, "Theological Education and Missional Leadership Formation" (chap. 1 of this book).

18. Cormode, "Cultivating Missional Leaders" (chap. 4 of this book).

In this section of my chapter, I want to reflect particularly on the contribution of the seminaries or theological schools to the ecology of vocation. I consider these questions: What does seminary or theological education offer congregations — or the people of God? How is theological education conceived in this instance, and is it reflective of or does it contribute to educating and forming missional leaders? Using the STM as a case study, I explore elements of Van Gelder's eight issues for current theological education.[19] First, I examine the mission and grounds of the school itself as having a particular posture within theological education. Second, I identify strategies that represent a particular missional posture with respect to spiritual and ministerial formation, theological education, and leadership development. I conclude the section with summary observations.

Telos of Theological Education at the School of Theology and Ministry

The mission of the STM at Seattle University is that "with God's help and in partnership with the churches of the Pacific Northwest, educates and forms women and men leaders to serve, heal and challenge communities, churches and all creation."[20] From its inception, the STM embraced as its primary emphasis the preparation of people for the ministry of the baptized. Therefore, most of the structures and curriculum emerged from a commitment to develop laypeople for deeper, more intentional service to the community of believers and to the universe. This perspective eventually led the faculty to shape a curriculum that would support a diverse group of people preparing themselves for Christian leadership.

While the STM was formally begun in 1996, many precursors contributed to the curriculum development. Since 1969, the curriculum emphasized the integration of spiritual formation, theological education, and ministerial skills. Most of the first students, laypeople responding to their baptismal call, gathered for eight intensive weeks that included formal

19. See Van Gelder, chap. 1. These eight issues are: use of a school model; the fourfold curriculum; the theory/practice split; patterns of theological education (*paideia, Wissenschaft,* vocation); cultural plurality and diverse contexts; *telos;* content; and key external forces as they are reflected in the school's mission and implementation.

20. http://www2.seattleu.edu/stm/Inner.aspx?id=3416&linkidentifier=id&itemid=3416 (accessed Dec. 3, 2008).

classroom instruction, opportunity for personal and spiritual growth, intentional community worship and play, and residential life. Mostly Roman Catholic in its orientation, the early curriculum sought to incorporate the emerging theologies in the early aftermath of the Second Vatican Council.

Within a decade, the profound redefinition of the ministry of the baptized in the documents of that Ecumenical Council impacted the church's leadership in ways that were not anticipated. For instance, in 1965 the Center for Applied Research in America recorded a total of 58,632 priests active in ministry in the United States.[21] At the time of that documentation, no lay ecclesiastical ministers were recorded. By 1992, however, a new study of lay ministry in the United States reported the surprising phenomenon of 21,569 lay parish ministers.[22] Responding to the impact of these national trends — decreasing numbers of priests and increasing interest in ministry by the baptized — the Archdiocese of Seattle closed its seminary.

Anticipating further reductions in the number of ordained to serve the growing numbers of Roman Catholics in western Washington, the archdiocese initiated a study to determine what might help it educate and form new leaders for the church.[23] That effort suggested competencies that new leaders would have to demonstrate to meet the needs of the people of God. The archdiocese turned to Seattle University, a Jesuit institution, to collaborate in preparing lay ministers to lead in western Washington. Consequently, on December 8, 1985, Archbishop Raymond Hunthausen and Seattle University President William Sullivan entered into formal agreement to establish at the university the Institute for Theological Studies, the predecessor to the School of Theology and Ministry.

This innovative venture sought accreditation from the Association of Theological Schools and was granted full standing for its master's degrees in 1993. A consortium of Protestant, Episcopalian, and Unitarian leaders immediately entered into negotiations to expand the school to include seminary education for preparing ordained ministers. Thus, by 1996, the

21. Center for Applied Research in the Apostolate, Georgetown University, 2007. http://cara.georgetown.edu/ (accessed Dec. 3, 2008).

22. Philip Murnion, *New Parish Ministers: Laity and Religious on Parish Staff* (Cincinnati: St. Anthony, 1993).

23. Michael J. McDermott, ed., *Promoting Viable Faith Communities: A Planning Guide for Faith Communities, Deaneries, and the Archdiocese of Seattle* (Seattle: Catholic Archdiocese of Seattle, 1989).

STM had developed the capacity to form men and women for leadership as lay and ordained. This history suggests that the very foundation of the STM lies less in the need to prepare ordained persons for a specific ecclesiastical community and more in the school's purpose: to educate and form leaders to serve, heal, and challenge. While all parties valued an educational approach related to a university, they designed a response that sought to integrate the polarity of *Wissenschaft* and *paideia*. [24]

From the beginning, then, partnerships formed to prepare the baptized for a variety of leadership roles both in ecclesiastical contexts and in the universe. Based on that, traditional steps toward accredited education followed: a faculty emerged with expertise in specific theological fields; students were screened for their preparation within their ecology of vocation; and disciplines for instruction followed somewhat the classical divisions of history, systematic theology, Scripture, and praxis.

Within this structure, however, the evolving curriculum sought to develop a new kind of theological education, requiring all courses to integrate three emphases: theological reflection, ministerial skill, and spiritual/personal formation. Faculty members needed to demonstrate their academic excellence in keeping with the standards of a Jesuit university. Moreover, they engaged pastoral ministry as they developed pastoral skills and experience, as well as their own personal and spiritual depth. This emphasis on integration shaped the core, even as the school intentionally included people from eleven partnering ecclesiastical bodies and over twenty additional denominations.

As it differed, then, from the traditional emphasis of a separated, fourfold curriculum, the STM described its task as shaping Christian leaders who showed a deep relationship with the triune God in call and practice; lived with integrity out of a deep faith in God, with primary focus on the the life of Jesus as revealed in Scripture; and possessed a variety of skills to serve, heal, and challenge communities, churches, and the world. As the vignette showed, the school necessarily participated in a complex network of relationships with people, pastors, ecclesiastical judicatories, faculty, administrators, and the geographical context of the Pacific Northwest Rim.

In this context, the school showed aspects of the Western emphasis on the *sentness* of the church. The school aspired to develop leaders who

---

24. For an understanding of polarities, see Barry Johnson, *Polarity Management: Identifying and Managing Unsolvable Problems* (Amherst, MA: HRD Press, Inc., 1996).

would serve and challenge communities, churches, and the world. At the same time, the school stressed the *in-relation* aspect of the Eastern tradition.[25] They did so by inviting students and constituencies to enter into genuine nonhierarchical relationships with others, and to root their spiritual commitment in deep personal and communal worship and prayer.

This emphasis has allowed the school to thwart some of the restraints other institutions face in their need to cater to theological guilds, academic advancement, and division of theological disciplines. As the school expanded to include formal agreement with eleven ecclesial communities and culturally diverse constituencies, it argued that it was "doing something new" in the context of traditional professional ministerial education. That new something was always defined in terms of organic, integrative, communal language that moved people from interior conversion toward external mission.

Theory-Practice Integration: A Missional Approach

Cooperating with the mystery of God calling humans is not an exact science. Rather, good people, trying to become more like the people God is calling them to be, develop strategies for action as they enter into a process of learning and discernment that they hope will respond faithfully to God's activity. This faith process is filled with ambiguity and mystery.

Practically everyone writing about pastoral leadership argues that the pastoral leader must show a personal relationship with God. Many authors also insist that the leader integrate this relationship in observable ways.[26] These two competencies or fundamental requirements for missional leadership challenge the entire ecology of vocation to support, nurture, foster, and demand growth in these areas.

Unfortunately, academic institutions often rebel at trying to invest in something so unmeasurable, indefinable, and essentially nonacademic.

---

25. Craig Van Gelder, "How Missiology Can Help Inform the Conversation about the Missional Church in Context," in *The Missional Church in Context: Helping Congregations Develop Contextual Ministry*, ed. Craig Van Gelder (Grand Rapids: Eerdmans, 2007), 27-30.

26. Sharon Callahan, "Leadership in Ecclesial Contexts: Art and Competence," *Journal of Religious Leadership* 2, no.2 (2003): 47-90. In this article I develop the two main competencies of deep relationship to God and integrity by including references from multiple competency lists as well as a scan of relevant religious- and business-related literature.

However, from its inception, the STM drew on its Jesuit roots to support the processes of spiritual formation, discernment, and faith that does justice. Thus the STM implemented specific strategies to further cultivate these two fundamental leadership competencies: they required all students to participate in a variety of spiritual practices, which are offered both on and off campus. These practices address elements of *paideia,* or character formation; *Wissenschaft,* or research and knowledge; and, most of all, *vocation,* professional ministry preparation.[27]

Like Dorothy Bass, Craig Dykstra, and Miroslav Volf, who are writing prolifically about the process of nurturing spiritual practice, the STM incorporates the wisdom of the mystics into formation requirements. To this end, students must participate in required days of reflection and retreat; spiritual direction, or coaching, or counseling; and corporate worship. These processes help people identify and clarify their baptismal vocation, and they also assist students in developing their pastoral imaginations.

The Association of Theological Schools (ATS) incorporates such requirements into the accrediting standards for all theological schools and seminaries.[28] As Van Gelder indicates in his introductory chapter of this book, the accrediting body can recommend and assess because it is the voice of the bodies choosing to be governed by it. However, the questions remain: What can a school or seminary really do? What outcomes do they address? The STM does encourage students to develop a relationship with God and to integrate their spiritual lives in four ways: first, it strives to teach people a spirituality of attending; second, it invites people to develop personal spiritual practice; third, it insists that spiritual practice necessarily engages a person in community; fourth, it emphasizes strategies for lifelong discipleship.

Attending

The prophets called the faithful to open their eyes, ears, and hearts to receive God in their lives. Jesus often exclaimed, "Let those with eyes see and

---

27. See Van Gelder, chap. 1.

28. *Bulletin 47,* Part I, The Association of Theological Schools (Pittsburgh: The Commission on Accrediting, 2006), 192. This document states in Standard A.3.1.3 that the program related to the master of divinity degree "shall provide opportunities through which the student may grow in personal faith, emotional maturity, moral integrity, and public witness."

those with ears hear." L. Gregory Jones and Kevin R. Armstrong, both leaders in seminary education, argue that a "vocation, whether lay or ordained, is fundamentally a lifelong task of listening attentively and obediently to the prompting of God's Holy Spirit."[29]

Retreats, spiritual directors, daily prayer and worship — all these help open minds, ears, hearts, and wills to God's activity in life. Together they invite participants to reconnect with the love that is in all of God's expression. They equip the baptized to recognize God in their lives and in the lives of their communities. They prepare people to sustain their baptismal call even when, as in the case of the pastoral associate in our vignette and the vowed religious in Vietnam, God doesn't appear to be listening. As Thomas Merton warned, the person "who attempts to act and think for others or for the world without deepening his own self-understanding, freedom, integrity and capacity to love, will not have anything to give others. He will communicate to them nothing but the contagion of his own obsessions, his aggressiveness, his ego-centered ambitions, his delusions about ends and means, his doctrinaire prejudices and ideas."[30] Thus does the STM emphasize the lifelong task of forming self to God.

Spiritual Practices

It is particularly Luke's Gospel that describes Jesus drawing away for prayer (Luke 4:42; 5:16; 6:12; etc.). Jesus' stories show that he observes nature and reflects on it in terms of how it teaches about God. Jesus also seems to observe and speak to human personality and refers to the Spirit of God enlivening, healing, teaching, and empowering for service. He listens carefully to the words, actions, and hearts of speakers and responds to them as he hears them.

Dorothy Bass defines Christian practices as formative activities that "Christian people do together over time in response to and in light of God's active presence for the life of the world."[31] These activities, documented in the letters of Paul to the various Christian communities, in-

---

29. L. Gregory Jones and Kevin R. Armstrong, *Resurrecting Excellence: Shaping Faithful Christian Ministry* (Grand Rapids: Eerdmans, 2006), 103.

30. Thomas Merton, quoted by Danaan Parry, *Warriors of the Heart: A Handbook for Conflict Resolution* (Cooperstown, NY: Sun Publications, 1991), 89.

31. Jones and Armstrong, *Resurrecting Excellence,* 54, citing Dorothy Bass, ed., *Practicing Our Faith* (San Francisco: Jossey-Bass, 1997), 5.

clude individual prayer, praise, song, communal prayer, interpreting Scripture, and speaking and interpreting tongues. Jones and Armstrong propose that these practices also include hospitality, forgiveness, and creating and caring for institutions. They contend that these additional practices open people up to better recognize the work of God in themselves, others, and the world.

Yet, in contemporary pastoral life, our baptismal *sent-ness* often equals busy-ness. Thomas Merton warns about this trap when he says that "there is a pervasive form of contemporary violence to which the idealist fighting for peace by nonviolent methods most easily succumbs: activism and overwork. The rush and pressure of modern life . . . destroys the fruitfulness of his own work, because it kills the root of inner wisdom which makes work fruitful."[32]

In light of this temptation to the violence of busy-ness, STM sets aside days for reflection and communal prayer; it teaches and fosters practices of discernment; and it invites people to understand their gifts and limits. As Episcopalian priest Eric Law says, returning people to their core experience of the liberating action of God requires ongoing connection to the Scripture texts accompanied by worship.[33] These times away help students experience the Western *sent-ness,* which they can balance with the Eastern emphasis on *perichoresis,* or indwelling.

Community

Next, the school intentionally fosters networks to support people in their ministries. Jesus called disciples and sent them out two by two (Mark 6:7). Paul set up house churches and left groups of people to lead them. Since missional leadership is rooted in the Trinitarian relationship, these images of collaborative discipleship necessarily impact leadership models.

These collaborative models of leadership challenge current U.S. dominant culture ideas of community. For example, the most recent DeLambo study of Roman Catholic lay ministry found that dioceses, regions, and deaneries often offer systems of support, but fewer than half of the lay min-

---

32. Thomas Merton, quoted by Parry, *Warriors of the Heart,* 41.

33. See Eric Law's many books, which include forms of Scripture sharing, information dissemination, and worship activities. Some examples may be found in *The Wolf Shall Dwell with the Lamb* (St. Louis: Chalice, 1993), *The Bush Was Blazing but Not Consumed* (St. Louis: Chalice, 1996), and *Sacred Acts, Holy Change* (St. Louis: Chalice, 2002).

isters avail themselves of the support.[34] Similarly, the Lilly Foundation recently offered significant grants to ecclesiastical bodies, congregations, and schools for the purpose of sustaining pastoral excellence. After five years of work among over sixty institutional grant recipients, the results indicated the most significant contribution of the grant was to create opportunities for pastoral leaders to work with each other. These findings further demonstrate that the era of the "lone pastor" attempting to meet the chaplain-type needs of the members of a congregation is fading.[35]

Building on the research connected with this pastoral excellence effort, Jones and Armstrong cite similar findings in the 2001 Pulpit and Pew national survey. They report that pastoral leaders considered "loneliness and isolation" to be the "single greatest predictor of overall dissatisfaction among Protestants and Catholics [pastoral leaders]."[36] They lamented the failure of schools and seminaries to prepare people by establishing patterns of networking and collaboration among ministers.

Working through its curriculum, both formal and informal, the STM fosters spiritual formation and skill practices that engage students in forming strategies of collaboration and network-building. In addition, students discover methods of listening to others that lead them to compassion and action for the community of believers. They apply critical social analysis to their communities of faith and discover obstacles to embodying the beloved community that was envisioned by Paul and written about by many. The school's emphasis on multicultural and ecumenical theology and practice challenges students, staff, and faculty to always increase circles of inclusion so that the unity of baptism (Ephesians, Galatians, Colossians, Romans) draws ecclesiastical communities together in service of the gospel toward living in confidence of the imminent reign of God.[37]

Theological Integration

As Van Gelder outlined in his analysis of education for ministerial leadership (chap. 1 above), seminaries and schools historically emphasized theological preparation for ministry. The accreditation standards of the Associ-

---

34. David DeLambo, *Lay Parish Ministers: A Study of Emerging Leadership* (New York: National Pastoral Life Center, 2005), 114.

35. Sustaining Pastoral Excellence Project: Conference Findings (August 2007).

36. Jones and Armstrong, *Resurrecting Excellence,* 74.

37. Eric Law, *Inclusion: Making Room for Grace* (St. Louis: Chalice, 2000), 42.

ation of Theological Schools (ATS) simply outlined "theological areas to be covered in the curriculum."[38] When faculty and administrators of theological schools and seminaries developed their curricular content, these vague standards often guided their choices. They reflected the fourfold curriculum initiated by the first seminaries in the United States. There are key questions that need to be addressed concerning these guidelines and their implementation for school curricula by accrediting agencies like the ATS.

In fairly postmodern terms, the STM often described its process of education as one of deconstruction and reconstruction. Accordingly, it expected students to alter core understandings of God, self, and the world through the education process. The Hebrew Scripture faculty often taught students that when one encounters God, one also encounters a particular worldview and person-view. As any dimension changes (God-view, person-view, or worldview), they all change.[39] In some ways, these shifts evolved from, reformed, and then reshaped various ecclesiologies, some of which are more missional than others.

In the late twentieth century, Catholic theologian Avery Dulles delineated six models of church based on his understanding of the tension between form (institution) and dynamism (spirit).[40] Dulles declared that each image emphasized specific aspects that ecclesiastical communities

38. *Bulletin 47*, ATS, Sections A.3.1-A.3.1.2.2, 191-192. These standards include: Scripture; broad historical heritage of the Christian tradition as well as specific understanding of a particular ecclesiastical tradition; exploration of varying cultural contexts and their significance for ministry; and global, multicultural, and cross-cultural nature of ministry in the U.S. and other contemporary settings.

39. Prof. James Eblen of the Scripture faculty teaches this in every introduction course in Hebrew Scriptures. Other members of the faculty often draw on this in their own teaching; it is related in content to many scholars' work.

40. Avery Dulles, *A Church To Believe In: Discipleship and the Dynamics of Freedom* (New York: Crossroad, 1982), and *Models of the Church* (Garden City, NY: Doubleday, 1974). This tension can be seen as related to the polarities Paul Tillich describes in *Systematic Theology*, vols. 1 and 2 (Chicago: University of Chicago, 1951, 1957). Recently I taught these models to a graduating group of master of divinity students to engage them in identifying their own emphases and their theology of pastoral leadership as it related to their ecclesiology. Our systematic theologian, Rev. Mike Raschko, observed my class session in the formal faculty "peer review" process for rank promotion and tenure. He was intrigued by the congruence between my class that week and his segment on Tillich's polarities in the foundational systematic theology course he was teaching that week, Oct. 10, 2007. Our own conversation increased our collaboration, and the insights impacted the content of our synthesis year, so that our students reaped the benefit of our work together.

embraced. More recently, Craig Van Gelder has challenged theologians and practitioners to rethink ecclesiology and missiology by combining insights from the two disciplines so that each is informed by the other.[41] Both Dulles and Van Gelder consider aspects that connect baptized believers with a community of faith; both contend that the church is to participate in God's mission in the world. These authors propose complementary and different God-views, person-views, and worldviews.

Van Gelder claims that missiology focuses on "how to proclaim the gospel and grow the church in different cultural contexts." He pays attention to such matters as "mission theology, world religions, cross-cultural communication, training missionaries, mission methods, church planting, and evangelism. All of this is framed in light of the mission of the Triune God in the world" (*Essence,* p. 25). He suggests that ecclesiology, on the other hand, "focuses on understanding the church in terms of its nature, ministry, and organization. Attention is given to such matters as biblical and theological foundations, historical ecclesiologies (different views of the church in different periods of time), and church polity (how different churches have been organized). All of this is related to God's redemptive purposes in the world" (pp. 25-26).

Van Gelder goes on to explain that "those who start with a theology of the church and proceed to mission usually make mission a functional task of the church . . . (where) the church is viewed in institutional terms, with mission being one of several tasks the church undertakes on God's behalf." In contrast, "those who start with a theology of mission and proceed to the church usually approach the church as something developed through the work of missionaries . . . . This perspective often fails to incorporate an adequate understanding of the historical existence of the institutional church." Furthermore, he argues, the ecclesiology that understands church as missional by its nature assists learners and leaders in rethinking mission in terms of Trinitarian theology (pp. 25-26).

Van Gelder proposes a God-view rooted in Trinitarian relationship. STM connects people's God-views to their worldviews and seeks to integrate their experience in ministry and leadership with their ongoing reflection on God's work in life. Every faculty member participates in some kind of pastoral work and strives to connect this work with the theologies being

41. Van Gelder, *The Essence of the Church: A Community Created by the Spirit* (Grand Rapids: Baker Books, 2000), 25.

studied. Fundamentally, the school purports to prepare people who can think theologically, act with integrity, and work toward justice. Faculty members attempt to model this integration even as they teach aspects of it in a differentiated curriculum.

Just as Paul encouraged the Philippians to embrace Jesus' sacrifice (Phil. 2:5), so the STM eventually must educate and form women and men as leaders who, with God's help, impact the entire universe through their actions. Most important, the school itself must image itself as a collaborative venture that relies on the triune God and collaborates with the ecology of vocation.

Leadership Development

The ATS accreditation standards require that all seminaries address the "capacity for ministerial and public leadership." Within this broad category, the standards further specify that the curriculum include: theological reflection; education for the practice of ministry within supervised ministry settings; constructive relationship between the practice of ministry courses and other courses in the curriculum; and leadership experience in congregations, as well as broader public contexts.[42]

While many authors emphasize multiple essential competencies for effective missional leaders, in this section I focus on those most attended to by the STM. DeLambo's recent study of Roman Catholic lay ministry delineates twenty-two specific ministry skills that lay parish ministers agreed were essential to their ministries.[43] The overall emphasis on administration, conflict negotiation, and chaplain-related skills suggested that the ecclesiology of the churches these ministers served relied on maintaining structures and values that were already entrenched. As Van Gelder shows (in chap. 1 above), these skills equip ministers to be combinations of all four previous historical moments in pastoral preparation. The question now is: How does the STM prepare missional leaders?

The STM provides classroom activities and leadership opportunities for the student body, as well as supervised internship placements. Theological reflection groups require weekly writing — giving and receiving feedback — and they connect people's experience to their evolving theology.

---

42. *Bulletin 47*, ATS, Section A.3.1.4, p. 193.
43. DeLambo, *Lay Parish Ministers*, 83.

Students enter a disciplined pattern of lived integration over twenty-seven weeks, in which the primary question is: Where is God in the midst of this?

Additional courses in leading small communities, cross-cultural ministry, immersion experiences in global contexts, preaching to culturally diverse groups, leading worship, and leading change additionally equip these students to "serve, challenge, and heal communities, churches and the universe" when they graduate. Increasingly, social analysis of specific locations situated in global contexts challenges people to consider a sea change occurring in the United States.[44] As every aspect of life struggles to adapt to multiple perspectives, the Christian church in the Pacific Northwest Rim finds itself losing influence in its traditional constituencies. Indeed, as Patricia Killen observes, people widely share the view that religious institutions are social utilities providing social services.[45]

Yet, as the opening vignette depicted, an upper-middle-class, dominant-culture congregation thrives and grows under the leadership of a pastoral team that preaches the gospel in the context of missional leadership. In their vocational ecology they invite and encourage young people and older adults to engage with a wide variety of experiences for encountering the other, where they expand the physical borders of their water-surrounded location to more permeable communal borders that ultimately extend to the entire world. The relational-team leadership approach allowed them to succeed in this endeavor because it embodies the newly emerging emphasis on interdependent or collaborative leadership. To accomplish this, the senior pastor limited his use of power and control, and he was supported in this effort by the entire staff and congregation. Together, lay and ordained leaders contributed their gifts toward equipping all the congregants for participation in God's reign. This mission reflected both the Western emphasis on being sent to proclaim and live the good news and the Eastern emphasis of recognizing and living with the Spirit dwelling in the community of believers.

As faculty members from the school interacted with the people of the congregation, they also participated in the healing, reconciling extension of God's Trinitarian love to those separated by ideology, geography, economic

44. A simple perusal of the daily newspaper leads one to recognize each of these in the Pacific Northwest Rim context. For a *global* view of these and other implications for the contemporary social context, see Thomas Friedman, *The World is Flat* (New York: Farrar, Strauss and Giroux, 2005).

45. Killen and Shibley, "Surveying the Religious Landscape," 13.

status, or ecclesiastical affiliation. Their collaborative leadership style designed the original curriculum and constantly renews it within the changing context. An outside consultant to the school's staff once described the whole school as alternating an outside reach with an internal contemplation. As Dwight Zscheile recently noted for a group of religious leadership faculty, the leadership called forth by the Trinity through baptism includes this same outward-reaching, generative movement *(ekstasis)*, which simultaneously draws all creation into divine communion through Christ.[46] Together, these outward and inward dynamics create the kind of *koinonia* Paul describes specifically in 1 Corinthians 12–14, but which he also uses throughout his letters to various communities. Grounded in this understanding, leadership development insists on both movements.

Margaret Wheatley articulates this very notion with respect to leadership. She says that new understandings of the laws of the universe have evoked new emphases in leadership skill development. Like STM, Wheatley calls for a return to the art of *autopoesis,* or self-knowing, an art that centers the person or organization in its own identity. The previously described emphases on attending, spiritual practices, and theological reflection represent curricular responses to help develop this critical inward dynamic. Wheatley also suggests that the universe and all elements of it are closely related. Thus, she says, connections between what were previously thought to be separate entities are the fundamental elements of all creation.[47] Speaking of the shifts in leadership that these insights demand, she further argues that leadership must change its fundamental emphasis on individual power toward facilitating processes that increase power of influence through communal relationships.

This unbroken wholeness, described by quantum science and linked to leadership by Wheatley, resonates with that unity in diversity that Paul so profoundly theologized in 1 Corinthians 12–14. In other words, to form and educate missional leaders, schools, congregations, and leadership teams, we must attend to the connectivity of the Spirit, the unity of matter, the very bond of baptism that our theologies proclaim.

46. Dwight Zscheile, "The Trinity: Leadership and Power," a presentation to the Academy of Religious Leadership, May, 2007. Power-point slide 15 (citing John 1, 2 Cor. 5, and Col. 1). This presentation has been published as an article, "The Trinity: Leadership and Power," *Journal of Religious Leadership* 6, no.2 (2007): 43-65.

47. Margaret J. Wheatley, *Leadership and the New Science* (San Francisco: Berrett-Koehler, 1992), 18.

Conclusion

As our biblical faculty members so aptly declare to every student entering STM, our God-images are related to our self-images, which are related to our world-images. The reintegration of Trinitarian God-images suffuses our understanding of God as being relational, as one who creates in love. Love necessarily relishes the one who is loved in an internal residing in the presence of the loved, while compelling the lovers to generate new life out of that love. If we are caught in that love as God's creation, we are compelled to generate life out of love. This movement necessarily involves us in relating to others and to the world, to reconciling and repairing brokenness, and to moving toward increased unity in the midst of unique diversity.

Edward P. Hahnenberg has observed that ordained leaders serve as catalysts and coordinators of diversely gifted members of a believing community.[48] Similarly, theologian Thomas O'Meara has said this: "The leaders of the local churches, bishop and presbyter, find their identities in leadership, but this leadership is not purely administrative or liturgical. . . . The pastor directs Christians through enabling them in their own ministries — that leadership is expressed in preaching and made manifest in leading the eucharistic liturgy."[49] These two theologians call for a renewed leadership of all the baptized. They urge the church to move from the Christologically centered approaches of earlier centuries toward a Trinitarian emphasis that makes ministry fundamentally relational.

Our opening vignette depicts a single example of this: an embodied Trinitarian theology being practiced through missional leadership. STM engages with many churches and denominations throughout the Pacific Northwest as it attempts to educate and form women and men to lead the communities toward justice and to participate in the reign of God. As theological schools and seminaries, including the STM, integrate these theologies and new leadership approaches into their practice and curriculum, they may come to cooperate more fully in an ecology of vocation that is preparing missional leaders for communities, churches, and the world in the twenty-first century.

48. Edward P. Hahnenberg, *Ministries: A Relational Approach* (New York: Crossroad, 2003), 75.

49. Thomas F. O'Meara, *Theology of Ministry,* rev. ed. (New York: Paulist, 1999), 12.

CHAPTER 6

Vision-Discerning vs. Vision-Casting: How Shared Vision Can Raise Up Communities of Leaders Rather than Mere Leaders of Communities

Dave Daubert

Introduction

A pastor recently wrote me to share his dilemma about working in a struggling congregation. He had been there only a short time when he learned that the congregation had already been in trouble before he arrived. However, his operating assumption — and that of most members of the congregation — was that if he was the right leader for the job, then he should just fix it. Both he and they had internalized this reality from many sources: life experience in the church, seminary education, professional role models, and the expectations that laity had placed on the pastor in previous experiences.[1]

As he struggled to make sense of the mess they were in, he sent me the statement he gave to the congregational leaders:

> You as the council have responsibilities, and that begins by realizing that the office of the pastor means something in the Lutheran tradition, and I am the pastor of this congregation. I have authority that you do not, and I am called to discern vision for the spiritual life and direction of the congregation, and that is just the way it is, whether you like it or not.[2]

1. See Scott Cormode, "Cultivating Missional Leaders" (chap. 4 above), for a discussion of this point.

2. This thought process is not unusual when vision in a community is gone. It often

I am not quoting from this statement to cast blame on the pastor. After I received that letter, I followed up by meeting with him. I consider him to be a friend, and I consider him an asset to the church's work. He is truly committed and is trying to do his best to make a difference. I know that he believes the church exists to be useful to God. But his "mental model" of leadership and vision hindered his ability to live that out effectively in the context of his congregation.[3]

When I spoke with him, it became clear that, deep inside, he knew that he didn't believe what he said in that statement. It was merely his fallback position in the crisis of working in a dysfunctional system that had lost vision. He assumed that vision only comes from a person who holds a position of power by virtue of an office, rather than vision being possible as the result of the power of the Holy Spirit poured out on the community. His mistaken understanding was that, if the congregation is smart, the members will align themselves with the pastor's vision and be made well once again.

That is the concept that I seek to challenge in this chapter. I propose an alternative approach, one that is grounded in discerning vision by way of dialogue among the majority rather than by having a vision cast by a strong individual. The process I am discussing here has been developed over the past six years through work that has involved the Transformational Ministry Team of the Evangelical Lutheran Church in America and its work with teams of congregational leaders.[4]

I am challenging the supposition that vision is something held in trust only by effective leaders. I propose to lay a foundation for an alternative way of building communities of leaders who work together to discern and cast a vision. These communities find ways of working that are communal in nature, are grounded in a missional commitment at their core, and are able to replicate and create new ministries that are continuous and consistent with their missional character. At the same time, leadership in

---

leads to the placing of unrealistic expectations on pastors by both laity and the pastors themselves. In addition, as you can sense in this letter, power to enforce vision and compliance based on office rather than engagement with the vision itself is assumed. If a congregation has lost its way, the way back to the right road is often assumed to be someone in authority with an idea, someone who is also strong enough to wrestle it back on track.

3. Cormode, "Cultivating Missional Leaders."

4. For more information, see: http://archive.elca.org/outreach/renew/abouttransformation.html (accessed Dec. 3, 2008).

these communities is more egalitarian and more broadly owned than what is often modeled in numerous other leadership patterns.

The Systemic Nature of the Problem

Confusion about this issue is systemic. In the denomination I serve, the Evangelical Lutheran Church in America, we believe in communal identity and leadership in our work. Yet we often speak to leaders in ways that seek to build their self-esteem, doing so out of the notion that a significant ministry will require an excellent (usually ordained) leader. The assumption is that these leaders are special and have unique abilities that most persons don't have. Many of us hold an underlying belief, which is still operative, that is often expressed this way: "We believe that only about 5 percent of our leaders can do this work [new church development or congregational redevelopment]."[5]

This mind-set is grounded primarily in the "Great Man" theory often credited to Thomas Carlyle.[6] This is not to deny the important role that key individuals can play. But the sense of that kind of leadership casting a vision and simply having people follow seems rare; furthermore, it is a poor model for congregations to try to pursue in order to be useful to God. The fact that we still work this way reveals an underlying belief in the Great Man (or Woman) theory that is partly responsible for this problem. In this sense, the church has failed to check its prevailing practice against Scripture and its own theology.

In the renewal work that I engage in, it is likely that most congregations have few people who are gifted in this special way. This is especially

---

5. I must confess that, even though I don't believe that this 5 percent figure is relevant, helpful, or even accurate, I found myself still mentioning it in some settings, in fact, even after I was sure that it was a bad paradigm for leadership and vision for the church. That is, though I have now stopped saying this to new leaders, I found that I had stopped believing it before I stopped saying it.

6. Thomas Carlyle was a Scottish philosopher who interpreted the rural-to-urban shift during the Industrial Revolution. His insights were grounded in the rise of wealthy industrial leaders, whom he viewed as strong individual leaders ("great men"). For a good summary treatment of Carlyle's work and life, see Michael Moran, "Thomas Carlyle," *Encyclopedia of Philosophy,* ed. Donald Borchert, vol. 2, 2nd ed. (Farmington Hills, MI: Thomas Gale, 2006), 32-35.

true in declining congregations where vision has been weak or missing for long periods of time. The median size of a worshiping community within the Evangelical Lutheran Church in America is 97 persons (those who attend worship every week). Seventy-eight percent of these worshiping communities have a low or moderate sense of openness to change in their purpose.[7] If visionary leaders were once present, their impact was minimal; they often became disillusioned and went elsewhere in search of a place where vision and engagement were welcomed and encouraged. To assume that vision means "someone gets it and tells us what it is" is to say that these congregations can only renew if a visionary person can be identified and convinced to come from the outside and restore vision to them.

Within the ELCA and other denominations, we use a process known as "behavioral interviewing." It is a process of exploring the previous behaviors of a person based on the premise that the best predictor of future behavior is past behavior. The assumption is that there are certain characteristics of effective missional leaders, one of which is referred to as "visioning capacity." Two aspects of visioning capacity are the ability to "project a vision into the future beyond the present" and the ability then to "persuasively sell it to other people."[8] I do not wish to completely reject these abilities; but they are too often assumed to reside primarily within individuals and to represent the "knockout factors" in our process: if you don't have them, then mission development and redevelopment is not for you.

I agree that leaders need to be able to be in touch with and communicate the vision: because a pastor's role is centered in preaching, his or her ability to communicate the vision is certainly important. In most systems this is fundamentally assumed to be part of the pastor's job — for good or ill. But I wish to challenge the notion that the pastor needs to be the one to see the vision before most others do. It is my premise that *only in community* is it possible for this work to be done with any real *integrity*.

---

7. Kenneth Inskeep, executive director of the ELCA Department of Research and Evaluation, provided these statistics in his presentation at the Southwest California Synod Transformational Ministry Conference, Sept. 2005.

8. Charles Ridley and Robert Logan, *Training for Selection Interviewing* (St. Charles, IL: ChurchSmart, 1998), 92.

Jesus' Ministry: Engaging the Present

Jesus began his ministry in the Gospel of Mark with these words: "The time is fulfilled, and the kingdom of God has come; repent, and believe in the good news" (Mark 1:15).[9] Despite the fact that the reign of God was at hand when Jesus arrived on the scene, apparently it was not always easy to see. He had to announce it over and over. Many still saw only brief glimpses or missed it altogether. Frustrated by the inability of people to recognize the work of God in the present, Jesus said, "Do you have eyes, and fail to see? Do you have ears, and fail to hear?" (Mark 8:18). It was vision in the present tense that Jesus was most concerned about in his ministry.

The impact for our work here is that our eschatology informs vision. While I want to recognize the tension and the truth of the "already and not yet" aspects of eschatology, it seems that Jesus comes to emphasize the "already" aspect of this in a world where it is often so easily missed.[10] The tendency is to think of eschatology (and with it, "vision") primarily as something off in the future. But the radical call of Jesus was to recognize the reign of God that is already breaking in on us in the present. Jesus' attitude toward the future was that we are to trust God for it. This is clearly the case in his response to the disciples' question about the future of Israel (Acts 1:7-8): rather than helping them see the future, he was more concerned with conveying to them the kind of eyes with which the power of the Holy Spirit enables us to see regarding what we are to be doing in the present. Jesus prepares us to look out into the present world in which we find ourselves being sent in order to bear witness to what God in Jesus is up to now.

A Missional Starting Point

There has been increased attention to the mission of God in the U.S. church as it has struggled to adapt to changing conditions in the culture. This attention has been caused by many factors, many of them misplaced

9. All Bible quotations are from the New Revised Standard Version (Nashville: Thomas Nelson, 1996).

10. Herman Ridderbos, *The Coming of the Kingdom,* trans. H. De Jongste (Philadelphia: Presbyterian and Reformed, 1976), 104-84.

motives that primarily find their source in systemic and institutional anxiety. Even Mark Hanson, the presiding bishop of the Evangelical Lutheran Church in America (ELCA) has taken to joking that ELCA stands for "Expectations Low — Climbing Anxiety."[11] Missional concerns are not so much about the *missio Dei*, but about keeping the ship afloat.

In spite of this anxiety, there is much to celebrate in the missional thinking of the church and its impact on ministry. Lesslie Newbigin helped the church wrestle with a recovery of domestic mission in the Western world, which had long assumed that it was and would always be Christian, a worldview in which it was generally assumed that mission was somewhere else. In *The Finality of Christ,* Newbigin expresses it in a particularly helpful way:

- The reign of God has come near in Jesus;
- To accept it means to be able to understand and direct all of your action — both public and private;
- There is an apostolic fellowship of those who are already committed and at work;
- This is the call to you to life commitment.[12]

This reminds us that the work of Jesus is to bring the reign of God as an expression of God's commitment to the work of redeeming all creation. Belief in this truth confronts human beings with a life-changing reality for all who believe that this is not just a dream but rather is the reality that has come near in Jesus.

This transformation is the charge to be disciples, both communally and individually, and to be committed and at work in a world in which the reign of God has come near in Jesus. The choices that communities and individuals make when the work of Jesus is their foundation will be directed by a different set of values from those made by people without this faith. This directs the community's public actions and the individual's private actions, and this also forms a community that is at work because of this re-

11. Mark Hanson used this phrase in several talks during 2007, including at the ELCA Churchwide Assembly in Chicago, Aug. 6-11, 2007. It is important to note that Bishop Hanson uses this humor to name the anxiety and to relate it to the low expectations in hopes of engaging people to be more serious about their commitment to mission and to higher expectations of effectiveness in the church.

12. Lesslie Newbigin, *The Finality of Christ* (London: SCM Press, 1969), 57.

ality. To "accept it . . . is to direct all your action"; it is thus behavioral by definition.[13]

A key to discerning vision is the assumption held by Christians that the reign of God is a defining reality. Within God's reign, pointed to and embodied in the ministry and person of Jesus, is the ultimate vision for humanity and for all of creation. Participation in the mission of God is a commitment to the content of this reign in the present — the church serving as a foretaste of what is to come.

Martin Luther, in his *Small Catechism,* sees the reign of God as a promise on which the Christian life rests and for which the Christian life longs. He says: "To be sure, the kingdom of God comes of itself, without our prayer, but we pray in this petition that it may also come to us."[14] Here we see two key elements of Luther's contribution to mission. The first is the confident assumption that the *missio Dei* is a given — and a successful one at that. We do not hope that the reign of God will come; we *trust* that it is so. But Luther held a second insight in tension with the first: he understood that we pray for the kingdom because we know that it is a coming reality, and that we desire to participate in it and not to miss it. We want the kingdom to also come to us.

Walter Brueggemann, in *Mandate to Difference,* makes a strong case that the only vision that matters is the one that is witnessed to in Scripture and revealed in Christ. In reflecting on the work of Jesus and the vision already pointed to in the Psalms, he urges his audience to "go deep into the vision of the psalm(s) concerning a new governance, a new heaven, and a new earth . . . to bring your life and our common life more fully in response to this regime."[15] The vision that God gives is the only one that ultimately matters in the life of the church and the world. Our task is to seek to bring our lives into alignment with it on a daily basis.

One thing that this means is that the church will necessarily need to define its values as well as operate from the vision God has laid before us of the new heaven and new earth. These images and values may often conflict with the dominant cultural values of the society in which the church finds itself. This is no easy proposition. As Diana Butler Bass noted when she left

13. Newbigin, *Finality,* 57.

14. T. G. Tappert, *The Book of Concord: The Confessions of the Evangelical Lutheran Church* [Small Cat.: III, 7-8] (Philadelphia: Fortress, 2000).

15. Walter Brueggemann, *Mandate to Difference: An Invitation to the Contemporary Church* (Louisville: Westminster John Knox, 2007), 6.

a congregation that she believed was simply too grounded in the values of the surrounding culture, "I needed to be part of a community that understood the difference between the City of God and the City of Man."[16]

J. C. Hoekendijk was a Dutch theologian who shared a radical vision of a renewed church for a new time. Two critical insights in his work are these: "The professional churchman can in general no longer be the best-suited organ for the apostolate," and "The organs of the apostolate will have to distanciate themselves as far as possible from everything that looks 'churchly.'"[17] Despite the criticism that Hoekendijk's ecclesiology is being lost in his commitment to send people into a secular world, he still has important insights and challenges for the church today.

I am a bi-vocational pastor: I work as a church executive for my full-time living, and I work in a congregation as a part-time lead pastor with a team of lay staff people, all of whom are also part-time workers. The images of clergy who equip laity — and of laypeople who are the primary apostolic missionaries — are essential ones for me. But what is striking is Hoekendijk's assertion that the clergy are placed in the church system in a place where their apostolic effectiveness is in question, and that apostolicity will be the work of the laity *almost exclusively* — as they serve as missionaries in this new day. I take this to mean that (1) laypeople need to be better equipped theologically for mission; (2) they need to be given practices and a framework within which to make decisions in a world that may not share their values and priorities; and (3) they need to be able to discern how best to serve as intentional, conscious instruments of God in the various places to which they are sent.

Hoekendijk saw this as redefining the work of the church. If the work of the church was to appeal to what he called "the middle class man" in the old way of working, then today's church will have to redefine itself more clearly and do so on theological and missional grounds rather than simply copying what he called "the bourgeois pattern of church life." He perceived that the Western church was too similar to the elitist patterns of the surrounding culture and that its images and roles have been too uniformly patterned with this assumption at their root. Rather than drawing from God's vision of the reign of God, the church has simply looked to the aspirations of

16. Diana Butler Bass, *Broken We Kneel* (San Francisco: John Wiley and Sons, 2004), 112.

17. J. C. Hoekendijk, *The Church Inside Out* (Philadelphia: Westminster, 1964), 54.

the dominant culture for its direction. Hoekendijk proposed a "post-bourgeois" church where ministry and leadership are engaged in more life-changing ways and where discipleship is not only an outcome of mission but the primary means for witness and engagement with the world (p. 55).

If Hoekendijk is correct, the values held by this new kind of church will often be in tension with the values of those held by the culture around it. One example of this can be seen in a common tension in church pension matters: some clergy members threaten to sue over the church's investing funds in socially conscious investments if the return might be even slightly lower than that of less ethical investments. Values clarification (and accountability) is thus an essential function that leadership must make sure takes place for a ministry to function effectively in this new day.

Much has been written about the Trinitarian nature of the mission of God and its purpose for the church. We owe much to David Bosch for his helpful way of stating this clearly: "[T]he classical doctrine of the *missio dei* as God the Father sending the Son, and God the Father and the Son sending the Spirit was expanded to include yet another 'movement': Father, Son and Holy Spirit sending the church into the world."[18]

It is now generally agreed that it is God who has both a mission and a church: the church is in service of the sending mission of a Trinitarian God, who fulfills that sending character by coming in Jesus and then entrusting the Holy Spirit to humankind and sending people forth in mission to participate in the service of God's mission to "bless and save the world."[19] This is essential as the long-thought mission to send for saving is augmented to remind the church that it also exists to bless the world. The church needs to see that it is an extension of God's own Trinitarian character to be a community that shows care and concern for all people and all of the creation that God has made.

Finally, if the work of the Holy Spirit is to bring power and to send God's people forth in mission to love their neighbors and to bear witness to what God is doing in Jesus Christ, then the giving of that same Spirit is instructive to our work. Of great significance is the Pentecost event: the Holy Spirit rested upon many people from many places, and they began to speak

18. David J. Bosch, *Transforming Mission: Paradigm Shifts in Theology of Mission* (Maryknoll, NY: Orbis, 1991), 390.

19. This quote is from Kelly Fryer's presentation in South Carolina Synod, Columbia, SC, Sept. 5, 2007.

and be heard in the languages of their audience. The result was both amazement and confusion. In explaining this, Peter quoted from the book of Joel:

> In the last days it will be, God declares,
> that I will pour out my Spirit upon all flesh,
> and your sons and your daughters shall prophesy,
> and your young men shall see visions,
> and your old men shall dream dreams.
> Even upon my slaves, both men and women,
> in those days I will pour out my Spirit;
> and they shall prophesy. (Acts 2:17-18)

This text opens up the work of the Holy Spirit to include "all flesh." Males and females, young and old, slaves and free — all are to be included in giving voice to God's work in the world. If there was ever a sense that only a few should plan, articulate, and shape the actions of the many, with the coming of the Holy Spirit that day was gone. Although it will take until the fulfillment of the reign of God for the church to fully embody this reality, everyone gets a voice in God's economy. This is not simply based on humanistic egalitarianism. Rather, it is grounded in the nature of the Spirit to work in and use anyone and everyone for God's mission in the world.

To summarize the impact of the above reflections on our work here, it is clear that the call for the church to be missional and to participate in what God is doing is firmly established in the theological foundations of the church. The following conclusions are critical for taking our next steps forward: (1) the horizon is the world; (2) we must be grounded in Jesus; (3) we are a called community; (4) involving the laity is crucial; and (5) we must rely on the leading of the Spirit.

Contrast this perspective to the common view that vision is primarily not about the direction of our looking (which is out), but that it is primarily preoccupied with time (trying to look forward). It is my contention that this way of looking out more than looking forward is more accessible to the majority of church members and also is more faithful to the primary witness of Jesus, who emphasized engaging the world and God's action in the present. To do so will result in a vision that will emerge and unfold in front of the watchful eyes of those who have eyes to see. This way of a community sharing in the discernment of the vision now opens up leadership to become a community responsibility rather than a task for a select few.

The Importance of Communal Processes: Theoretical Perspectives

My journey in this direction started when I heard Walter Brueggemann lecture on preaching. My view of communication and involvement in the parish was radically changed when he said this: "It all begins with utterance which invokes real conversations among the faithful, and that leads to mission."[20] The move to assume that mission requires conversation was a radical insight. It is not the pastor's job to announce the last word (the vision and goals); rather, the pastor is called to announce the first word (God's) and to foster a conversation where people own, process, and apply the word to the lives and mission in which they participate.

Adding this dialogical component to the very heart of mission, the theoretical basis for this essay rests on the conviction that vision emerges from within a community of faith. That vision is to be discerned in the community in the midst of an environment of missional dialogue. This is not a matter of simply hoping that something will emerge. Rather it is an intentional process of engagement, reflection, and conversation to discern and articulate a position and a direction for the ministry to act.

Jürgen Habermas and Communicative Action

Jürgen Habermas made a significant contribution to understanding the elements involved in such an intentional and dialogical way of engaging this as he shaped thinking about discourse ethics. In *Moral Consciousness and Communicative Action,* Habermas seeks an alternative to strategic action, which he defines as being where "one actor seeks to *influence* the behavior of another by means of threat of sanctions or the prospect of gratification in order to cause the interaction to continue as the first actor desires."[21] In this understanding of engagement, the goal is to win over the other, and one applies power in order to do so.

Often the "Great Man" theory assumes that this is how leadership

20. Walter Brueggemann, Lecture to the ACTS Doctor of Ministry in Preaching Program, Chicago, July 3, 1996.

21. Jürgen Habermas, *Moral Consciousness and Communicative Action,* trans. Christian Lenhardt and Shierry Weber Nicholsen, intro. Thomas McCarthy (Cambridge, MA: The MIT Press, 1990), 58.

functions and how vision is communicated. The intrinsic ability and power in the leadership discerns the direction and then influences a community, most often based on the authority and perceived giftedness of the leader. While this is not always coercive and may generally not be malicious, it is this understanding that we hope to avoid. In contrast to this, Habermas defines communicative action as "a circular process in which the actor is two things in one: an *initiator*, who masters situations through actions for which he is accountable, and a *product* of the transitions surrounding him, of groups whose cohesion is based on solidarity to which he belongs" (Habermas, p. 135).

Communicative action is grounded in a more mutual understanding of outcomes and sees discourse as the medium by which decisions are made. It is a process that involves relational work and is impacted by both the individual and the social dimensions in which the process takes place. Habermas defined it as where "one actor seeks *rationally* to *motivate* another by relying on the illocutionary binding/bonding effect *[Bindungseffekt]* of the offer contained in his speech act" (p. 58).

What is important about this is that Habermas saw communicative action as involving more than the mere exchange of ideas; it is grounded in a broader sense of trust and relationships. Therefore, it is not just the content of the speech that engages but also the credibility and the reliability of the speaker (pp. 58-59). In other words, there is more than just the accuracy of information at stake when a claim is made. There is an underlying trust, a sense of shared values, and a relationship that can be counted on.

Habermas sees three central elements in all such discourse: claims of truth, claims of rightness, and claims of truthfulness. Claims of truth deal with what the participants in a dialogue would see as objective and verifiable; claims of rightness deal with issues of values that lie within a shared social world, which are justifiable based on commonly held values; and claims of truthfulness deal with the integrity of the speaker sharing honestly from his or her own subjective view of the world. The actions and the words of the speaker are congruent. What is important for our argument is Habermas's insight that discourse about both truth and rightness can give clear reasons that are accessible to both the speaker and the hearer in any dialogue. They are shared points of contact. But the third aspect, claims of truthfulness, can only be meaningfully supported through *consistent behavior*, in which "a person can convince someone that he means what he says only through his actions, not by giving reasons" (p. 59).

What is essential here is that this means that all meaningful discourse to shape a congregation's vision must result, not simply in ideas, but must ultimately translate into behaviors. A vision cannot settle for capturing the imagination if it does not, even more, capture the hands and feet of those for whom it exists and do so in such a way as to change the behaviors to be consistent with it.

I wish to suggest a key move here: it is my belief that the shaping of mission in the congregation will best be accomplished in systems that work to help people discern missional behaviors. These must provide people with the accountability to pursue these behaviors with vigor and intentionality, and then to allow this vision to emerge. This means that the congruence of communal behaviors and our message will often — dare I say always? — precede the vision to some degree.

Hans-Georg Gadamer and Interpretation

Hans-Georg Gadamer's work also contributes to our thinking here. In critiquing the problem of hermeneutics in his book *Truth and Method*, Gadamer notes that the Romantics sought to unify understanding and interpretation, noting that to some degree "understanding is always an interpretation, and hence interpretation is the explicit form of understanding."[22] While recognizing the reality of this at one level, Gadamer rightly saw that the result was that the application became separated from hermeneutics. As a result, "[t]he edifying application of scripture, for example, in Christian proclamation and preaching now seemed quite a different thing from the historical and theological understanding of it" (Gadamer, p. 274). Gadamer rightly reintegrated the witness of Scripture, the community's understanding and interpretation of it, and the application in the present by going "one stage beyond romantic hermeneutics, by regarding not only understanding and interpretation, but also application as comprising one unified process" (pp. 274-75).

This "unified process" of understanding is essential to the work that I will propose for congregations to use in discerning a scripturally informed

---

22. Gadamer, *Truth and Method*, ed. Garrett Barden and John Cumming (English translation copyright held by Sheed and Ward Ltd. [1975]), 2nd ed. (New York: Crossroad, [1965] 1985), 274.

and communally shared way of being missional in the world. Later in this chapter I will define a process way of being church together, guided by mutual engagement in ways that are consistent with Habermas's communicative action theory, while at the same time reintegrating elements in a process of trying to both clarify discrete elements within a vision and also to reintegrate them into the whole, much as Gadamer has done with hermeneutics.

The Nature of Vision

As I have observed above, the focus of this work is not to try to see far into the future with a sense of foresight. Rather, the focus is to engage and recognize the activity of God and to see and understand the faith community's role in it — within the present. In many cases, as we will see, no one knows what is to come, but there can be agreement when it happens that this is what God wants.

Vision is thus not something that draws us forward in this definition; it is this engagement with the present and the insight that it brings that propels the ministry forward into the future. Vision understood in this way actually pushes us forward *into* the future rather than drawing us forward *from* the future. While both the push and the pull of vision are, of course, realities, this emphasis on contrasting the two is more than mere semantics. Too many congregations have shriveled up and become ineffective because no one was visionary enough to see the future. But if vision is a communal enterprise, recognizable by the masses and articulated by a community working missionally and dialogically together, then the willingness to engage with integrity in the process and in the present is often enough for vibrancy to be renewed.

Although vision is not needed in the sense of seeing the future clearly (which is not to say that in some cases it might not still be helpful), what is needed is the confidence that God in Jesus Christ has a future for us, promises to be with us on the journey, and intends for us to be engaged and useful on the way to finding the vision. It is my contention that if we place missional impulses deeper within the system than traditional leadership models have often permitted, we will mobilize the church for mission in new ways. This will be because vision arises when the community of faith engages with its context from a missional impulse shaped by what God is already doing and where God is already leading.

Vision, then, must *emerge* from this engagement with the context rather than be foreseen and laid over it. Gadamer points out how significantly our ability to see and articulate our vision is shaped by the limits of our experiences and the worldview from which we have come. If we take this insight to its logical end, the reality of vision is always shaped by the limits placed on vision by those charged with seeing and articulating it. Traditional models of leadership often fail to account for this: the result can be leaders who are effective in the short-term work of advancing a cause but who struggle with long-term effectiveness.

When the driving force behind the vision departs from the scene — for whatever reason — the community is at risk of losing the vision altogether. Within the Evangelical Lutheran Church in America we often witness this in what we call the "after pastor" effect in mission development and redevelopment: this is a system that has had relatively good health and missional effectiveness on the surface but suddenly goes into decline when the leader leaves. The sense of vision, the gifts and ownership of ministry, and the ability to sustain it apart from the gifts of the leader are inadequate to overcome the centrist approach to leadership that served the system but did not equip it for ongoing work when the one who was the keeper of the vision departed.

What if leadership is the work of the community in a broader way? What if vision is a function that emerges and is discerned in community rather than cast out from "visionary leadership"? What would such a community of faith look like, and what key practices would it need?

Purpose and Guiding Principles: Key Practices for the Work

The practices used in this process include *purpose* and *guiding principles.* These assist a congregation to articulate its commitment to the mission of God and to their nature, identity, and essence as the church within the *missio Dei.* These things are dialogically discerned through prayer and Scripture study and are articulated to aid in the decisions that must be made on the journey ahead.

The goal of this engagement with God and Scripture is to discern locally why God has a church and to press toward the people owning their role in God's economy. The biblical study needs to be grounded in various missional texts in Scripture, all of which point to behavior as being central and help God's people move from intellectual assent to a recognition of the importance of reconnecting application in a more holistic way. This is what Gadamer saw as essential for recovering a hermeneutic that would be truly helpful.

In addition, this study process is grounded in discourse. Habermas reminds us that a conclusion that is truly agreed to in a noncoercive way is grounded in a genuine sense of participation by each participant. True conversation allows people to both speak and listen, to weigh the value of the ideas that are shared (in this case using Scripture as a key barometer for rationale), and to come to a shared group conclusion with regard to what is ultimately most important. Genuine dialogue is difficult in large group settings: it generally requires, in practical terms, multiple small groups that allow all participants to find their own voices. Even then, providing time for people to reflect on and write out their thoughts can allow for those who are more quiet to participate in a way that pure oral discourse often truncates. This group work can then be brought together with the work of other groups, refined, discussed again, and modified until the larger group can reach some sense of consensus or agreement.

Purpose in this process is defined as our role in the mission of God. This is intentionally not called "mission," which is to remind all of us that there is only one mission, and that belongs exclusively to God. We are invited to participate in God's mission, and our acceptance of this participation is our purpose.

Guiding principles are defined as values that are biblically grounded and that further the purpose: they provide clarity about what is most important, and thus they should be behaviorally defined (in sentence form with active verbs). They should also, with accountability, provide the basis for decision-making as a community proceeds. If they are not just words, then Habermas's test for truthfulness as "congruence between words and actions" will be a stressor that presses members of a congregation to either reject their purpose because they do not own it or engage in new behaviors in order to increase the integrity of their witness. It is the framework of intentional dialogue, as well as the use of the principles that underlie communicative action, that allow the purpose and guiding principles to be both discerned and owned by a congregation. This ownership allows for accountability to be willingly taken up by the congregation *from within* rather than being imposed by a leader *from above*.

A brief example may help. In the congregation where I currently serve as pastor, we engaged in a several-month process of Bible study, prayer, and conversation to engage the ministry regarding the missional questions of purpose and guiding principles. One of our principles was: "We deepen our faith to strengthen our discipleship." Agreeing to this meant that the congregation would work on changing its corporate behaviors to better match this value. An example of this was the relocation of adult education on Sunday mornings: people had to choose to relocate in order to participate, and the result was that only a minority of people engaged the work. Since the principle was to define a norm, we decided that the congregation should assume that they were to be involved, and we made it so public that people would have to opt out. The class was moved to the fellowship space, the space where refreshments are served. Class sizes have quadrupled and people have increased their involvement; however, we also have had to change the content of what happened during that time. Since the goal was not only knowledge, but ultimately increased discipleship, the move toward application was now mandatory. This, too, we have done dialogically, using guided table discussions to apply insights and to help people make the move from Sunday to Monday in the process.

A Process to Discern Vision

We will now take all that we have discussed and attempt to apply it in practice so that we may process this work in a communal way. The goal is to discern a vision that is close at hand, is grounded in what God is doing in the congregation and the community, and is lived out in concrete behaviors in accountable ways.

This process requires us, therefore, to begin missionally and to turn prayerfully to Scripture and to the creative, redeeming, and sanctifying work of the triune God as the basis from which a congregation begins to define what God is up to in the world. I intentionally say "prayerfully" because I have observed that this kind of work takes a significantly different turn when groups pray together for discernment before entering the discourse. Prayer that asks for God's direction seeks answers to the questions "What is God up to?" and "What does God want us to do?" Furthermore, it produces a radically different environment for group work. This allows groups to be centered on God's work rather than arguing over their own ideas.

Purpose and guiding principles are tools to help shape one aspect of vision. When the ELCA's Transformational Ministry Team began its work in this area, we thought that a sense of purpose that arose from discerning a role within the *missio Dei* with respect to the reign of God would be joined by values discernment (articulated as guiding principles for mission). We taught vision as being a function of purpose, guiding principles, and time: that is, engage the work and over time the vision would come.

While this view was correct to a degree, it was also limited in its effectiveness. It was assumed that those of us outside the congregational systems were providing contextual engagement, because articulating a purpose assumed engagement within a context. But we found that, in practice, if we did not help congregations to be directed with intentionality into their context, a high percentage of cases tended to turn back inward.

We found that we not only needed to help congregations own the *missio Dei* in principle, but we also needed to integrate the truthfulness of that commitment *behaviorally* into the process. To be missional in truth and understanding without being missional in action left the process incomplete and ineffective. If God is doing something in the world and we are to participate in it, then a congregation has to engage the world around it. It must do mission with as much energy and accountability as it has engaged its internal life, and it must develop a missional identity and self-understanding of its call to participate in God's mission.

Contextual engagement needs to happen in two ways. The first is informational. Information from census data and other demographic suppliers, agency statistics, and other sources can help in this work. These are important aspects of investigating the field. But because the integrity of the church's work is grounded in its truthfulness and based on the integrity of its demonstrated actions, a second and very important aspect of this work is relational. There is little to be found in demographic information about a community that does not need to be verified relationally. Christian people need to be out in the world and relationally engaging the people in their community.

This is best done with a genuine desire to know the people within the church's context and to discover what is really happening in the surrounding community. In addition, because a commitment to *missio Dei* means believing that God is already at work in the world, it also means that we are trying to discern what God is already pleased with and/or is doing in the community. Questions such as "What do you see that makes God rejoice?" and "Where do you see God already at work?" are the basis for this discovery work. Again, this element of the process is dialogical in character. Outcomes will involve not just the identification of problems to be solved, but also glimpses into the reign of God, which are to be celebrated, and the discovery of partners to connect with in doing God's work.

The vision that finally emerges relies on the following ingredients. The first is a missional commitment that includes engagement with the context. Without this conviction that God has a mission and that we, as the church, are to play a part in this, everything else in this process is reduced to mere exercises — helpful exercises but incomplete in their usefulness. It is essential that this commitment to the *missio Dei* and the reign of God be more than intellectual assent; it must also include a strong passion for the work and a willingness to get involved behaviorally.

If biblical and theological foundations are in place to frame the essence and identity of the church within the ongoing mission of the triune God, then the remaining elements come together organically in a fusion of work in which each element has integrity of its own. Like Gadamer's hermeneutical understanding, no part can stand on its own; each part only finds its fulfillment in the interrelationship of all the elements pressing together. These elements are: (1) purpose and guiding principles; (2) contextual engagement that is relational and invitational, and the awareness of its assets, gifts, and passions — as well as its needs; and (3) the faith community with all of its assets, gifts, and passions — as well as its needs. A vision will emerge when these three elements press against each other in missional ways. The diagram below suggests what this might look like:

Vision: What's Involved?

(Note: This assumes that God can and is doing amazing things in the church and in the world)

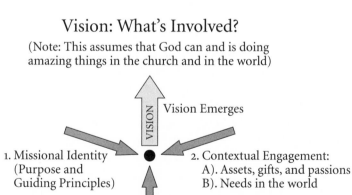

VISION

Vision Emerges

1. Missional Identity (Purpose and Guiding Principles)

2. Contextual Engagement:
A). Assets, gifts, and passions
B). Needs in the world

3. Faith Community:
A). Assets, gifts, and passions
B). Needs in the church

In this image one can see that each of the contributions to vision is engaged fully and simultaneously in the present. The missional commitments mean that each is always operating beneath the primary questions "What is God doing and how can we help?" and "What is God dreaming and how can we get involved?"

The simultaneity of these elements means that this is not a linear process. It is more like elements that are poured into a crucible, mixed and heated, and something new comes out as a result. When a ministry's purpose and principles, contextual engagement, and its gifts, assets, and passions are all pressed together and forced to interact, a vision for ministry will emerge. It will not be far away, nor will it take special gifts to see it: it will be visible to many and, within community, discernible to all. This process of vision-discernment is replacing vision-casting in many healthy ministries, calling forth new energy for mission and allowing the many to be involved in leading rather than the few.

Implications for Leadership

A ministry that sees vision in this way will discover something quite dramatic. Suddenly, armed with basic tools to see and engage the present, everyone will be more qualified to see. Vision stops being the property of the few and becomes the property of the many, as leadership is redefined in terms of what everyone can contribute to it.

The basic question for everyone in a ministry is simply this: "Based on what you understand us to be about, what do you care about and have the ability for that God could use to do something meaningful?" To become leaders, maturing people of faith need only ask one additional question: "Whom can I get to accompany me and help me in this work?" The answer can involve people from both inside and outside the church. The successful engagement of these two questions in the lives of people of faith is the breeding ground for vision and the basis for ministry.

This means that leaders in this new way of seeing will ensure that proper building blocks are in place: a commitment to participate in the *missio Dei;* scripturally discerned purpose and guiding principles; genuine contextual engagement that honors the gifts, assets, and passions as well as the needs of the world; and the gifts, assets, and passions of the faith community, as well as its needs. They will do so, not primarily by telling, but by engaging a process and involving people in answering questions. To be a leader, one will not need nearly as much vision as was once assumed. Rather, one will need a commitment to engage the context and a willingness to ask questions and develop accountability for the answers to those questions.

With these criteria (obviously, limited space does not allow me to flesh out this with more detail), any person who has basic ministry skills, has a maturing faith, and can engage relationally with a group of people can serve as a leader. This service may be in a ministry subsystem, as people form missional groups to pursue particular ideas based on how their particular gifts, assets, and passions can be linked with others to do something specific. Or it may be to engage the larger system to provide the same accountability to answering missional questions on a more macro level. In either case, the focus of the questions will be the same; only the scale of those who are to answer will change.

Our experience has verified what Edgar J. Cahn has expressed in his book *No More Throw-Away People,* where he makes the case that anyone and everyone can be useful to God and that leadership is more readily attainable by the many rather than the few.[23] Although vision in the sense of seeing the future clearly is not necessary (which doesn't mean that it isn't helpful!), what is needed is the confidence that God has a future for us, that Christ promises to be with us on the journey, and that through the empowerment of the Holy Spirit we can be led on the way to discerning it.

Peer Coaching as a Fundamental Communal Skill

Mission is now viewed as a way of entering a journey with and for the sake of God's reign, and our ability to ask key questions is the primary method of advancing the congregation's purpose. In light of this, an essential skill in this new way of being church is not to have the right answers but to have the right questions. Peer coaching, a skill that facilitates the ability of a person or group to process information, now emerges as a key aspect of this new leadership paradigm.

Within the Evangelical Lutheran Church in America, one of the ways that we have embraced coaching is through training a network of peer

23. Edgar Cahn, *No More Throw-Away People* (Washington, DC: Essential Books, 2004), 200.

coaches. These peer coaches learn to ask questions that help others go deeper in understanding and ultimately to address the question "What will you do about it?" This behavioral emphasis is essential to the values of the process we have explored above. Much of the expertise for most ministries is already present in the context and the congregation. Peer coaches are trained within congregations and are there to honor, facilitate, and draw this out and to encourage the individuals or groups to pursue what they are called to do.

The coaching that has been the most helpful for the unit in which I work has been implemented by CoachNet, under the leadership of Robert Logan.[24] Drawing heavily on insights from *Co-active Coaching,* this process assumes that the best basis for finding good answers lies in the context.[25] Using a relationally based process, CoachNet's method helps people assess where they are, what God is calling them to be about, and to commit to what they will do. It is accessible and can be taught and used in a variety of contexts to a variety of people; clergy and laity together are being taught to use this simple skill effectively. Some congregations are now realizing that their ability to raise up leaders rests primarily on believing that people can use the practices for mission described above, and through giving them coaching support to transform within their congregations and ministries. As such, it levels the playing field and expands the leadership base from a few individuals to a larger pool of people who are ready and able to implement the vision that they were already a part of discerning.

In the congregation where I serve, this has meant improved Vacation Bible Schools, mission trips successfully led by people who otherwise would have struggled or failed to lead, and a general sense of mutual accountability that expects and encourages people to act. It has also meant the bubbling up of a "Green Team" to address environmental issues (including a wonderful midweek Bible study on creation that was led by someone who would never have done it using vision the "big" way), a Justice and Advocacy Group (JAG) to deal with issues in public life, an upcoming Fair Trade Fair, annual parties for the neighborhood, and a number of other grassroots and highly involved ministries.

24. For more information on CoachNet, go to www.CoachNet.org; see also Bob Logan, *Coaching 101* (St. Charles, IL: ChurchSmart Resources, 2003).

25. Laura Whitworth et al., *Co-Active Coaching: New Skills for Coaching People Toward Success in Work and Life,* 2nd ed. (Mountain View, CA: Davies-Black Publishing, 2007).

An exciting development has come about as a team of people from the congregation begins its third year of tutoring in the elementary school. Because of the congregation's involvement and relationship with residents in the neighborhood association, this year the tutoring will begin to involve unchurched people we have met in the neighborhood who want to help the church do something good. Experience tells us that some of these people may come on Sundays and become active and engaged members of our congregation, while others may not. But God is most surely pleased that we have been a vehicle for their gifts and talents to find a way into the lives of children after school each Monday afternoon.

The result has been a vibrant congregational system in which people are asking how they can see and be a part of what God is doing, and how they can do something about it now. Coaching, while still being more situational than systematic, is giving them the support to move from talk to their efforts to put that talk into action.

Summary: Putting the Pieces Together

To help a system discern an emerging vision, the work I have discussed in this chapter uses the following elements:

1. *Group Process:* a group learning process grounded in prayer, Scripture study, and intentional conversation
2. *Key Practices:* three key practices are intentionally pressed by leaders to form creative tension:
   a. *Missio Dei:* intentional grounding in *missio Dei* and attention to how the congregation's understanding of "purpose" relates to what God is doing in the world, as well as attention to values-clarification and a focus on articulating these in behavioral terms, here referred to as "guiding principles"
   b. *Discovery of Gifts:* the discovery of assets, gifts, and passions present within the congregation — as well as awareness about its needs
   c. *Intentional Engagement:* an intentional engagement with the context to begin understanding and imagining what God is already doing and what God desires to have occur there, and to discover its gifts, assets, and passions — as well as its needs

3. *Peer Coaching* is used to facilitate a communal and accountable system in order to ensure the use of the process and to ensure that essential, missional questions are always asked. This also models shared responsibility for long-term culture change to become a community of leaders who together discern vision and work to embody it.

These elements, when pursued and intentionally held together, provide the basis by which visions emerge in ministries. As the context and gifts provide raw material for ministry and imagination, the commitment to the *missio Dei* and the congregation's sense of purpose and guiding principles provide tools for discernment. The nature of this work is much like a journey. When travelers take a trip to a place where they have not been before, they do not need to see fully the destination ahead of time. In fact, the desire to "see what we have not seen" is the primary reason for taking many trips in the first place. To quote Paul, "For now we see in a mirror, dimly, but then we will see face to face. Now I know only in part; then I will know fully, even as I have been fully known" (1 Cor. 13:12-13). It is the confidence that we have from what we know now that encourages us to press forward.

Therefore, I would contend that the most helpful thing is to have a definition of vision that is immediate, as being at hand, and as appearing on the scene as it unfolds. It is essential that we recognize the signs along the journey and respond to them appropriately. Just as the traveler needs only to recognize the next turn before passing it by as the journey unfolds, it is not necessary for a congregation and its leaders to see the entire journey unfold before they set out. In fact, the more they do see of it in advance, the more they will be likely to miss what is actually happening along the way.

The task of leadership is to keep the journey before us and to facilitate our moving ahead in such a way that all people will keep their eyes open — engaging the context as real partners in the journey; sharing gifts, assets, and passions in ways that meet each other's needs; and staying focused on the purpose for their trip and the behaviors they will hold to along the way. When this happens, a few might see far ahead, but all of us will be better prepared to engage in ministry and have the eyes to see that Jesus calls us to have now.

One day, perhaps, pastors will write letters different from the one I quoted at the beginning of this chapter. Instead of pulling rank on people, they will say, "I am the pastor here. That means that my work, along with all of you, is to be sure that we are not paralyzed by our anxiety; that we spend time in prayer, Scripture, and conversation; that we continue conversing with our neighbors; and that we ask, 'What is God doing?' and 'How can we participate?'" When that day comes, the result will be a people who, rather than wondering what God might do in the future, are better able to participate energetically, passionately, and effectively in what God is doing now.

MISSIONAL LEADERSHIP FORMATION IN RELATION TO RECENT RESEARCH

This third section consists of two chapters that provide the reader with insights into missional leadership formation gleaned from recent research in the field. Many readers who have followed the missional church conversation have asked this question: "What does this actually look like within real congregations?" These chapters offer some perspective in helping answer that question.

Terri Elton's interest is in what the practices and characteristics are of those congregations that appear to be more fruitful than others in forming missional leadership. Since there is little published literature available on this subject, she utilized a grounded-theory approach in studying five very different Lutheran (ELCA) congregations, all of which, however, had a reputation for producing missional leadership for the church. Elton used informed sampling to initially identify the congregations she would study, and then she conducted interviews and focus groups on site. Through extensive narrative coding, she eventually was able to identify eight dynamics of leadership-formation practices that were evident in each of these congregations. Her chapter here reports these findings and also proceeds to offer a biblical and theological argument for understanding them within a missional framework.

Kristine Stache's interest was in what progress has been made toward embedding a missional understanding of leadership within a number of diverse denominational systems that have been trying to engage the missional church conversation. She had access to a database of extensive qualitative research that had been conducted within four denominational systems. Specific judicatories or regional units of these denominations had been seeking to innovate missional church identity and practices for several years. Within this research database, there were specific questions about how people were engaging the missional conversation and how they were understanding leadership in light of this conversation. By analyzing the responses of these relevant questions, Stache was able to identify — and reports here — distinct patterns in missional leadership formation that were becoming evident in each of these denominational systems, some of which are quite surprising.

CHAPTER 7

Characteristics of Congregations That Empower Missional Leadership: A Lutheran Voice

Terri Martinson Elton

Introduction

Imagine this: doctors, lawyers, firefighters, teachers, students, and parents all believing that their ordinary lives are opportunities for living their faith every day. Imagine this: communities of faith welcoming the lonely, serving meals to the hungry, speaking out against injustice, and partnering with other organizations seeking to transform individuals, neighborhoods, regions, and the world. Imagine this: congregations actively discerning how to participate in God's creative and redemptive mission in the world. Imagine God's people living for the sake of the world.

Why should God's people in community live for the sake of the world? Because God's gathered people exist not for their own sake but to join God in what God is already doing in and for the world. To put it differently, the church has no other mission than to participate in God's creative and redemptive mission *in the world*.

The Evangelical Lutheran Church of America (ELCA) professes to be a church that exists for the sake of the world. However, the lived reality of the ELCA has not always embodied this commitment. Yet, could the ELCA be a church that lives for the sake of the world? Could ELCA Lutherans allow God's mission to define their identity and their actions — both their being and their doing?

"Faithful, yet changing" is how Mark Hanson, the presiding bishop of the ELCA, described the current state of the ELCA when he began his term in 2001.[1] What does a faithful, yet changing ELCA look like? Currently, mainline churches, including the ELCA, have become overly instrumental: that is, their actions are substantively driven by their policies and structures — what is primarily a functional view of church — and the result is ministry that is often stalemated as the church seeks to respond to the diverse contexts present in the United States today. So, what is being faithful and what needs to change? The answers, I believe, are located within our ecclesiology.

The structures and patterns of church both inform and are informed by our particular views of church, ministry, leadership, and the world.[2] Structures and patterns are certainly needed, but they can become limiting and restrictive at times. If the church is to faithfully and effectively engage in ministry in the twenty-first century, it is time for the church to evaluate its ecclesiology once again. While an instrumental view of church tends to permeate the ELCA, missional impulses are also present, and the place where we can best observe these impulses is within numerous congregations. Many ELCA congregations are attending, implicitly and explicitly, to the dynamic relationship between God and God's people — and within their contextual realities. What can be learned from these congregations is worth mining, and that is the specific focus of this chapter. It is crucial that we explore the contribution of such congregations, placed in conversation with the richness found in Lutheran traditions and theology, as a Lutheran missional ecclesiology is formed and reformed.[3]

---

1. Mark S. Hanson, *Faithful, Yet Changing: The Church in Challenging Times* (Minneapolis: Augsburg Books, 2002).

2. For example, a view of church that focuses on practices and functions often translates into ministry as programs, leadership evaluated pragmatically, and the world as the environment from which to draw people into the church and the place where the church serves. A missional view of church has at its core a dynamic relationship among God, God's people, and the particularities of being located — geographically and historically. Structures and forms enhance these relationships and are flexible and secondary in nature. Ministry and leadership are varied and diverse, often reflective of the contexts.

3. For a discussion of forming and reforming, see Craig Van Gelder, "How Missiology Can Help Inform the Conversation about the Missional Church in Context," in *The Missional Church in Context: Helping Congregations Develop Contextual Ministry*, ed. Van Gelder (Grand Rapids: Eerdmans, 2007), 37.

Part 1: A Study of Missional Leadership

I set out to study missional leadership in the ELCA by paying attention to the three-way dialogue concerning context, God's activity in the world, and God's people participating in God's mission in the world. With the belief that missional leadership is needed, that communities of faith are significant in shaping missional leaders, and with a curiosity about why some ELCA congregations cultivate more missional-minded people than do others, I asked two research questions:

- What are the cultural dynamics within a congregation that are vital to empowering missional leadership?
- What commonalities, if any, exist between various ELCA congregations with regard to these vital cultural dynamics?

Using a grounded-theory, qualitative-research method, my study focused on identifying common cultural dynamics for empowering missional leadership in a purposeful sample of five ELCA congregations.[4] I collected four sources of data for each congregation: a congregational profile, an on-site ethnographic visit over an extended weekend, four focus groups, and my own research journal. I analyzed the data from each of the sources separately and then comparatively. All four sources of data served to create narrative findings on each congregation, and the focus group transcripts served as the primary source for the deeper analysis where I had identified the cultural dynamics.

Key Definitions

Two concepts are important to define for this study. The first is *missional leadership*. Mission, according to David Bosch, is undergoing a transfor-

---

4. I selected the five ELCA congregations in a three-stage process: I solicited nominations for ELCA missional congregations from various ELCA leaders; once the names of congregations were submitted, I created a preliminary list and e-mailed a letter to a select group of congregational systems stating the purpose of my research and inviting them to consider being a participant. I conducted phone interviews with the lead pastors of the churches that responded positively, in which I clarified the purpose of the study and the expectations of the congregation's participation, and determined their availability within the given timeline of the research. After I had completed the phone interviews, I selected five congregations.

"Missions" has been a word that was used to refer to a particular of the church, primarily ministry working across various boundaries, be they geographic, cultural, or socioeconomic. Church leaders who have used "missions" in this way have often referred to missionaries being sent to particular locations or to particular populations.

The concepts of "mission" and "missional," however, are understood more broadly today: they focus on the *identity* as well as the *activity* of the church. A view of God that is missional declares that God is a missionary God inviting all people into communion with God's self and sending God's people into the world to share God's transforming message. "Missional" describes both God and the church's very nature. The new missional self-definition sees a missional imagination as an imperative for all Christian communities, and it considers missional leadership the call of all Christians.[5]

A basic definition of missional leadership has been developed based on this rationale, and it includes persons who understand their calling as disciples of Jesus Christ, see themselves as equipped by God with certain gifts to be shared with the larger body of Christ, and believe that they are empowered by the Spirit to engage the world by participating in the creative and redemptive mission of God.

A second concept worth defining is that of *cultural dynamics.* Culture, according to Clifford Geertz, "denotes a historically transmitted pattern of meanings embodied in symbols, a system of inherited conceptions expressed in symbolic form by means of which men communicate, perpetuate, and develop their knowledge about and attitudes toward life."[6] These varied — and often abstract — dynamics are significant in understanding a culture and are at the heart of what my research set out to discover. Richard Shweder says that a cultural account assists "in explaining why the members of a particular cultural community say the things they say and do the things they do to each other with their words and other actions."[7] It is through identifying and naming cultural dynamics that one begins to discover why particular congregations do what they do and what gives them life.

5. David Bosch, *Transforming Mission: Paradigm Shifts in Theology of Mission* (Maryknoll, NY: Orbis, 1991), xv, 9.

6. Clifford Geertz, *The Interpretation of Cultures: Selected Essays* (New York: Basic Books, 1973), 89.

7. Richard A. Shweder, *Why Do Men Barbecue? Recipes for Cultural Psychology* (Cambridge, MA: Harvard University Press, 2003), 11.

Margaret Wheatley adds that there is much to be learned from the space between and the relationships of one part to another.[8] Space, in addition to words and actions, defines and shapes congregational culture. This fluid yet powerful aspect plays into meaning-making and sustaining life. Therefore, the concept of cultural dynamics refers to this: any dynamic (words, action, space, or relationship) that shapes the meaning of the culture, influences its members, and perpetuates its life together.

Describing the Five Congregations

I studied five ELCA congregations in five different contexts. This section highlights both the unique dynamics of each congregation and those they shared in common. Each congregation had unique cultural dynamics that shaped it for empowering missional leadership. In summarizing their stories and highlighting some of their key characteristics, the summaries below provide a glimpse into these congregations.

Congregation No. 1: Casa para Todos

Not a proud people, but a purposeful community with a particular calling, the Casa para Todos faith community is growing not only in membership but also in diversity and as a community on a mission. (All names in this section are pseudonyms for the actual congregations studied.) One of the members put it this way: "We are not called to be comfortable. . . . I think it's . . . good to remember where the focus is. . . . It's not on what we do . . . but what God does through us. If we lose that, we are not the church."

A gracious and active view of God draws this congregation into the world. The changing world serves as their horizon as they continually discern where God is leading them. The heart of this community of faith is to be a people who are shaped by a Lutheran identity, but not necessarily by Lutheran traditions. Leadership is shared between the ordained clergy and staff, the elected lay leadership, and the community of faith as a whole.

This church has several key characteristics:

---

8. Margaret J. Wheatley, *Leadership and the New Science: Discovering Order in a Chaotic World,* 2nd ed. (San Francisco: Berrett-Koehler Publishers, 1999), 10.

- This congregation is Christian first and Lutheran second: that is, they are Christian in that Christ is their center, and they are Lutheran in that a theology of grace clearly lives and breathes within this community of faith. Their mission is: "God's love comes *to* the church in order for that same love to flow *through* the church to the world."
- "A Home for All" was not only the theme of their recent building campaign, but it is a metaphor for their life together (and was a phrase used many times by focus group participants). It is a home for all the members, and those members are also meant to contribute as if it were their home. It is a home for all, not just those who are members, but also to those outside their doors as they continually open their building to the greater community.
- The people in this congregation live within a tension of being leaders and followers, or in their words, being *servant leaders*. Worship is the most public way this attitude is shaped and formed, but it is also modeled and lived within the people themselves as they lead and serve within the church and the world.

In summary, this congregation is a community of God's people who live with and for each other, and who are centered by a gracious God at work in their lives, a God who is calling them into mission in the world. In worship and through leading together, they engage in ministry with eyes toward the future and the changing world.

Congregation No. 2: Bread for the Journey

One participant said: "It is not about our politics or social issues or comfort zone, it is all about a community that is growing in faith and taking the message of Jesus to the world." This congregation is a community of disciples with an active faith in a living, Trinitarian God, disciples who participate in God's mission in a changing world. They believe that this living God continues to create, redeem, and sustain life, both within their faith community and in the world. They participate in God's mission by being a storied people, seeking to be a vibrant presence within their greater community and around the world. Seeking to engage their diverse context with resources and power, this congregation has accepted its call to be a church for the world, and it has a story to tell.

This story is informed primarily by the Christian story, but it has a

Lutheran flare. Planted in an area where Christianity is in the minority, the people of this congregation have attempted to create a fresh, Christian community that draws on Lutheran theological roots, while it also recognizes the particularities of its context.

This church has several key characteristics:

- It is rooted in the Word of God, as witnessed in its preaching and learning opportunities, has a high value on discipleship and equipping people for a life of faith, and holds the sacrament of Holy Communion in high regard. With Christ at its center, the congregation's posture of welcoming catches people on their first encounter and draws them into a deeper discipleship journey.
- Relationships are critical to the people in this congregation. The sacraments are social, the welcoming is social, the missional initiatives are social, and the people of this congregation value being social — mainly by being connected through small groups.
- The passion and commitment of the people within this faith community are contagious. They truly are living out their mission "to *invite* people to faith in a living God; to *grow* and *equip* people to become fully devoted followers of Jesus Christ; to *serve* others by the Holy Spirit."

In summary, this is a community of Christian disciples who are following an active and living Trinitarian God. They are narrating their life together, sharing power and leadership, and participating in God's mission in a changing world.

Congregation No. 3: Mission Central

One member summed up the spirit of this congregation this way:

> The Lutheran theology keeps our focus on the center, which is Christ, and seeking first the kingdom and all else will follow. . . . That is what drew us to this congregation, the focus on the center. There's one thing in our life that's rock solid, and that's this congregation. It's the most humble group of people.

This congregation is located in an area in which Lutherans are a minority, but it has established itself as a vibrant ELCA mission outpost. It has done so by being a community of God's people joined together in a journey with a living God.

As a congregation of humble saints and sinners, their belief in God deeply and variously connects them — not only to God but also to each other. They see themselves being tied to the ELCA and to the greater history of the Lutheran church, which means that *Lutheran* is part of this community's DNA. However, their identity is not passive but active, as they seek to participate, influence, and shape it both now and in the future. It's most evident expression is in its planting of several other ELCA congregations in their area.

This church has several key characteristics:

- This community is a group of sinners who believe in something greater than themselves. They come together to refocus their lives, and with this overarching view, their worship and ministry continue to significantly shape their thinking and way of being.
- The congregation has a story to tell, a story that is continuous and is being added to as it moves into the future. People know the story, share the story, are humbled by the story, and want to continue the story.
- The community has a social agenda: that is, being in relationship with one another is important and needs tending to. Whether it be on Sunday mornings, during special events, at small groups, or while serving together, this is a group of people who value each other.

In summary, this congregation is a Lutheran community of God's humble people who are connected to each other on a journey with a living God, and who are seeking to live their faith in the world. They are both willing to respond to the realities of their context as well as influence and shape the community's future.

Congregation No. 4: New Wine

This congregation is undergoing a transformation, just as its people are. One member expressed it this way: "It is a process for people to come to faith, it's a relational process, and we try to build relationships wherever they are." Talking about the ministry of this congregation, another member added: "We try to remove speed bumps when people come to faith. We try to make the main thing the main thing." The main thing for this faith community is to be faithful followers of Jesus living in and for the world.

This congregation is a welcoming community that believes in an active, relational God; the people in it come together to share in the journey of discipleship, spiritual growth, worship, and prayer, and then they are sent into the world. Within this process they openly accept one another, allow each other to be authentic, and are willing to risk and forgive.

Keeping a Lutheran identity at their core, they have also learned that they need to be willing to adapt and be flexible as the world around them continues to change. One of the biggest changes has been the diversification of their immediate neighborhood. This reality has provided both challenges and opportunities.

This church has several key characteristics:

- A doctrine of incarnation is present here. It is a come-as-you-are, grace-filled community that seeks to keep discipleship the main thing. Simply stated, in whatever way they can they try to share Jesus with those who do not yet know him.
- The congregation has had a roller-coaster history, but the small remnant of it that remains seeks to be a welcoming presence in its changing and mobile community. For many, this community of faith is the connective tissue for them in the greater neighborhood.
- As a praying church, this congregation is living *into* being a people fueled by learning and growing in faith and *out of* their passion for reaching out to others. The Spirit moves freely through this faith community, surprising many, igniting passion, and empowering all.

In summary, this congregation is a group of God's people who are living as a discipling community, discerning God's leading as they are open to and sent into the world. They are a small faith community poised to make a significant mark in the world.

Congregation No. 5: Cross in the Road

"This church is the first church I've been to that's given me a way to live my faith," one member confessed. Mature and confident in its ministry and mission, this congregation won't allow itself to become too comfortable or complacent.

Grounded in Lutheran theology and tradition, this community of faith is equipping God's people to be mission-minded followers of Jesus. As a community of the baptized, they are Spirit-led and mission-shaped. Operating within a Lutheran framework, they have developed a missional theology that weaves together discipleship, service, and worship. The leaders of this congregation believe that when learning and service come together (and people of all ages are engaged), missional discipleship and Christian community emerge. In other words, there is both a sense of belonging to something and a responsibility to reach beyond.

Leadership is centered on the pastors and council, as they set the direction; but it is also decentralized as participants become involved, are empowered, and take ownership of the ministry. This shared leadership is made up of veteran members and new people.

This church has several key characteristics:

- The congregation operates within a Lutheran frame and takes seriously Lutheran traditions; it is also relentless in proclaiming that every congregant has a call. There is a fervent belief that God is alive and active in their midst as a congregation, in the lives of their people, and in the greater community.
- Service is prevalent among the ministry of this congregation and among its people, and it is more than charity work. Service is framed theologically and is seen as part of a Christian way of life. As several said, "From those to whom much is given, much is expected."
- Baptism centers and directs this community. Rituals are created around this journey, and people of all ages are invited to participate.

In summary, this congregation is a Lutheran community with a missional identity. It is a ministry of the baptized, who are led by the Spirit into the world, and who seek to faithfully worship, learn, and serve together.

Comparing the Five Congregations

Having now briefly described each congregation, in this section I want to compare them contextually, numerically, historically, and programmatically.[9] Contextually, the five congregations are dispersed across the United States, located in three different states and four different metropolitan areas. While all are located in some kind of metropolitan area, the population of those areas range from 361,000 to 3.6 million. When seen from the perspective of U.S. averages, four of the five congregations are located in areas that are above average economically.[10] Four congregations are located in counties that are average or above the national average in education.[11] Three of the congregations are located in counties that are more ethnically diverse than the U.S. average.[12] This diversity translated into diversity in language: four of the five congregations are located in counties that had more than the U.S. average of people whose primary language is something other than English.[13] Finally, all these congregations are located in areas in which they are a religious minority.[14]

With regard to congregational makeup, by ELCA standards these congregations are large, ranking between the 69th and 99th percentile.[15] Three of the congregations are similar in size, representing the higher end

9. It is worth noting that the sample was purposeful in that I sought ELCA congregations that were empowering missional leadership. Secondarily, in my selection of congregations I was seeking diversity, but this diversity was limited and not the primary lens.

10. Only one of the five congregations is located in an area that was above the national average in the level of poverty and below the national average in median income.

11. The congregation referred to in note 10 had a lower percentage of people with a high school diploma than did the national average and a higher percentage of dropout rates for 16- to 19-year-olds than did the national average.

12. Two of the five congregations are located in counties in which the percentage of whites is higher than the national average, but one of those counties has a higher percentage of Hispanics than does the national average. The other three congregations are located in counties in which the percentage of whites is lower than the national average. The areas higher than the national average varied in each county: one was higher in African-American, all were higher in Asian, and all were higher in Hispanic.

13. Four of the five congregations were located in counties that had higher than the United States average of people whose primary language was Spanish.

14. One congregation listed mainline Protestant as the third most represented group, after Unclaimed and Roman Catholics. The other four had it listed fourth or fifth (out of five).

15. Three of the congregations were in the 99-99.6 percentile based on placement within ELCA congregations in 2004, which translated into between 166 and 804 in weekly worship. While a range in size was one of the secondary factors that I used in selecting congregations from the initial list, I should acknowledge that there is an opportunity for further study that would address congregations smaller than the ones in this study. Comparing the findings would allow the chance for deeper reflection on missional leadership.

of the scale; one congregation is small, representing the lower end of the scale; and the fifth one is in the middle.[16] In the 1998-2005 period, all five congregations grew in confirmed membership, and all but one grew in baptized membership. Two congregations reported a high percentage of members worshiping, over 50 percent, while the others were closer to 33 percent. Many factors influenced these numbers: during that period, one congregation birthed another ELCA congregation; another had facility constraints and then moved into a new building; and two experienced lead pastor transitions. All five congregations experienced an increase in giving; all but one also increased their mission support. All in all, these congregations have demonstrated vitality and growth.

Historically speaking, these congregations ranged in age from twenty-two to forty-seven years.[17] Pastoral tenure ranged from one year to sixteen years; the number of paid staff ranged from six in the smallest church to twenty in the largest one, including both part-time and full-time employees. All but one congregation had a first-call pastor currently serving on the staff. These congregations also varied in their programs: three had preschools; two had ethnic-specific worshiping communities that were sharing their facilities and partnering with them in ministry; and another was at the beginning stages of starting a Hispanic ministry. In addition, one congregation had recently birthed another congregation, and another was exploring the possibility of adding a second site. Overall, all five congregations are finding ways to be intentional with respect to engaging their particular location.

Part 2: The Findings: Eight Common Cultural Dynamics for Empowering Missional Leadership

All of these ELCA congregations have unique expressions of ministry and different personalities. But a deeper analysis brings several commonalities to the surface, and eight cultural dynamics become evident, which I will examine in this section.

16. The three large congregations, based on baptized/worshiping membership in 2005, are: 1,348/804, 1,825/515, and 1,449/556. The numbers for the one small congregation, based on baptized/worshiping membership in 2005, are 253/166.

17. This is a factor worth acknowledging. There exists an opportunity to study congregations that were begun in different eras and compare the findings with this study. This comparison would deepen the learnings on missional leadership.

Dynamic No. 1: An Active and Present God

At the core of these five congregations is a view of God that is *active and alive* in the world, in their community of faith, and in the people as individuals. God is identified as being at work leading, guiding, challenging, and empowering these communities of faith and the individuals within them. Not surprisingly, worship is the main communal encounter with this active God: it provides the compass that keeps each of these faith communities focused. Worship serves as the central, focal point of these communities, informing and shaping their life together.

While worship is at the core in shaping each church, the congregations' worship experiences are remarkably different. Yet, in all five congregations, God is expected to show up and be present in worship, and people anticipate their worship time together. One of the tangible ways God is present in worship is through the sacraments and the proclaimed Word of God; but I must note that this usually includes a brief teaching that explains the meaning of these practices for those not familiar with them. One unique thing about worship is that it is not only about the people's life together as a community, shaping and forming them into God's faithful people; it also has an outward turn that equips people to see the world through God's eyes and challenges them to exercise their faith in their daily living.

While worship is the primary place where the active God is witnessed, this view of God accompanies the people into their various ministries — both within the congregation and in the world. This view of God allows the people in these congregations to see that God is active in the world in which they go to school, work, and share their lives together. Sometimes this results in seeing community needs that the congregation can respond to; other times it means one person caring for her or his actual neighbor; and at other times it impacts how the congregants care for members of their immediate families. But for all of them, God does not live in a box, nor is God simply part of history. God is alive and present in their world, in their lives, and in the faith community in which they participate.

Dynamic No. 2: The World as the Horizon

With an active view of God at the center, the changing world marks the horizon. Each congregation has an *outward focus,* an eye to the *future,* and each exists for the sake of the *world.* Each incorporates into its self-understanding an identity shaped around reaching out to people outside the church. They exist to love their neighbor and welcome others, and loving the neighbor happens both inside and outside the walls of the church building.

Welcoming others is primary and something they strive for when they gather together as a community. Each congregation arrived at this conclusion, thus blurring the lines between church and world. People in these congregations see real needs in the world and they, as individuals and communities, seek to engage the world in God's name and participate in God's mission in real and tangible ways.[18]

Dynamic No. 3: Discipleship as a Way of Life

With God as the center and the world as the horizon, discipleship defines the way of life together for these congregations. The people in each of these

18. It is important to note two critical reflections on how these systems see their relationship to the world. First, being a church with the world as the horizon is one of the critical elements of what it means to be a missional church; yet the language of "missional church" was not prevalent among the people in these faith communities. Some of the leadership used missional language when they articulated what they were about, but most of the people within these systems used other language, such as "neighbor, inviting others, serving the needs of people, or living for the sake of the world." This is worth noting because the people within these systems are not consistent or clear about this aspect of their life together. This leads me to believe that they are in the early stages of their missional understanding.

Second, the majority of the language that is used to articulate this aspect was about *doing* rather than *being* missional. From my perspective, it seemed that the doing of acts of mission was the first part of the transformation of a congregation toward being missional. People were able to get their minds around helping others, serving tangible needs, and inviting their neighbors. However, a shift in attitude — that the church exists not to add more members to its roster but to share the good news of Jesus Christ with others through one's words, actions, and attitude — is a deeper shift. For some of these systems that deeper shift has taken place across the majority of the faith community; for others it still rests primarily within the leadership. For these reasons, we can conclude that these congregational systems are at various points in making the transformation toward being a missional church.

congregations are *passionate* about their faith and about being on a journey, both individually and communally. The discipleship way of life within these congregations has some common characteristics. First, there is a humble spirit present in the people and an understanding that they are both saints and sinners. People are aware of their brokenness, but they are also aware of the gracious gift they have received from God. Second, the people are curious. While they have confidence that God is among them and active in their lives, they are also open to the mystery of God and interested in learning and growing in their faith.

Third, diversity within each of these faith communities provides an enriching and dynamic atmosphere, forcing these communities to continually redefine themselves. People within these systems come from diverse faith backgrounds: from lifelong Lutherans to people new to the church; from those with European backgrounds to those from Hispanic and Asian cultures; and from people who know the language of the Christian faith to others who are just learning it. Framed theologically, these congregations have a lived practice of being the priesthood of all believers, of being called and sent, and of being God's presence in the world through their various vocations.

Dynamic No. 4: The Congregation as a Network of People

Life in these congregations is messy, and it was difficult to figure out how this discipleship as a way of life became embedded in the people. Ironically, the answer was obvious: it was the people themselves. These congregations are communities of people who operate as a *network,* or a human system of relationships. In networking language, people are the "nodes."[19] Clues about this network come from the variety of relational words: empowering, growing, welcoming, inviting, connecting, supporting, loving, and encouraging. Focus-group participants often refer to their shared life together.

This networking aspect, so natural to the people themselves, is not often talked about directly. Yet these relationships have a rhyme and reason to them. The people of these congregations have multiple ways of relating

19. "Node" is a networking term that refers to one element or unit within a network. Networks and nodes will be defined in more detail later in this essay.

to one another for various and multiple purposes. This relationality is fluid yet intentional, as people pass on the congregation's DNA to others. Certain people clearly serve primary roles as the hubs, but relationality as a whole is the foundation undergirding each congregation.

Dynamic No. 5: The Dance of Leadership

Each congregation had formal leadership roles, but all of the people within these faith communities had a part in the leadership dance: leadership was *communal* in nature. It was clear across the board that pastors had a critical role in creating the tone, were expected to lead, and were expected to proclaim God's Word. Yet all of these congregations also had strong lay leadership, both in official capacities and among the people in general. There was a leadership dance occurring within these congregations, a give and take between clergy and lay leadership and between formal and informal leaders.

Woven into this leadership dance is the paradox that people, who are both saints and sinners, boldly assert themselves as God's people leading within their congregation and the world. They do so within a culture that allows imperfection and that practices forgiveness. In the end, leadership sets the communal tone, articulates the mission and vision, and creates an atmosphere that sets people free to lead and serve.[20]

20. One important finding was that there was no uniform organizational structure across these five congregations. While there could be many different reasons for this, including their various sizes, in the end it was clear that the organizational structure was less important than the core understanding of this leadership dance. A second and related finding was that very few of the focus group participants could clearly articulate the leadership process within their system. Over the course of the focus group time the leadership process questions were answered, but not when they were asked directly. Yet in all of the systems, people were confident in the leadership of their congregational system and knew how to make their way through it. Even in systems where the leadership process was changing, or had changed, there was little doubt in the leadership. In the end, leadership was more about planting the DNA within the people and creating an environment in which that DNA could be lived out. While the pastor, staff, and lay leadership all had roles, ultimately what emerged was created by and credited to God.

Dynamic No. 6: The Tension of Ministry and Mission

Within the network of people, ministry and mission provided the connective tissue.[21] Ministry and mission exist in tension and move people back and forth between their *internal, communal* life together and their daily encounters with their *neighbor and the world.* In some congregations the combination was missional ministry, or internal ministries with an external focus; in others the focus was ministry partnered with mission, side by side yet influencing each other; in still others it was mission that turns into ministry, like Alpha with a twist.

Whatever the makeup, these two foci created formal opportunities in which people in these congregations could gather and engage in discipleship, while they were also attentive to the greater culture. With worship as the primary hub, mission and ministry serve as secondary hubs: they provide people with places to grow in their faith, to exercise leadership, and to connect with the world in intentional ways. However, it was clear from my study that the mission activities and ministries were not ends in themselves. Interestingly enough, it didn't matter what the ministry or the missional activity was, because all served these purposes.[22]

Dynamic No. 7: A Vibrant Lutheran Identity

Lutheran identity is important, yet it is a Lutheran identity in which the Christian and Lutheran parts *inform each other* within the context of the world. Some participants stated this notion explicitly, while others simply lived it. The primary focus of these congregations is to help the people in their midst grow in their discipleship journey. While all the congregations

---

21. I use "ministry" and "mission" here in the following way. "Ministry" refers primarily to attending to the discipleship journey of the people of God. While the particulars vary from congregation to congregation, this might include Christian education, support ministries, age-specific ministries, and so on. "Mission" refers primarily to engagement with the other — in the context, in service, and so on. One tends to be focused internally (though certainly not exclusively), and the other tends to be focused externally (though certainly not exclusively). The point here is that *both* focuses (internal and external) and impulses (to sustain community and to expand community) were present and significant.

22. One example was the choir at one of the churches, which served as an outreach ministry even while its primary role was to lead worship.

have various Lutheran elements in their DNA, these Lutheran elements are more about core Lutheran theological commitments than about loyalty to the ELCA or Lutheran traditions.

Word and sacrament are important Lutheran components, as is the notion of grace. All of these five faith communities consciously hold these elements as the core dynamics among their people. Preaching is vibrant, relevant, memorable, challenging, and accompanied by the study of Scripture. The sacrament of communion is defining for all members as they strive to become a confessing community seeking to share their life together. Being the baptized people of God shapes these communities on their faith journey, but in a less prominent way.

Dynamic No. 8: A Changing and Adapting Posture

Finally, these congregations are *fluid, living systems* that keep an eye toward the future and maintain an *adaptive posture*. They continually seek to discover what it means to be church as they live within a changing world. Many participants noted that change was part of their DNA. All of these congregations live with an attitude that change happens and, over time, they have come to expect and recognize it.

This is partly because all five congregations have experienced some kind of significant change in their recent history (be it a new building, new staff, or a new leadership structure), and change is real in their lives and systems. As a result, people have gained a confidence in God and their congregation: they know that neither can be restrained by any particular form or way of being. God has proven to be bigger than any one particular congregational issue. In the end, this points right back to the first cultural dynamic: a God who is active and alive in the world, in these congregations, and in the people themselves.

Part 3: A Proposal for Missional Leadership from a Lutheran Voice

"[T]he Lutheran posture toward missiology in North America can be characterized as 'reactive reform.' We let other theological traditions innovate missiological programs, ideas, and theologies," declares Richard Bliese.

"While others innovate . . . we constantly reform their work by making it 'more Lutheran.'"[23] Historically, Lutherans have not set out to be key players in the missional church conversation.[24] "But 'reform,'" Bliese continues, "as a permanent theological posture is insufficient for mission vitality. Every church must discover, finally, some basis for its own tradition's missiological genius. The key for Lutheran missiology in the future is to move from 'reactive reform' to some kind of 'innovative initiative.'"[25]

Some missional thinking has recently taken place among some Lutherans, but overall Lutherans are late in the game and underdeveloped in providing a missiology that draws on Lutheran tradition and theology.[26] What might a Lutheran voice contribute to the missional church conversation? Might the findings of this study provide a base for developing such an innovative Lutheran missiology? What is missional leadership at the dawn of the twenty-first century?

As others have already established in this volume, missional leadership involves working a hermeneutical process that brings the gospel, church, and world into conversation. This study of congregations empowering missional leadership affirms that hermeneutical work. Van Gelder has developed a hermeneutical process of leading in mission that brings lived experience, theology, and theory into conversation.[27] Drawing on his framework, on Lutheran theology, and on the cultural dynamics identified

---

23. Richard H. Bliese, "Lutheran Missiology: Struggling to Move from Reactive Reform to Innovative Initiative," in *The Gift of Grace: The Future of Lutheran Theology*, ed. Niels Henrik Gregersen et al. (Minneapolis: Fortress, 2005), 216.

24. Yet, there have been Lutheran missiologists: some examples are Carl Braaten, James Scherer, and the work of those in the Lutheran World Federation. However, few are actively working on a Lutheran missiology for North America.

25. Bliese, "Lutheran Missiology," 217.

26. Richard Bliese and Craig Van Gelder, eds., *Evangelizing the Church: A Lutheran Contribution* (Minneapolis: Augsburg Fortress, 2005); Richard Cimino, ed., *Lutherans Today: American Lutheran Identity in the 21st Century* (Grand Rapids: Eerdmans, 2003); Patrick Keifert, "The Return of the Congregation: Missional Warrants," *Word and World* 20, no. 4 (2000); Cynthia D. Moe-Lobeda, *Public Church: For the Life of the World* (Minneapolis: Augsburg Fortress, 2004); Craig L. Nessan, *Beyond Maintenance to Mission: A Theology of the Congregation* (Minneapolis: Fortress, 1999); Cheryl M. Peterson, "The Question of the Church in North American Lutheranism: Toward an Ecclesiology of the Third Article," (Ph.D. diss., Marquette University, 2004); and Gary Simpson, *Critical Social Theory: Prophetic Reason, Civil Society, and Christian Imagination* (Minneapolis: Fortress, 2002).

27. Craig Van Gelder, "The Hermeneutics of Leading in Mission," *Journal of Religious Leadership* 3, no. 1/2 (2004) 139-72.

in this study of five ELCA congregations, this final section presents the seeds of a Lutheran hermeneutic for missional leadership.

Communicatively Discerned

A process of communicative discernment is taking place within these congregations. People exist within a web of relationships, namely, within the church and the world. Discernment is taking place within these webs, which allows congregations to live their unique calling within their particular context. How can this communicative discernment be explained? As a way of unpacking the communicatively discerned aspect of missional congregations, I offer three perspectives below.

Congregations as Complex Systems

The first perspective is that missional congregations are *open, complex* systems. Open-systems theory provides a general framework for looking at congregations, and within open systems there are varying levels of complexity.[28] The missional congregations that I studied are not only open systems; they are also highly complex. In addition to relying on the environment for their survival, they also seek to be countercultural, to exist only by the volunteer exchange of resources, and to vary in form.

Congregations Create a Cultural Identity

A second perspective focuses on a congregation's work of creating its own *cultural identity.* Kathryn Tanner, a theologian who draws from cultural anthropology, offers insight into how congregations create identity.[29] Tanner says that common investments are what bond a culture and serve as its reference point; they determine how it lives and what sense it makes

28. Systems theory looks at things holistically and helps explain how systems survive. Within systems theories there are closed or self-maintaining systems and open systems, which rely on the environment for input and support to sustain life. Mary Jo Hatch, *Organization Theory: Modern, Symbolic, and Postmodern Perspectives* (New York: Oxford University Press, 1997), 36-37.

29. See Kathryn Tanner, *Theories of Culture: A New Agenda for Theology* (Minneapolis: Fortress, 1997).

of its social action (Tanner, p. 57). What makes any culture what it is involves the process of defining and redefining elements that have been transported across boundaries from other cultures. In reality, all cultural identity is a *hybrid*, a relational affair that lives as much between cultures as within them (pp. 57-58).

Congregations are open, complex systems, and they are cultures that are always working to create meaning within their context. This reality means that congregations must develop the ability to be self-critical, both outwardly against other cultures and inwardly in creating and re-creating their own identity (p. 58). Ironically, this process of creating identity and the congregation's ability to be critical of itself does not threaten the culture's identity, but actually strengthens it. The congregations I studied have developed the ability to do this work.

Theology as a Way of Life

The final perspective is that theology becomes a *way of life*. The question that finally has to be answered is this: How is the truth of the gospel to be lived in this time and place? Discerning God's work within a specific community requires attending to the particulars of a context, as one also tests and seeks understanding of previous claims about God. This reality means that God's people can no longer separate their church life from their home life. Since culture refers to the whole social practice of meaningful action, then Christian theology has to do with the meaning dimension of Christian practices.[30]

This understanding pulls theology in two different directions: in one sense, theology defines a culture of people and their way of life; in another sense, people challenge theological claims as they press against them in an effort to create meaning in their particular location. Congregations live in the midst of this tension, constantly wrestling with creating and re-creating their hybrid identity. The cultural dynamics of an active view of God and discipleship as a way of life have at their core this issue of the meaning-making of Christian practices.

---

30. Tanner, *Theories of Culture*, 70: "Christian social practice essentially involves making theological affirmations about God and Jesus and about human life in their light."

Biblically/Theologically Framed

Communicative discernment highlights two voices within the hermeneutical process. The church has another key dialogue partner, the gospel,
which must be biblically and theologically framed.[31] This section highlights four perspectives: views of church, God, ministry, and leadership.

View of the Church

Church is a loaded word, holding various meanings. The mainline church
can no longer assume a shared understanding of what it means to be
church. This reality provides both a challenge and an opportunity. The
mainline church has been an *ecclesiocentric* church, a church centered on
structure. This ecclesiocentric focus is now being challenged by the idea of
a *theocentric* church, a church centered on one's view of God. In an
ecclesiocentric church, God's mission is synonymous with the church's
mission, collapsing the two into one. The church was placed in the center,
with God working only through the church, not outside it. In a theocentric
church, the church exists to participate in God's mission, the *missio Dei*,
with God working through the church yet keeping a distinction between
the two. A theocentric view of church translates into God's being active in
and through the church, but also in the world. Using the language developed by the "missional church," the church's calling and vocation is to represent the kingdom of God in the world.[32]

Seeing God's mission as larger than the church reorients the
church's focus toward the world. Simply stated, God and the church exist
for the sake of the world. Therefore, *missio ecclesiae* must follow *missio
Dei:* that is, the church's structure must follow God's mission. It was clear
that the congregations I studied saw themselves in this way. While there
was no uniform perspective, the commitment to the world and their
communal discipleship journey kept the tension between mission and

31. Hunsberger describes this three-way dialogue between the gospel, culture, and
church in George R. Hunsberger and Craig Van Gelder, eds., *The Church between Gospel and
Culture: The Emerging Mission in North America* (Grand Rapids: Eerdmans, 1996), 8-9.

32. Darrell L. Guder, ed., *Missional Church: A Vision for the Sending of the Church in
North America* (Grand Rapids: Eerdmans, 1998), 80-81. Matthew 16 is an illustration of this.
Here the *ekklesia* and the *basileia* are separate — but closely related — concepts (*Missional
Church*, 97-98).

ministry alive in these congregations and kept them open to new opportunities for dialogue.

View of God

Currently, there is a renewed focus among many theologians on understanding God from a Trinitarian point of view. Recent scholarship has lifted up two aspects of the triune God: God's *sending* nature and God's *perichoretic* nature. The sending nature, traditionally connected with the Western line of Trinitarian thought, has God the Father sending God the Son, and the Father and Son sending the Spirit (see, e.g., John 20:21: "As the Father has sent me, so I send you" [NRSV]). This view highlights the particularities of God: God creates, redeems, and sanctifies. Within this view, the triune God sends the church into the world to participate in God's mission.

The periochoretic nature, traditionally connected with the Eastern line of Trinitarian thought, has the Father, Son, and Spirit dwelling in relationship within the Godhead (see, e.g., John 14:11: "I am in the Father and the Father is in me" [NRSV]). All of God indwells in the Father, Son, and Spirit, with each completing who God is. Each is in relationship with the other two, being equal but not the same. God, in God's self, is a God in relationship. The triune God moves together, creating a three-way circulation of love based on equality. This view highlights the kenotic nature of God: the emptying of the persons, one to another, and in turn to humanity and all of creation.

Humankind, created in the image of God, is created with both a communal and sending nature, created for mutuality and interdependence, as well as for being open to the other. Christian community seeks to live with this perichoretic, relational identity *and* with this sending — for the sake of the world and reality. Both the perichoretic and sending natures suggest movement, one internal and one external. These movements were present in the congregations that I studied. The people of these faith communities were continually shaping their life together by emptying themselves to one another, and by going out as people sent into the world to participate in God's mission.

View of Ministry

While the previously stated views of God and church are more broadly Christian, what would a missional view of ministry influenced by Lutheran theology look like? We need to address two broad themes: the creative and redemptive aspect of God's mission and the community of the baptized.

God's Creative and Redemptive Mission   God created the world and continues to create in the world. Luther sets this forth in his explanation of the first article: "I believe God had created me and all that exists." God "provides me with food and clothing, home and family, daily work, and all I need from day to day."[33] This is not a one-time event in the past, but God continues — and will continue — to actively create and sustain life. God, the creator of the universe, enlists humanity to join in this ongoing creative process and the congregations I studied believe that (see, e.g., Gen. 1–2).

Yet sin exists in the world. Not only has the Fall taken place, but a power encounter exists in the world. Humanity lives in "a situation in which there are two kingdoms (earth and heaven, in Luther's terminology), two contending powers (God and the devil) . . . in which Christians are involved in constant struggle."[34] But this is not the end. God so loved the world that God sent God's son, Jesus, to save it. "The death of Jesus on the cross is the centre of all Christian theology. . . . All Christian statements about God, about creation, about sin and death have their focal point in the Crucified Christ."[35] This focal point of the Christian faith is the gospel message, which is good news.

The Baptized Community   What is the role of Christian community? Christians are baptized into Christ's death and resurrection and joined in community. In baptism, Christians become a new creation, dying to their

33. Martin Luther, *The Small Catechism in Contemporary English with Lutheran Book of Worship Texts: A Handbook of Basic Christian Instruction for the Family and the Congregation* (Minneapolis: Augsburg, 1979), 11.

34. Marc Kolden, "Luther on Vocation," *Word and World* 3, no. 4 (Fall 1983): 383.

35. Jürgen Moltmann, *The Crucified God: The Cross of Christ as the Foundation and Criticism of Christian Theology,* trans. R. A. Wilson and John Bowden (New York: Harper & Row Publishers, 1974), 204.

earthly will and rising to a heavenly one.[36] Yet this one-time event is the call to a lifetime journey. How does this happen?

In baptism God is the primary actor; in baptism God extends and invites humanity into God's self; in baptism God creates anew, forgives sins, promises life eternal, gives the Spirit to each baptized person, and releases the Spirit into the world.[37] God does all of this; the one who is baptized simply receives. Baptism is God's free gift to humanity. In its most inclusive ways, baptism is the opening up of God's self to the world, so that people will come together and be united.[38]

The faith community receives the baptized and professes to faith on their behalf. This is most clearly seen in infant baptism. Although this is a practice that has not gone unchallenged, it is both theologically sound and symbolic of a Lutheran understanding of baptism. Baptism is not about the proclaimed faith of the one baptized; it is a gift from God to the baptized, which is received by the Christian community for the purpose of the creation of faith in the one newly baptized. In baptism, faith, not works, orients the Christian way of life.[39]

In baptism, the baptized receive a call to a new way of life. This new Christian way of life is lived in community and committed to serve the world. "Baptism clearly articulates that we are not our own. . . . [R]elationships mark the Christian life."[40] This community of the baptized has two

36. "In baptism the recipient is buried with Christ; he must die with him that he may rise and live with him (Rom. 6)." Gustaf Wingren, *Luther on Vocation,* trans. Carl C. Rasmussen (Evansville, IN: Ballast Press, 1999), 28.

37. "Baptism as reception into the Body of Christ is a divine act independent of man's action, one which, in and with his being set within the Body of Christ, confers on the baptised person the grace that he 'be clothed with Christ' (Gal. 3:27; Rom. 6:3ff.) just at this particular place within the Body of Christ. In this Body the resurrection power of the *Holy Spirit* operates." Oscar Cullman, *Baptism in the New Testament,* trans. J. K. S. Reid (London: SCM Press, 1950), 39.

38. Cullman puts it this way: "At Golgotha, the prevenient grace of God in Christ is appropriated to *all* men, and entry into Christ's kingdom is opened to them. In Baptism, entry is opened up to . . . the 'inner circle' of this Kingdom, that is, to the earthly Body of Christ, the Church. Golgotha and Baptism are related to one another as are the wider all-inclusive Kingdom of Christ and the Church." Cullman, *Baptism in the New Testament,* 34.

39. "This is the Christian liberty, our faith, which . . . makes the law and works unnecessary for any man's righteousness and salvation." Martin Luther, *Three Treatises,* 2nd rev. ed. (Philadelphia: Fortress, 1970), 284.

40. Martha Ellen Stortz, "'The Curtain Only Rises': Assisted Death and the Practice of Baptism," *Currents in Theology and Mission* 26, no. 1 (1999): 14.

movements: internally, it is both forming and reforming its members and their way of life together (as sign and foretaste); externally, it is witnessing to and engaging the world, participating in God's mission (as agent and instrument).

View of Leadership

Christians, communally and individually, have agency. Ignited in worship, empowered through ministry, and lived daily in the world, agency was a powerful source within the congregations I studied. Agency was present both in individual persons and within the faith communities as a whole. As baptized Christians they had discovered that they had been transformed into "agents of Christ's love"[41] by the Holy Spirit. This agency was communal and aimed at serving the neighbor.[42]

For Luther this call, both general and particular, is best articulated in the notion of the priesthood of all believers. Developing a theology of vocation can help the baptized people of God understand their particular callings on earth and the particular, concrete ways in which they can love and serve their neighbor. Home, work, faith community, and civic community are all places where Christians are to be God's presence in the world and to give witness to the gospel. These are the places where the gospel is discovered and the ways in which the baptized are dispersed throughout the world. Therefore, vocation belongs to the Christian's life between baptism and resurrection, and it is what connects God's people with the *missio Dei.*[43]

---

41. Cynthia D. Moe-Lobeda, *Healing a Broken World: Globalization and God* (Minneapolis: Fortress, 2002), 87.

42. Moe-Lobeda, *Healing a Broken World,* 75, quoting Luther, "Third Sermon on Pentecost," in Lenker, 3:321.

43. Wingren, *Luther on Vocation,* 250. It is worth noting that the relationships that constitute the Christian way of life not only are with those within Christian communities, but also include relationships in other communities in which God's people are stationed in the world. Christians are always located within the world and are God's presence — God's agents of love — in the world. In varying degrees the people within the congregations I studied have discovered not only a communal identity as baptized believers, or the agency they have received in baptism through the Holy Spirit, but they have also claimed their particular vocations as stations in which they can participate in — and are participating in — God's creative and redemptive mission in the world.

Theoretically Informed

Congregations are communities of faith that need to be framed theologically; but they are also organizations and thus need to be understood theoretically. Organizational and leadership theories are fruitful conversation partners for understanding congregations. I will now address the theoretical informing of our ecclesiology in four broad themes: change and adaptivity, congregations as networks, leadership as a dance, and lifting up the gifts of people.

A New Worldview Requiring Change and Adaptivity

Margaret Wheatley challenges leaders to adopt a new worldview, for the "old ways of relating to each other don't support us any longer."[44] To get to this new worldview requires looking at connections, seeing energy in relationships, acknowledging the power in what is unseen, and leaving behind the Newtonian worldview, which sees the world as a machine with separate parts. In this new worldview, chaos and change are givens. Leading requires new leadership skills around adaptability and the ability to deal with change. Leadership looks at the whole rather than the parts, tends to the development and retention of the core identity, and fosters relationships inside and outside the organization.

Wheatley's findings describe the workings of the congregations I studied. As the church seeks to create missional communities, Wheatley's ideas highlight the work that needs to be done and give leadership guidance on where to focus (Wheatley, pp. 157-70). Organizations that operate within this worldview focus on participatory management, tend to relationships, work within networks, share information, and create meaning. The voices of the people in five congregations I studied would agree.

The Congregational System as a Network

Networks, a foundational reality in Wheatley's work, are seen to be critical in this new worldview. Alberto-Laszlo Barabasi predicts that "[n]etworking thinking is poised to invade all domains of human activity and most fields of human inquiry . . . [for] [n]etworks are by their very nature the

---

44. Wheatley, *Leadership and the New Science*, xi.

fabric of most complex systems."[45] As I have noted above, networks were the primary topology in the congregations I studied.

We can learn many things from networks. Networks are made up of nodes, links, and hubs. Within a social network, *nodes* represent the individual persons, *links* are the things that connect these persons or nodes, and *hubs* are the key people (or nodes) who represent dense populations and diverse connections that create shortcuts to other parts of the network. Identifying the nodes, hubs, and links within a network illuminates key information about a network. Hubs are the "generic building block[s] of our complex, interconnected world" (Barabasi, p. 63), and are created when a large number of nodes attach to one particular node. In a network, the greater the number of large hubs, the more effective and robust that network becomes.

Connectivity is key for networks, for vulnerability comes when networks are not interconnected (p. 130). "Achieving robustness is the ultimate goal" for networks, since it is their greatest protection against failure (p. 111). Without robustness, a network can be dismantled by the disabling of only a few hubs (p. 118). Scale-free networks are a key way that networks organize themselves for robustness, because they increase the number of large hubs strategically throughout the network. Each of the congregations I studied not only had networks as their topology, but they were robust, scale-free networks.

The Dance of Leadership

"Leadership would be a safe undertaking if your organizations and communities only faced problems for which they already knew the solutions." These kinds of problems, according to Ronald Heifetz and Marty Linsky, are technical ones.[46] Treating problems as technical ones has been a common approach for church leaders in dealing with change. Yet the new worldview suggests seeing change differently: "[T]here is a whole host of problems that are not amenable to authoritative expertise or standard operating procedures. . . . We call these adaptive challenges

---

45. Alberto-Laszlo Barabasi, *Linked: The New Science of Networks* (Cambridge, MA: Perseun Publishing, 2002), 222.

46. Ronald A. Heifetz and Marty Linsky, *Leadership on the Line: Staying Alive Through the Dangers of Leading* (Boston, MA: Harvard Business School Press, 2002), 13.

because they require experiments, new discoveries, and adjustments from numerous places in the organization and community" (Heifetz and Linsky, p. 13). This approach to change requires both shifting one's perspective and posture of leadership.

Most organizations look to leadership, or, more specifically, to individual leaders, to solve their problems. However, "[w]hen people look to authorities for easy answers to adaptive challenges, they end up with dysfunction" (p. 14). For too long organizations have relied on technical responses — restructuring, new leadership, changing methods, or adopting new styles — for the answers to problems that require major shifts (p. 14).[47] However, the leadership within the congregations I studied operated with a different posture. These systems did not rely on quick fixes, but were able to dig below the surface: they sought to discover the core issues, and they changed not only programs but attitudes.

As the church is called to shift from an ecclesiocentric view to a theocentric one, church leaders will have to shift their thinking from technical to adaptive change and from solo to shared leadership. With an adaptive posture to change, leaders are not the experts who handle the problems but the conveners of the people who are directly affected by the problem. As one pastor said, "You don't shape congregations rationally but behaviorally. Modeling is how you shape people. . . . It's shaping the culture. . . . Our job is to shape the culture."[48]

Lifting Up the Gifts of the People

The congregations I studied operate as complex, open systems made up of robust networks with shared leadership, and they have an active, missional view of God as the source of their life together. They find the energy for their life together in the work of the Spirit and in the people themselves. People, called and gifted, are what make up these congregations. Equipped by the Spirit and empowered by communities of faith, these baptized people of God live out their particular callings in the world and within their

47. This issue is not only common within the church but in organizations as a whole. Heifetz and Linsky say: "The single most common source of leadership failure we've been able to identify — in politics, community life, business, or the nonprofit section — is that people, especially those in positions of authority, treat adaptive challenges like technical problems."

48. Interview participant from congregation No. 1.

communities of faith; they are the invisible force field present within each community of faith.[49]

Many theories have been developed — within both secular and Christian literature — that highlight human potential and help people discover their unique gifts and design.[50] For the purposes of this missional view of leadership, the particulars of these various theories are secondary to my main point, which is the empowering and lifting up of God's gifted people. The work of discovering and empowering the gifts of God's people will be done within the holdings of one's individual vocations, located within community, and with an eye to the world and the *missio Dei*.

Strategic Action

The reality is that the church will need to live into this new worldview at the same time that it is discovering it and certainly before it can fully understand it. This can be unnerving, yet it is the work of current church leaders to lead in the midst of this real dilemma. Within this liminal time, church leadership will need to act, and to do so strategically, helping faith communities make their way forward.[51] I want to address here one final

49. The concept of force fields has to do with the "invisible forces that occupy space and influence behavior." Wheatley, *Leadership and the New Science*, 15.

50. Within the Christian literature, resources have emerged from teaching congregations such as Willow Creek, and their own gifts ministry called Network. One of their current resources is Bruce Bugbee, *Discover Your Spiritual Gifts the Network Way* (Barrington, IL: Willow Creek Association, 2007). In addition, Saddleback's gift ministry is named SHAPE. See more at www.saddleback.com. Individuals working this area include Jane A. G. Kise, David Stark, and Sandra Krebs Hirsh, *Lifekeys: Discovering Who You Are, Why You're Here, What You Do Best* (Minneapolis: Bethany House Publishers, 1996); Peter Wagner, *Your Spiritual Gifts Can Help Your Church Grow* (Oxnard, CA: Regal Books, 1995). Within the secular literature, the resources are multiple. Here are some examples: Renee Baron, *What Type Am I? Discover Who You Really Are* (New York: Penguin Books, 1998); Renee Baron and Elizabeth Wagele, *The Enneagram Made Easy* (New York: HarperSanFrancisco, 1994); David Keirsey, *Please Understand Me 2* (Del Mar, CA: Prometheus Nemesis, 1998); Otto Kroeger and Janet M. Thuesen, *Type Talk* (New York: Tilden Press Book, 1998); Don Richard Riso, *Personality Types: Using the Enneagram for Self-Discovery* (Boston: Houghton Mifflin, 1996); and Marcus Buckingham and Donald O. Clifton, *Now, Discover Your Strengths* (New York: Free Press, 2001).

51. I use "leadership" here to intentionally note that this is a shared, communal view of leading rather than an individual's sole responsibility.

aspect — strategic action — by looking at missional leadership from four perspectives: as cultivation, as agent of change, multidimensionally, and as fostering Christian community.

Missional Leadership as Cultivation

Alan Roxburgh and Fred Romanuk, in *The Missional Leader,* have set out to be bridge builders. Deeply committed to the missional church, they are helping congregations become missional. For them, missional leadership is about cultivation. Cultivation describes leadership that "works the soil of the congregation so as to invite and constitute the environment for the people of God to discern what the Spirit is doing in, with, and among them as a community."[52]

Leadership focused on cultivation is organic and fluid, more of an art than a skill. Cultivation is not a linear process; rather, it is the ongoing work of missional leadership. Cultivating awareness, co-learning networks, fresh ways of engaging Scripture, and new practices, habits, and norms are four key elements.[53] The congregations I studied exhibited cultivation as part of their ongoing work. At times a large part of the faith community was involved, while at other times a smaller group was involved; but over all, leadership as cultivation was prevalent.

Missional Leadership as Agent of Change

Leadership in a missional church also guides and leads change within an ever-changing, complex set of systems. Roxburgh and Romanuk recognize three zones in the change process.[54] This perspective provides a framework

52. Alan Roxburgh and Fred Romanuk, *The Missional Leader: Equipping Your Church to Reach a Changing World* (San Francisco: Jossey-Bass, 2006), 4, 28, 31-32.

53. These three types are: awareness of what God is doing among the people in the congregation; awareness of how the congregation can imagine itself as the center of God's activities; and awareness of what God is already up to in their context. The co-learning networks "create an environment that releases the missional imagination of a congregation." The scriptural element deeply connects God's people to God's work in fresh ways as they put into practice their new awareness. These practices are not based primarily on programs and traditions, but on Christian formation and the disciplines of discipleship. Roxburgh and Romanuk, *The Missional Leader,* 31-34.

54. Roxburgh and Romanuk, *The Missional Leader,* 41. These zones are: reactive leadership, performative leadership, and emergent leadership.

to "assist leaders in understanding the adaptive shift in leadership style required amid such change; identify the skills and competencies required in each zone; and help congregations understand their own location in massive change" (Roxburgh and Romanuk, p. 40).

The preferred zone for missional congregations is one of pioneering and experimenting/emerging (pp. 41-44). Working this change process creates both an understanding of the current situation and helps an organization find a new way, with new language and common commitments (p. 114).[55] Roxburgh and Romanuk's emergent zone leadership is descriptive of the congregations I studied. All were on a journey, with an unforeseeable end, and they allowed for ambiguity and failure. They were also about the work of creating new language with clear meaning.

Missional Leadership as Multidimensional

As I have already revealed, leading a missional congregation requires navigating multiple complexities. Missional leadership requires being a cultural anthropologist, a contextual theologian, a student of organizational leadership theory, and one who empowers others. Roxburgh and Romanuk acknowledge these complexities as they highlight both the personal attributes and skills that leadership within a missional congregation must have. The leadership skills are about cultivating people, forming mission environments and congregations, and engaging context. The personal attributes are personal maturity, conflict management, personal courage, and developing trust (Roxburgh and Romanuk, p. 114).

These four clusters of work and/or skills are vital for missional congregations and align with the cultural dynamics explored in this study. For example, the cultural dynamic of discipleship as a way of life focuses on cultivating people, attending to the particularities in the congregation and their context, and requires a commitment to the leadership's own discipleship journey.

---

55. To do so, the change process includes five aspects: awareness, understanding, evaluation, experiment, and commitment This model of change is a five-step process based on Everett Roger's *Diffusion of Innovations.*

Missional Leadership as Fostering Christian Community

Missional leadership, however, is about fostering Christian community and helping God's people live into and out of Christian disciplines. Programs within missional congregations are present, but only as mechanisms for something greater, a vibrant relationship with God. Diana Butler Bass, in *The Practicing Congregation,* discovered that congregations that experienced a renewed sense of identity, vocation, and mission were intentionally attending to and embracing particular Christian practices.[56]

Bass is not alone. Craig Dykstra and Dorothy Bass add: "The distinctive understanding of *Christian practices* . . . [represents] the constituent elements in a way of life that becomes incarnate when human beings live in the light of and in response to God's gift of abundant life."[57] Christian practices of missional congregations are Christian practices of Christian communities. Missional Christian practices tend to the forming of faith communities as well as the ever-changing translatability of contextual realities. Hence, this hermeneutic ends back at the beginning, communicatively discerned.

---

56. This study included fifty congregations from various mainline denominations, including the ELCA, Presbyterian Church (USA), United Methodist, Episcopal, United Church of Christ, and Reformed Church in America. Congregations were large, medium, and small; they were diverse geographically, pastorally, and in class, race, and ethnicity. Diana Butler Bass, *The Practicing Congregation: Imagining a New Old Church* (Washington, D.C.: Alban, 2002). Bass describes these congregations as: "Communities that choose to reword denominational tradition in light of local experience to create a web of practices that transmit identity, nurture community, cultivate mature spirituality, and advance mission. These practices — as varied as classical spiritual disciplines such as *lectio divina* and centering prayer, or moral and theological practices like householding, Sabbath keeping, forgiveness, doing justice, and hospitality — are drawn from, recover, or reclaim individual and corporate patterns of historic Christian living that provide meaning and enliven a sense of spiritual connection to God and others. In these congregations, transmission of identity and vocation does not occur primarily through familial religious tradition, civic structures, or the larger culture. Christian identity is neither assumed nor received. Rather, transmission occurs through choice, negotiation, and reflexive theological engagement, in community, by adopting a particular way of life as expressed by and sustained through historically grounded Christian practices."

57. Craig Dykstra and Dorothy C. Bass, "A Theological Understanding of Christian Practices," in *Practicing Theology: Beliefs and Practices in Christian Life,* ed. Miroslav Volf and Dorothy C. Bass (Grand Rapids: Eerdmans, 2002), 21.

Conclusion

This chapter plants the seeds of an innovative Lutheran missiology with a view toward identifying a Lutheran hermeneutic of missional leadership. Rooted in a grounded-theory approach, the research of this study, combined with current theoretical and theological resources, has offered a missional Lutheran ecclesiology for these changing times. I have proposed a hermeneutical approach, one that takes into consideration texts, both biblical and theological; culture, and the forming of it; Christian community, God's people working out their Christian way of life together; and strategic action, the lived practices.

What I am finally suggesting can be summed up in two words: *intentionality* and *openness*. The changing times are real, for the landscape is changing at rates faster than ever before. Yet the opportunities and the need for missional leadership in these changing times are also real. So the question needs to be asked: Are we as church leaders willing to be faithful, yet changing, as we seek to participate in God's creative and redemptive mission in the world?

CHAPTER 8

Leadership and the Missional Church Conversation: Listening In on What Leaders in Four Denominational Systems Have to Say

Kristine M. Stache

Introduction

"Missional church" has become a catchphrase for congregations and denominations in the twenty-first century. Grounded in a theology that the church is defined primarily by what it *is* rather than what it *does,* missional church focuses on the core issue of congregational identity — regardless of denominational affiliation. But many people today appear to be confused about what missional church means, and some mistakenly view it as merely new language that is trying to reclaim an older emphasis on missions.

A recent research project that was a collaboration of The Gospel and Our Culture Network and Church Innovations Institute provided insights into these contrasting views.[1] It included national leaders, mid-level judicatory leaders, administrators and teachers in theological education, and pastors and laypeople from congregations in four different denominational systems. All four systems declared that they were striving to become missional churches. This chapter draws on insights I gained from this re-

1. Innovating Missional Church was a project that was conducted collaboratively by The Gospel and Our Culture Network and Church Innovations Institute. It was funded by the Lilly Foundation and completed in 2005. A consultation was held in October 2005 at Luther Seminary, in which its findings were presented to systems leaders from around the world. For information on these two organizations, see: http://www.gocn.org/ (accessed Dec. 3, 2008); see also http://www.churchinnovations.org/ (accessed Dec. 3, 2008).

search as to how leadership is or is not functioning in each of the four systems in their efforts to become missional churches.

Theological Perspectives and Methodological Approach

Ecclesiology

Though it did not emerge until the late twentieth century, missional-church theology draws on two thousand years of church history. Ecclesiology, the study of the nature, ministry, and organization of the church, is as extensive as the history of Christianity itself. From the early Christian church of the first few centuries up to the time of the Reformation, the church was constantly evolving as it encountered ever-changing cultures. It was through the Reformation in the sixteenth century that the church further diversified into multiple ecclesiologies and polities.

Roger Haight identifies five "distinctly different churches and ecclesiologies" that came out of that period: Lutheranism, the Reformed tradition, the Church of England, Anabaptism, and the Baptist Church.[2] Four of those five ecclesiologies discussed by Haight as having their roots in the Reformation constitute the focus of my research.

Missiology

It was not until the middle of the nineteenth century that missiology, the study of how to proclaim the gospel and grow the church, became a discipline in theological education.[3] It emerged initially as part of the modern missions movement, and it reflected an understanding of mission as being primarily a task of the church. Interestingly, missiology as a discipline struggled to find its place in theological education, primar-

2. Roger Haight, *Christian Community in History: Comparative Ecclesiology* (New York: Continuum, 2005), 3.

3. David Jacobus Bosch, *Transforming Mission: Paradigm Shifts in Theology of Mission*, American Society of Missiology Series 16 (Maryknoll, NY: Orbis, 1991), 491; Stephen Bevans and Roger Schroeder, *Constants in Context: A Theology of Mission for Today*, American Society of Missiology Series 30 (Maryknoll, NY: Orbis, 2004), 221.

ily due to its focusing on the practice of mission.[4] However, mission in the last fifty years has undergone a significant shift from its definition primarily as a task of the church, to its new definition as inherent in the very nature of the church. A theology of mission is being replaced by "missional theology."[5] Here mission is understood as being inherent in the very nature of the church because the triune God is seen as a missionary God.

But what do we mean by the nature of the church? Without an understanding of God as a divine community in which the church participates, it is difficult to understand mission as being inherent in the church's nature. It was at the International Mission Council gathered in Willingen, Germany, in 1952 that this shift began to take place: from an ecclesiocentric view of mission to one focused on the nature and personhood of the triune God. The gathering's summary paper, written after the meeting, rejected a church-centered view and brought forth a new understanding of mission that was focused on the *missio Dei*.[6] This understanding of the mission of God — one in which the church participates — provided a new basis for a Trinitarian understanding of mission.[7]

Missional Church and the Doctrine of the Trinity

The language of "sending," "receiving," and "bearing the message" abounds in today's literature that discusses mission.[8] But how God acts in God's world still appears to be open to debate. Lesslie Newbigin argues that the *missio Dei* is made known in God's world via multiple methods at the same time: proclamation of the Word, presence of God, and proveni-

4. See Kyle Small, "Missional Theology for Schools of Theology" (chap. 2 of this volume).

5. Craig Van Gelder, *The Essence of the Church: A Community Created by the Spirit* (Grand Rapids: Baker Books, 2000), 33.

6. Norman E. Thomas, *Classic Texts in Mission and World Christianity*, American Society of Missiology Series 20 (Maryknoll, NY: Orbis Books, 1995), 101-2.

7. Thomas, *Classic Texts*, 114; Bosch, *Transforming Mission*, 390; and James Scherer, *Gospel, Church, and Kingdom: Comparative Studies in World Mission Theology* (Minneapolis: Augsburg, 1987), 98.

8. See Bosch, *Transforming Mission*, 390; see also Van Gelder, *Essence of the Church*, 125; Darrell L. Guder, ed., *Missional Church: A Vision for the Sending of the Church in North America* (Grand Rapids: Eerdmans, 1998), 77-109.

ence of the Spirit.[9] David Bosch argues that mission is not something that the church does, but the *missio Dei* actually constitutes the church.[10] Others note that the church is not the goal of the work of God, but rather its instrument and witness.[11] Even in this view, the doctrine of the Trinity tends to be relegated, at least by some, to the position of model and mentor.[12] These views all call us to imitate both the communal nature and the activity of the Trinity.

Further development is needed to understand just how the Trinity and the church are related. Historically, the Trinity has been understood on two separate fronts: its activity in the world (the Western perspective) and the interrelationships within itself (the Eastern perspective).[13] Most recent literature is beginning to open a new door for our understanding of the relationship between humanity and the Trinity. As members of the church, we are invited to participate in the social reality of the Godhead, or what is known as *perichoresis.*[14]

Feminist Theology and Missional Church

The studies noted above help us understand the Trinity more fully, but our understanding can be further developed. Feminist theologians have contributed much over the years in bringing forward the lost voices and experiences of women to help us better understand the life and activity of God. Serene Jones refers to feminist theology as "a collection of critical texts and a conversation . . . [that] share a common goal, namely, the liberation of women."[15] Feminist theology contributes to a revisioning of Christian cat-

9. Lesslie Newbigin, *The Open Secret: An Introduction to the Theology of Mission,* 2nd ed. (Grand Rapids: Eerdmans, 1995), 56.

10. Bosch, *Transforming Mission,* 389-392.

11. Guder, *Missional Church,* 77-109.

12. See George Cladis, *Leading the Team-Based Church: How Pastors and Church Staffs Can Grow Together into a Powerful Fellowship of Leaders* (San Francisco, CA: Jossey-Bass, 1999), 10-13.

13. See Karl Barth, *Church Dogmatics,* vol. 1, part 1, trans. G. T. Thomson (Edinburgh: T&T Clark, 1960); Karl Rahner, *The Trinity* (New York: Herder, 1970).

14. See Miroslav Volf, *After Our Likeness: The Church as the Image of the Trinity* (Grand Rapids: Eerdmans, 1998), 208-13.

15. Serene Jones, *Feminist Theory and Christian Theology: Cartographies of Grace,* Guides to Theological Inquiry (Minneapolis: Fortress, 2000), 14.

egories by informing and shaping a new language and new metaphors that take the experiences of women seriously.[16]

The voices of two women in particular, Elizabeth Johnson and Catherine LaCugna, bring this conversation into the subject arena of the Trinity. Not only do they say that the Trinity is both immanent and economic, but they claim that the Trinity indwells humans as participants in that relationship.[17] These voices — and the experiences of women throughout history — help us to shape a fuller understanding of God as a being in community.[18] By understanding God as a God who exists in relationship, we can begin to understand our relationship with God and with each other. God exists for us and with us. "The doctrine of the Trinity insists that God does not exist except as Father, Son, Spirit. . . . This means that every human being, and indeed every creature, has its origin in a person who by definition is not solitary but in relationship with another."[19]

This new view of community is what helps shape a missional imagination. We begin to see God's world as part of this community, where all participants are equal and exist because they are in relationship with one another. A missional church is something that exists together with the world, not on behalf of the world or over against it. Instead of merely taking the gospel to others, or giving it to another, we also become receivers and bearers of God's Word through the Spirit. Instead of merely being providers of hospitality to those in need, we also allow ourselves to become recipients of hospitality. In a missional church we recognize how all people's gifts fit together as one, holy, catholic, and apostolic church, where the "whole community enjoys a radical equality of relationship with the Holy One and as sacred each and every person has equal standing."[20]

---

16. Anne E. Carr, *Transforming Grace: Christian Tradition and Women's Experience* (San Francisco, CA: Harper & Row, 1988), 158-62.

17. Elizabeth A. Johnson, *She Who Is: The Mystery of God in Feminist Theological Discourse* (New York: Crossroad, 1992); Catherine Mowry LaCugna, *God for Us: The Trinity and Christian Life* (San Francisco: HarperSanFrancisco, 1991).

18. Johnson, *She Who Is*, 5-6.

19. Catherine Mowry LaCugna, "The Practical Trinity," *Christian Century* 109, no. 22 (1992): 681.

20. Elizabeth A. Johnson, *Friends of God and Prophets: A Feminist Theological Reading of the Communion of Saints* (New York, NY: Continuum, 1998), 63.

Methodology

The qualitative data I am citing in this chapter were collected from four different denominational systems, each of them seeking to become a missional church: the Evangelical Lutheran Church in America, the Synod of the Trinity of the Presbyterian Church USA, the Mennonite Church USA, and a fellowship of Church of Christ congregations associated with Abilene Christian University. I gathered the data in 2003-2004 from these four denominational systems on two levels for a study in which I was seeking to innovate missional church in each of these systems.[21]

The data consist of the answers to eight different questions that I initially presented to national leaders, mid-level judicatory leaders, and theological educators within each system. Later, I presented these same questions to pastors and laypeople from congregations in various locations around the country, congregations that were part of each denomination.[22] I interviewed 75 to 100 people in each denominational system, and they provided answers to the same eight questions.[23] While the data were originally collected for a larger research project, they are useful in this chapter because they represent the people's stories, opinions, and interpretations of how missional church is understood and lived out in each of the four denominational systems.

21. Leaders of each of these systems have granted permission to use this data for publication, allowing me as a researcher to further explore the language, stories, and metaphors used in these systems to talk about the relationship between their understanding of God and missional church.

22. This method of interview was designed by Pat Taylor Ellison and Patrick Keifert at Church Innovations, Inc., as a method for ethnographic research within congregations. It focuses on four major areas: attitudes and beliefs, minimum knowledge base, skills, and pass-on-able habits for innovating a missional church.

23. The questions were created to reflect four different components: capacity, attitudes, and beliefs; skills; minimum knowledge base; and habits. The questions were the following: When you hear the expression "missional church," what do you think that's about? When you think about this topic, what do you feel and what attitudes and beliefs are needed for innovating such a church in your system? What were the things that you already knew that made it possible for you to begin this work? What is the minimum knowledge base you're trying to teach people for innovating this system? What skills have you found most helpful for doing this work? What are the skills you have needed to develop in your system? What are the habits you grew up with that have made a positive difference in this work? What are the new habits you're trying to pass along, and where did you get them?

Evangelical Lutheran Church in America

The Evangelical Lutheran Church in America, and its various sister denominational bodies, is the result of Martin Luther's efforts to bring about reform in the Roman Catholic Church nearly five hundred years ago.[24] Individuals participating in this reform movement were soon given the name Lutherans, much to his dismay: Luther was not looking for a "new party name," just a return to what was purely Christian.[25] Luther's reform movement spread quickly across the continent in the wake of his defiance of the Roman Catholic Church. By 1522, Lutheran preachers were working in northern Europe. The Lutheran National Church of Denmark was already formed by 1537 (Gritsch, pp. 50-51), and the first Norwegian Lutheran bishop was installed in the same year (p. 53). In addition to Scandinavia, Lutheranism expanded to the Baltic states to the east, and it even made its way into some of the predominantly Catholic areas in the south (p. 56).

After a century of bloody territorial fighting and battles over the right to designate the religion of choice in a land, a lasting peace was finally achieved in 1648. In the midst of the upheaval during the sixteenth century and most of the seventeenth century, Lutheranism in Europe went through a period of the forming and formalizing of its confessional identity. The first formal book of teachings, *The Book of Concord,* was published in 1580, which attempted to forge unity among the Lutherans by focusing on orthodoxy and subscribing to the confessions. Toward the end of the seventeenth century, however, a new movement emerged that rejected orthodoxy and its focus on formal confessions. The movement was Pietism: it emphasized the religion of the heart and was "grounded in the renewal of the local parish" (Gritsch, p. 157). Meanwhile, Lutheranism also began to move across the ocean to the New World. While the first Lutherans[26] arrived in the Delaware

---

24. As of 2005, there were ten different Lutheran denominations in the United States, made up of nearly 20,000 congregations, with over eight million members. Frank Spencer Mead, Samuel S. Hill, and Craig D. Atwood, *Handbook of Denominations in the United States,* 12th ed. (Nashville: Abingdon, 2005), 116-24.

25. Eric W. Gritsch, *A History of Lutheranism* (Minneapolis: Fortress, 2002), xi.

26. Some sources cite the first Lutherans arriving in what is now Florida as early as 1564. However, those settling at that time were given the name "Lutheran" by the Catholic authorities because they referred to all Protestants as Lutherans. Those early Florida settlers were actually French Huguenots. See Gritsch, *A History of Lutheranism,* 172.

Valley in 1638,[27] it wasn't until the beginning of the eighteenth century that they began immigrating en masse. By the early 1700s, fourteen congregations had formed in the colonies, and by 1776 there were 150 Lutheran congregations located along the eastern seaboard of America.[28] The Lutheran organization grew quickly. New synods were formed, and by the middle of the nineteenth century there were nearly sixty different synods. As Lutherans grew in numbers, so did their creation of Lutheran educational institutions: dozens of colleges and several seminaries were formed to educate the Lutheran immigrants. This trend continued right up to the turn of the twentieth century.

Despite the tragic consequences of World War I and World War II for some Lutherans in the United States — especially German congregations — the twentieth century brought about a time of coming together of various Lutheran traditions in the form of mergers. The wars forced many of the former immigrant communities to move toward the use of the common American language, English, in their worship services.[29] This paved the way for more open forms of communication between the various Lutheran bodies and laid the groundwork for multiple mergers that would eventually form the American Lutheran Church (ALC) in 1960 and the Lutheran Church in America (LCA) in 1962. These two Lutheran church bodies and the Association of Evangelical Lutheran Churches (AELC), a group that broke away from the Lutheran Church — Missouri Synod in 1976, joined together to form the Evangelical Lutheran Church in America (ELCA) in 1988.[30] This group, which makes up 57 percent of the Lutheran churches in the United States, is the church body from which I collected the data for this study.[31]

27. Bret E. Carroll, *The Routledge Historical Atlas of Religion in America,* Routledge Atlases of American History (New York: Routledge, 2000), 47.

28. Roger Finke and Rodney Stark, *The Churching of America, 1776-1990: Winners and Losers in Our Religious Economy* (New Brunswick, NJ: Rutgers University Press, 1992), 25.

29. E. Clifford Nelson, *The Lutherans in North America,* rev. ed. (Philadelphia: Fortress, 1980), 435.

30. Edgar R. Trexler, *High Expectations: Understanding the ELCA's Early Years, 1988-2002* (Minneapolis: Augsburg Fortress, 2003), 6-9.

31. Mark Noll, "American Lutherans Yesterday and Today," in *Lutherans Today,* ed. Richard Cimino (Grand Rapids: Eerdmans, 2003), 4.

Data Observations

The Evangelical Lutheran Church in America is today made up of more than four million members in ten thousand congregations across the country. These congregations are grouped into sixty-five different synods that are organized into nine different geographic regions; in addition, the ELCA has eight seminaries. Data was collected for the ELCA from leaders and worshipers from four of these synods and one of the seminaries. I conducted a total of 109 interviews (25 on the first tier, and 84 on the second tier), with each interviewee answering the same eight questions: there were a total of 872 responses. References to leadership showed up in 36 of the first-tier responses (18 percent) and in 54 of the overall responses (7.3 percent). While the frequency percentage may seem low, leadership and references to it made the list of top-ten subjects mentioned across this system's data; it placed eighth in the overall list and sixth among the first-tier data. In fact, the subject of leadership in the ELCA's first-tier data showed the highest percent of frequency of all four denominational systems in the study.

Table 1: ELCA Data Results

	1st-tier data (% of responses out of 200)	All data (% of responses out of 872)
1	Communication (34%)	Gospel (20.3%)
2	Gospel (26.5%)	Community/Culture (18.2%)
3	Church Tradition (26%)	Outreach (18.1%)
4	Community/Culture (25%)	Communication (17.3%)
5	Outreach (22%)	Church Tradition (13.4%)
6	**Leadership (18%)**	Prayer (9.2%)
7	God's Movement (11.5%)	**Leadership (7.9%)**
8	Role of Family (11.5%)	God's Movement (7.6%)
9	Prayer (9.5%)	Role of Family (7.6%)
10	Relationship (8.5%) Worship (8.5%)	Evangelism (6.3%)

Leadership in the ELCA was discussed very positively. "Leadership is crucial," said one respondent. Others shared the hope and excitement they felt about moving forward as they strive to become a missional church. Yet these respondents were also aware of the challenges they had before them. "Our system and all leadership development," said one respondent, "needs preparation for carrying out this task." "It [missional church] requires a lot of knowledge on the part of leadership, constantly reforming the system." While somewhat daunted by the work before them, they moved forward with optimism and hope.

While several of the interviewees identified themselves as leaders in this system, many of those same people talked about other leaders across the denomination. One interviewee referred to them as "leaders in the field." The word "leader" was used to refer to both ordained and lay leaders in ministry settings. One interviewee even claimed that their 700-member congregation had 250 in active leadership positions. Another said that we need to put "an emphasis on shared leadership between clergy and lay, and between professionals and volunteers." Leaders come in many shapes and sizes in this system — and fulfill a variety of functions.

As expected, the first-tier data frequently mentioned the role of synods in becoming a missional church. This is not surprising since many of those interviewed for the first-tier data collection were people in a variety of positions in ELCA synods. However, the second-tier data frequently mentioned synods and other church structures as well. Regardless of one's leadership role, the place of church structure, church doctrine, and church history for Lutherans is fairly important, enough so that this qualified as the third most frequently mentioned topic in the first-tier data and fifth in the overall data for the ELCA. Lutherans take their Lutheran heritage and their Lutheran structures very seriously, and they connect their understanding of missional church to these systems. One respondent said that a portion of the skills leaders needed to develop was "to connect who they were as Christians and leaders with Christian doctrines of [the] Lutheran church."

Across the board, however, interviewees felt that all leaders were in need of training and education for preparation to "carry out this task" of missional church. A variety of skill sets, such as communication, organization, and management were seen as necessary for leaders. Some interviewees felt that leaders also needed to be vision presenters, whether or not they themselves developed the vision. "Our seminaries," said one respondent, "need to train our leaders in practical ways." Another said that it was the responsibility of leaders to do the teaching, "teaching their people at every opportunity that their faith makes a difference and that's a good thing."

"Pastors need to become equippers, not presiders." "Leadership needs to be learned from all sources (nonprofits, for-profits, etc.)."

Respondents also seemed to have a desire for more accountability on the part of the leaders. One interviewee said: "[We are] yearning for accountability — desire to have performance evaluated so that work can be affirmed and challenged. [We are] yearning for collegiality instead of silo mentality. [It is about] getting the best leaders into the right places." In addition to needing accountability, leaders were seen as needing to support pastors and other leaders, and to reach out to others. For this system, missional church was about reaching out to neighbors, and it was necessary for leaders not to be afraid to do this.

Finally, a few of the interviewees talked about the relational aspect of leadership. For these Lutherans, leadership is not an isolated activity to be done by one on behalf of the many. Leadership is for all, by all, and with all. Missional leadership is "not me-centered but about finding and releasing energy and creating ownership for their call. Everybody's a leader." "The church is an exciting, dynamic arena for practicing our faith life. For this work specifically, I know how important collegiality is to our lives as leaders."

No single interviewee referred to God as a triune God, nor did any one individual refer to the Father, Son, and Holy Spirit in any given answer. However, varied references to the three persons of the Trinity were evident — but with unequal use. Jesus — or Christ — was mentioned 48 times throughout the 200 responses from the Lutherans.[32] Respondents referred to God 89 times, though the third person of the Trinity, the Holy Spirit, showed up a mere 5 times. Despite the fact that the everyday use of language to refer to God varied, liturgy[33] and the creeds[34] of the Lutheran church unequivocally mention the Father, Son, and Holy Spirit. Formal

---

32. Unlike the tallies in the previous categories mentioned, those included in the count of words used to refer to the three persons of the Trinity include multiple references in each response. For example, if a respondent said Jesus three times in a response, all three references were included in the tally. Though it was possible for any one respondent to mention the Father, Son, and Holy Spirit in a response, it never occurred within the ELCA data.

33. Each of the ten settings for worship found in the ELCA's new worship book starts with an invocation or greeting that includes Father, Son, and Holy Spirit. *Evangelical Lutheran Worship*, ev. ed. (Minneapolis: Augsburg Fortress, 2006).

34. See the Nicene Creed and the Apostles' Creed in *Evangelical Lutheran Worship*, 126, 127.

language in the Lutheran church is highly Trinitarian, but the everyday language of the believer is not.

Conclusions: ELCA

There is a clear sense that the presence of God is alive and active in the world for these Lutherans. Many of them have experienced God as a transforming God, shaping both their lives and the lives of others. However, they did not experience or feel the presence of God internally as much as it came from that which is external. Worship, the holy sacraments, and the preaching of the Word were all occasions for experiencing God's presence. While some referred to their participation in God's mission, only two people equated it with God working in and through them. There was either a lack of understanding or an inability to articulate a perichoretic understanding of God's relationship with God's people, of being in communion with God, despite the overwhelming presence of community language in the data.

There also seems to be a disconnect between the rich Lutheran heritage, where the doctrine of the Trinity takes a prominent place, and the day-to-day practicality of being a Lutheran Christian. While Lutheran theology seems to be richly appreciated among the interviewees, there was a distinct lack of it in terms of its translation into everyday life as they described who they were called to be in God's world and how God the Father, Son, and Holy Spirit worked in their lives. There is a commitment — or, more importantly, a passion — for this triune God whom they confess in worship. It will be interesting to see whether a more practical, lived-out expression of the triune God, on behalf of those feeling called to become a missional church, will make a difference as this denominational system continues to examine leadership and its role as they become a missional church.

The Synod of the Trinity, Presbyterian Church USA (PCUSA)

The roots of the Presbyterian Church in the United States of America (PCUSA) can be traced back to the days of colonial America, but the PCUSA as a denomination is barely twenty-five years old, having been formed in 1983 from the merger of the Presbyterian Church in the United States (PCUS) and the United Presbyterian Church in the USA

(UPCUSA), the two largest Presbyterian bodies in the United States.[35] The historical roots of the PCUSA, as well as the Synod of the Trinity, go back to the time of the Protestant Reformation in sixteenth-century Europe. Martin Luther had initiated the movement for reforming Catholicism in Wittenberg, Germany. John Calvin soon joined him and led the way in developing the Calvinist (or Reformed) branch of the reforming movement in France and Switzerland. Calvin, a former Roman Catholic, understood the importance of the relationship between church and state, and thus he wisely dedicated his great work, *Institutes of the Christian Religion,* to the king of France at that time, reassuring the king that he had nothing to fear with the new kind of Christianity.[36]

Calvin developed a new form of polity for the church, which included representation by both pastors and laypeople. He focused on worship, relationships with the government, polity, and discipline. For Calvin, Christianity was a way of life, and it intersected with all realms of the civil community.

> In the Reformed view of the church, God calls the Christian community into being through the work of Christ and the Holy Spirit. The church is a community of faith and life that is called to share Christ's story with the world. As such, Christians belong to a communion of saints, not a hierarchical order in heaven but a community of the dead and the living, the number of which is known only to God.[37]

The Reformed movement initiated by Calvin spread throughout Europe, taking on an ethnic identity wherever it took root: Dutch Reformed, Swiss Reformed, French Reformed, and Scottish Reformed were but a few of the newly emerging groups. It was the last group, the Scottish Reformed, who eventually made their way to America to begin the Presbyterian Church in the New World. Presbyterians were worshiping in Jamestown as early as 1611, but it wasn't until 1683, with the arrival of Francis Makemie, that real growth began to occur. Beginning in Virginia, he started churches up and down the eastern coast, and he formed the first presbytery (the

---

35. Mead, Hill, and Atwood, *Handbook of Denominations,* 141.

36. John Calvin, *Institutes of the Christian Religion,* trans. and ed. Ford Lewis Battles (Grand Rapids: Eerdmans, 1975).

37. James H. Smylie, *A Brief History of the Presbyterians* (Louisville: Geneva Press, 1996), 23-24.

Philadelphia Presbytery) in 1706. Eleven years later the first synod, the Synod of Philadelphia, was formed by the union of the presbyteries of Philadelphia, Delaware, Newcastle, and Long Island.[38]

The Presbyterian Church in the United States continued to grow. Together with other denominations and agencies, the presbyteries developed organizations alongside their denominational structure to further missionary efforts. They also increased and strengthened education opportunities in the form of Sunday schools, colleges, and seminaries, which contributed "to the welfare of all peoples."[39]

The Civil War fueled conflict and divisions within the presbyteries as much as it did in the states themselves: by 1870 there were at least seven different branches on the Presbyterian Church family tree in the United States.[40] Then, during the decades following the Civil War, unique challenges emerged for all members of society. The country saw an explosion of growth in urban areas, with a move from a primarily agrarian culture to an industrialized one. In addition, the country saw an influx of immigrants like it had never seen before: those numbers went to over a million a year after the turn of the century.[41] Just as cities struggled to develop infrastructure to meet the needs of these new population groups, denominations struggled to keep up with the need for starting churches. *The Book of Common Worship* was adopted in 1906 to aid pastors in "comforting congregations in times of personal crises."[42]

Like many mainline denominations, the PCUSA has seen a significant decline in membership during the twentieth century. Between 1966 and 1988 alone, the PCUS and UPCUSA saw a membership drop of over 1.3 million, which represented more than 30 percent of its total membership.[43] Today they number 2.4 million members, with over 11,000 congregations

38. Carroll, *Routledge Historical Atlas*, 38-39.

39. Smylie, *A Brief History*, 77.

40. The seven included in this list are: Reformed Presbyterian Church in North America (1774), Presbyterian Church USA (1870), Presbyterian Church in the Confederate States of America (1861), Cumberland Presbyterian Church (1810), United Presbyterian Church of North America (1858), Associate Reformed Presbyterian Church (1822), and Reformed Presbyterian Church of North America (1833). Robert C. Walton, *Chronological and Background Charts of Church History* (Grand Rapids: Zondervan, 1986), 68.

41. Sydney E. Ahlstrom, *A Religious History of the American People* (New Haven: Yale University Press, 1972), 749.

42. Smylie, *A Brief History*, 98.

43. Smylie, *A Brief History*, 140.

grouped into 173 presbyteries and sixteen different synods.[44] The Synod of the Trinity, where I collected the data for this study, is the oldest and largest of the sixteen synods in the PCUSA. Serving over 10 percent of the congregations in the denomination, it represents only a fraction of U.S. geography: Pennsylvania, West Virginia, and a small part of southeastern Ohio. Leaders from the Synod of the Trinity and several of its presbyteries provided interview data for the first tier of this project, with the second-tier data coming from pastors and laity in their congregations.

Data Observations

Data was collected for the Presbyterian Church USA from synod leaders, presbytery leaders, pastors, and laity across the region within the Synod of the Trinity. I conducted a total of seventy-five interviews (fifteen on the first tier and sixty on the second tier); each interviewee answered the same eight questions, for a total of 600 responses. References to leadership showed up in 14 responses (11.7 percent) in the first-tier data and in 42 responses (7 percent) overall.

Table 2: PCUSA Data Results

1st-tier data (% of responses out of 120)	All data (% of responses out of 600)
1 God's Movement (25%)	Gospel (21.5%)
2 Communication (25%)	God's Movement (17.2%)
3 Church Tradition (25%)	Outreach (16%)
4 Gospel (20.8%)	Community/Culture (14.7%)
5 Community/Culture (18.3%)	Communication (14.2%)
6 Outreach (15%)	Prayer (12.8%)
7 Prayer (15%)	Church Tradition (12%)
8 Role of Family (12.5%)	Role of Family (8.3%)
9 Laity (11.7%)	**Leadership (7%)**
10 **Leadership (11.7%)**	Change (6.6%)

44. Presbyterian Church USA, "Who We Are," http://www.pcusa.org/navigation/whoweare.htm (accessed Apr. 12, 2007).

As a synod in the PCUSA, the Synod of the Trinity exists in the middle of a hierarchy of denominational structures and relationships. The local structure starts with the congregation: a congregation is part of a presbytery, presbyteries are part of a synod, and synods make up the national church body. With multiple levels of structure come multiple levels of leadership; yet there were surprisingly few references to leadership in the data for the Synod of the Trinity. When leadership was mentioned, it was often in the context of leaders who had influenced the interviewees throughout their lives. At other times, respondents spoke of leadership in general, such as "leadership of the church," without specific references to roles (sessions, pastors, executive presbyters, etc.). Yet, despite the general nature of this data, some interesting themes did emerge.

For these interviewees, leadership has a lot to do with character. Those talking about leadership often remarked on the need for leaders to be responsible and authentic: the "transparency of leadership" is important. Missional church is about leaders showing "humanness, struggles, [and] authenticity." Another interviewee said that we need to "teach leadership responsibility." For yet another, developing leadership skills was about the "integration of beliefs into leadership." These respondents saw the living of a transparent life, where authenticity and integrity are at the forefront, as crucial for becoming a missional church.

Along with these character expectations comes the belief that leadership is about coaching and mentoring. When it comes to attitudes and beliefs about missional church, one respondent said that the "leadership (clergy and laity) must model [it]." Another person shared her story of going back to college after having four children to become a new kind of leader, a role that involved mentoring and coaching. For another, leadership was a lifelong learning process in terms of inspiring others: "One needs to help the dream become their dream." Many of these same people mentioned leaders who had served as mentors for them; several of those stories came from their childhoods, when they had been mentored by their youth leaders.

Finally, the sense of leadership in these data was about leading others and creating space for others to participate in being missional church. "Pastors and leaders should really spearhead it, to allow others to do the work," said one. For another, leadership is about "helping the group do what they're about." One interviewee even talked about his own growth in developing this skill.

I've had to be a better administrator [to] organize people to go. I needed to develop the ability to be a good enough leader so that others will feel structure so that they will be involved. People want to see that whatever skills they have can be used.

In the view of many of the interviewees who mentioned leadership issues, leaders hold the responsibility for making it possible for others to do the missional church work.

Perhaps it is not surprising that references to laity were just as frequent in the first-tier data as were references to leadership — and almost as frequent as leadership in the second-tier data. There seems to be a consistent thought that the missional church is about the work and the role of the laity. The few references to clergy were often given within the context of what clergy needed to do to identify gifts, to equip, and to make space for the laity. One interviewee said: "I preach sermons that have to do with equipping the saints. Especially in the Reformed tradition of the priesthood of all believers, we are all ministers of Jesus Christ." "We are all ministers and missionaries," said another.

What was perhaps most surprising in the PCUSA data — compared to the other systems in this study — was the high frequency of language in which God was the acting subject. "God speaks," "God sends," "God is at work," "God is in charge," and "God cares" were just a few of the many phrases used to talk God. There is definitely an awareness of God's presence and activity in the world. "[I am aware of] God's presence both in and around me," said one participant. Another said, "[I am] looking for and claiming God's activity — a sense of spirituality — awareness of God's presence in and around us."

Despite the strong presence of data showing that these people were acutely aware of what God is up to, there was a lack of response data showing that they saw themselves as participating in that activity. The only two respondents to even use the language of participation related it to participating in God's mission, not God's activity or Godself. Missional church, said one respondent, is where "you are doing God's work together."

Several respondents talked of the importance of knowing that God was in and among people already. "God is here in every aspect of our lives, whether we go to church or not. God will never abandon us." Another said that we need to be "looking for and claiming God's activity —

a sense of spirituality — awareness of God's presence in and around us." Yet, despite this heightened awareness of God's presence and activity, there was little if any language about participation with God in this activity, let alone in the actual life of God. The few times that was mentioned, it was referred to almost as a response to God's guidance or call. Out of all the things people mentioned that God was up to, the most frequently mentioned activity of God was calling and directing people to do what God wants.

Conclusions: Synod of the Trinity, PCUSA

In a system that is highly structured, there is a surprising lack of emphasis placed on that structure with regard to leadership. Leadership in this system is personal. It is about one's character and how one relates to another. Leadership exists in order to create space for the missional work of God's people to be done. It would seem that leaders have the task of identifying and training others, then getting out of the way for the work to be done.

There is a significant amount of talk in this system about the activity of God, yet there is a lack of language to describe how people participate in that activity. God is present and among them, and God cares and loves all people. The voices in this data are filled with hope. They approach missional church with a sense of optimism, and this comes from the strong belief that God is present and up to something good.

Mennonite Church USA

The origin of the Mennonites also goes back to the Protestant Reformation in Europe. While somewhat pleased with how Martin Luther sought to reform the church, these were reformers who felt it just wasn't enough.

> The Anabaptists actually rejoiced at the work Luther had done but saw it as a halfway reformation. They did not feel that the Bible taught his sacramental understanding of the Lord's Supper or the saving power of baptism; but they were particularly disappointed with his definition of the church as the place where the Word of God was preached and

the sacraments were rightly administered. To them, the church, according to the New Testament, should consist of believers only.[45]

It was in January 1525 that the name *Anabaptist ("baptized again")* was officially given to this unique group of reformers after three individuals were "rebaptized" as adults even though they had been baptized as infants (Dyck, p. 33). Despite the protest of these believers that they were not rebaptizing, but carrying out their one and only true baptism, the name stuck to them and has been used ever since.

The persecution of the Anabaptists, which also began at about that time, put additional strain on the movement. Pressure from both Protestants and Roman Catholics sent many Anabaptists into hiding; those not so lucky were imprisoned or sentenced to death, and their leaders began to scatter. Despite the persecution, Anabaptism continued to spread. It soon took root in the southern and central parts of Germany, along the northern coast of the Netherlands, and over to the east in Moravia. It was the group of Anabaptists centered in the Netherlands that came to be known as the Mennonites. Menno Simons, originally a priest in what is now the province of Friesland, did not become an Anabaptist until the mid-1530s. Persecution still made this a difficult time for the group, but Simons kept them alive. "[I]t was Menno's leadership which saved the Dutch Anabaptist movement from fanaticism and possible disintegration" (Dyck, p. 105). His followers soon were called the Mennonists, and later the Mennonites. They continued to face persecution until 1577, when Prince William of Orange ordered that Mennonites be left alone as long as they continued to be "useful citizens" (p. 129).

Over a century later, in 1688, an English Quaker by the name of William Penn offered an invitation to Anabaptists living in the Dutch city of Crefeld. Penn had received 18,000 acres in the new colonies from the king of England, and in a quest to conduct what he referred to as a "holy experiment," he invited six men to come and settle on his land and create a village. Soon afterwards, thirteen families arrived. This settlement in Germantown, Pennsylvania, grew larger and larger, and Mennonites pushed their way further west to Lancaster, then down to Virginia, and to the Carolinas.

---

45. Cornelius J. Dyck, *An Introduction to Mennonite History: A Popular History of the Anabaptists and the Mennonites*, 3rd ed. (Scottdale, PA: Herald Press, 1993), 31-32.

Intent on forming communities with other Mennonites, they found themselves in similar situations and facing the same harsh realities that other settlers did. Out of necessity, they settled alongside other Protestant groups, such as the German Lutherans, the German Reformed, and the Amish, with whom they often shared buildings and meeting places. The Mennonites' practices and habits were like those of other denominations as they struggled to make a home in a strange new place.

The Anabaptist population continued to grow during the eighteenth and early nineteenth centuries, primarily because of high birthrates and continued immigration. More Swiss-German Mennonites arrived and settled alongside their Amish brethren in Ohio and Indiana. Other Mennonites emigrated from Russia and settled in Kansas. These latter settlers formed the General Conference of the Mennonites in the mid-1800s, thus splitting the Mennonites into two separate groups for the next century and a half.

The Mennonites continued to feel the pressure of external cultural influences. Instead of shutting the world out (as the Amish did), they formed a defensive posture by undergoing a process of restructuring and codification of their practices. Internally, they shifted from a mode of operation that was grounded in their belief in mutual consent to one of standardization and regulation of practices — right down to the role and authority of the bishop. Agencies and institutions within the church multiplied. A college was established in Goshen, Indiana, in 1902, and a publishing house and a mission agency were soon added to the structure.

By the mid-twentieth century, the Mennonites had given up on their defensive structuring. Where they once had fought hard to keep external cultural influences at bay, they were now living into their new context more fully. Most worship services were now conducted in English. Sunday school became a regular part of a church's curriculum; the Revised Standard Version of the Bible was introduced and accepted; and Mennonites began to engage and live in their present context and culture.

It was not until the beginning of the twenty-first century that Mennonites finally underwent an extensive merger of the Mennonite Church and the General Conference, when they formed the new Mennonite Church USA in 2002. Today, with over a million members, the national church body is searching for new ways to engage the changing culture in which they live.

Data Observations

Data was collected for the Mennonite Church USA from leaders and worshipers across the country. I conducted a total of 80 interviews (22 on the first tier and 58 on the second tier), with each interviewee answering the same eight questions, for a total of 640 responses. References to leadership showed up in 26 of the first-tier responses (14.8 percent) and in 57 (8.9 percent) overall. Leadership references made it on the list of top-ten subjects mentioned across this system's data, placing sixth in the first tier and ninth overall. In the overall data, leadership had the highest-percentage showing (9.1 percent), more than any of the other three systems in this project.

Table 3: Mennonite Data Results

1st-tier data (% of responses out of 176)	All data (% of responses out of 640)
1 Church Tradition (21.3 %)	Communication (21.7%)
2 God's Movement (21.3%)	Church Tradition (21.3%)
3 Gospel (20.9%)	Outreach (20.9%)
4 Community/Culture (19.2%)	God's Movement (20%)
5 Communication (21.6%)	Community/Culture (19.2%)
6 **Leadership (14.8%)**	Gospel (18.4%)
7 Outreach (13.1%)	Relationship (9.7%)
8 Calling (10.8%)	Role of Family (9.5%)
9 Role of Family (10.2%)	**Leadership (9.1%)**
10 Evangelism (8.5%) Laity (8.5%)	Evangelism (6.1%)

Leadership for members of the Mennonite Church USA system is something for the whole, not just for the individual. Those interviewed talked about leadership relationally: that is, it is something that happens in teams, groups, or in systems. One person talked about a situation at her church in which two people were installed for the sole purpose of looking at members' gifts. Their "leadership team is looking to find young new leaders to become pastors and other leaders," said one respondent. Others talked about their leadership team as needing to be guided in order to move toward a common vision.

[Missional Church is about] the ability to teach others what you know, not just doing it yourself. Do things in a way that can be reproduced. As we create leadership structures in the church, they can be replicated. Vision extension: impart to the people I am leading that [my] sense of call and purpose [should be] shared more widely than just me.

Gifts discernment appears to be crucial to this team approach. A few respondents talked about the importance of recognizing gifts in others for leadership. One even said that, once gifts were named and claimed, a congregation can "turn loose the Holy Spirit." Another said that "God has provided the congregation with so many gifts within lay leadership [it was] more than 'developing' them, [they] need to bless and encourage, help the congregation find ways to access its gifts." And another: "Congregations must shift from programs we give time to, to people finding their own story and gifts, who they are, and what they are called to do in mission. It's got to come up from persons, not down from leaders."

These people take seriously the idea that leadership is not just for pastors. Leadership and leadership development is a grassroots endeavor, and, as we have already heard, lay leaders come gifted in many ways.

Look at people as God sees them and see them as equals. If we take a strong position, we should be consistent and consider all the implications. Gently nudge people in areas where they need to grow. Encourage strong (but not dictatorial) leadership as being necessary to be missional. People want to be part of an organization that offers something for the whole family.

One final observation from the MCUSA data concerning leadership is about the role of spiritual practices. For Mennonites, leadership is about spiritual disciplines, particularly spiritual discernment. "Listening and being sensitive to the Spirit" and regular worship were important. "I've been practicing these habits in my congregation," said one respondent. "Dwelling in the Word, and calling for the gospel. God is at work in that, forming us through that practice. Good leadership [involves] discernment in congregations." Another, when asked what skills were necessary, said:

[We need skills of] listening. Being able to communicate. Being resourceful. Taking initiative as a leader. Being visionary and discerning.

Courage to stand firm with what you hear God calling you to do regardless of what friends and family think.

One respondent felt so strongly about this that she said leaders should be accountable to spiritual directors. Another said that this work involves intuition, "sensing what God might be calling us to." Still another cited the need to teach people to trust lay leadership to listen to God and ask questions, such as, "What is God up to?"

Interestingly, the role of church tradition was the most frequently mentioned topic for the first-tier data and came in second for the overall data. Mennonite structures, organizations, and institutions were frequently mentioned as partners and resources for this work. For some, their Anabaptist roots provide the operating theology for why missional church matters. "Mennonite church concepts [of discipleship]," said one respondent, "make Mennonites predisposed to understand that following Jesus is what we do all the time, not just on Sunday."

One more important thing to note is that, even though it didn't make the top ten, there were references to missional church as being about working together with God, not just for God. Participation language in the life and activity of God was fairly common to these interviewees' responses. "[Missional Church] is about getting on board with what God is doing in the world," said one respondent. Another said that it was about "living incarnationally . . . being sent to engage in God's mission." "In missional church we are to be engaged in what God is doing in the world."

Conclusions: Mennonite Church USA

The data gathered for the MCUSA shows more consistency between the first- and second-tier respondents. Both tiers discuss leadership generally, not with respect to specific titles. Both discuss the importance of laity and the need for identifying and encouraging the gifts of all.

What is unique to this church system is the role spiritual disciplines play in leadership. While other systems mention it, this data talks about it specifically in relationship to leadership. As we look more closely at leadership for the missional church that is shaped by a *perichoretic* understanding of the triune God and participation in that reality, we must further explore and better understand the place of spiritual disciplines in leadership.

Like the other church systems, MCUSA confesses a belief in the triune God; but here, too, while the Father, Son, and Spirit are rarely mentioned, there is conversation as to how the three persons of God matter in the day-to-day lives of believers, even though the language to articulate it is absent.

Churches of Christ, Abilene Christian University

The Churches of Christ is a self-professed nondenominational religious movement whose congregations are concentrated in the South and Southwest of the United States. It has no central headquarters and no official governing bodies. Yet the Churches of Christ have more than 10,000 congregations and a membership of about 1.5 million.

It was amid the ever-changing religious landscape of nineteenth-century America that the Churches of Christ as a movement began to form, emerging as one of many movements intent on restoring Christianity to its New Testament roots. During a time in history when America was experiencing a new sense of political freedom with its liberation from England, a new freedom of religious expression came about as well. A desire emerged among "restoration" groups during the late eighteenth and early nineteenth centuries to liberate Christianity from "institutions and denominational divisions"[46]

August 8, 1801 was the turning point for this movement. A Presbyterian pastor named Barton Stone held a "great meeting" in his small church in Cane Ridge, Kentucky.[47] This meeting ended seven days later, but only because they had run out of provisions for its participants, who numbered in the tens of thousands. This monumental event in American religious history was deemed the "greatest outpouring of the Spirit since Pentecost" (Ahlstrom, 433), as well as "the largest and most famous camp meeting revival in American history." Preachers represented the Methodists and Baptists, as well as the Presbyterians. This revival meeting is where Stone received his vision for true Christian unity.[48]

Following the revival, Stone was charged by his presbytery with "not only indecorous churchmanship and low educational standards, but for

---

46. Carroll, *Routledge Historical Atlas*, 70.

47. Ahlstrom, *A Religious History*, 432.

48. Gary Holloway and Douglas A. Foster, *Renewing God's People: A Concise History of Churches of Christ* (Abilene, TX: ACU Press, 2001), 33.

heresy as well." To avoid standing trial, he withdrew from the presbytery and, along with other leaders from the revival, organized the Springfield Presbytery in 1803. By that time, however, Stone and his followers had so distanced themselves from Presbyterian doctrine and polity that they disbanded their newly formed presbytery and adopted the name "Christian." The Bible became their "only creed and law" (Ahlstrom, pp. 445-46). This new Christian movement grew rapidly in Kentucky, and it made a lasting impression on the Presbyterian churches in southeastern Ohio as well, converting all but two.

Meanwhile, a similar movement was underway in western Pennsylvania. Thomas Campbell, also a former Presbyterian, formed a small group known as the Christian Association of Washington County. His intent was not to form another denomination, but he wished to "promote Christian unity by preaching a simple gospel which would rise above denominationalism" (Ahlstrom, p. 447). He was later joined by his son Alexander, and together they formed multiple groups and called themselves Disciples of Christ. This movement grew rapidly across the lower Ohio Valley and the upper South; by 1830, it had become the fastest-growing religious movement, with members numbering about 12,000.[49] Thus, in his efforts to undo denominationalism, Alexander Campbell unintentionally created a new denomination.

The Campbellites and Stoneites, as well as various other "restoration" movements, were working for the most part in isolation from one another, basically unaware that the other existed. It wasn't until Alexander Campbell came to speak in Kentucky that Stone and Campbell realized their commonalities. They soon joined forces, and their merged membership became the Disciples of Christ in 1832. In the midst of an expanding frontier they offered a simple message of Christian unity for Christians from dissenting churches of many Christian traditions. Despite their lack of desire to become a denomination, they had to form minimal organizational structures of some kind — at least enough for them to hold a national convention in Cincinnati in the mid-1800s.

The merger did not last. In about a half century the two groups split: the Northern, more urban churches continued as the Disciples of Christ, and the Southern, more rural (and more conservative) churches took a new name, Churches of Christ. This division left the Churches of Christ in

---

49. Carroll, *Routledge Historical Atlas*, 70.

a state of distress, both financially and in terms of numbers. "While thriving in rural areas, Churches of Christ were left virtually to begin all over again in many urban centers from Tennessee to Texas. Their comeback was, nonetheless, remarkable."[50]

In a system that professes itself to be nondenominational, the Churches of Christ have been able to maintain a semblance of unity in their theology — as well as in their structures and practices. Three particular vehicles served the Churches of Christ in that way: their religious schools, their papers and print journals, and their traveling evangelists. "The schools trained leaders, discussed issues, and formed an informal network of associations, all contributing to the identity of Churches of Christ."[51]

As a result, church membership for Churches of Christ continued to grow after the split from the Disciples that occurred around the turn of the century. By 1980, membership had grown to 1,240,820, and the group continued to see growth through the 1980s and up to the 1990s.

Data Observations

Data was collected for the Churches of Christ fellowship connected with Abilene Christian University from leaders and worshipers from across the country. I conducted a total of 86 interviews (20 on the first tier and 66 on the second tier), with each interviewee answering the same eight questions, for a total of 688 responses. References to leadership showed up in 20 of the responses (12.5 percent) in the first-tier data (out of 160) and in 51 of the 688 responses overall (7.4 percent). While the frequency percentage may seem low, references to leadership made the list of top-ten subjects mentioned across this system's data, placing eighth on both lists (see p. 235).

The data I collected within the Churches of Christ about the theme of leadership showed a surprising lack of understanding as to what missional leadership was or what it looked like. "What is church leadership in the missional church? That is the burning question," said one respondent. Others referred to congregational leadership as a skill that needed to be better understood.

---

50. Richard T. Hughes and R. L. Roberts, *The Churches of Christ* (Westport, CT: Greenwood Press, 2001), 3.
51. Holloway and Foster, *Renewing God's People,* 104, 106.

Table 4: Churches of Christ Data Results

1st-tier data (% of responses out of 160)	All data (% of responses out of 688)
1 Education (45.6%)	Community/Culture (23%)
2 Community/Culture (40%)	Gospel (19.6%)
3 Gospel (36.3%)	Education (18%)
4 Communication (32.5%)	Communication (14.8%)
5 God's Movement (23.2%)	Outreach (14.5%)
6 Church Tradition (16.9%)	God's Movement (9.9%)
7 Outreach (15.6%)	Church Tradition (8%)
8 **Leadership (12.5%)**	**Leadership (7.4%)**
9 Relationship (9.4%)	Relationship (6.7%)
10 Story (8.8%)	Models (6.3%)

Many expressed frustration with leadership and referred to it as problematic. There is a "disconnect," said one interviewee, "between church leadership and church body, due to lack of communication and education." Others said that there is "tension in church leaders" in that they "want to be missional, but [are] so overwhelmed with taking care of [the] church body." Another said that "church leaders don't spend time with people who don't know the Lord. [They] see that there is something wrong in leadership. . . . [There is an] absence in missional thinking among the leaders."

However, not all interviewees were negative about the issues of leadership in this church system. "We have a new wave of leadership," said one respondent, "and that excites me." Another felt a sense of hope: "Hope . . . it's a leadership issue. God will use leaders to help people discover their calling." Here lies one of the strengths of this system's understanding of missional leadership: while many are still confused as to what it is, there seems to be a common thread of missional leadership being linked with the idea of relationality.

Leadership is not for the one or for the few; leadership in this system is for all. Not one of the respondents mentioned a particular role or job description for a leader. Occasionally one might refer to a minister or an elder, but never in the context of that individual's serving as the one leader. This "takes people, not just one person or a charismatic leader," said one respondent. Another called preachers, elders, and all "who have surrendered to God" the leaders of the church.

In addition to missional leadership being the responsibility of all, respondents identified missional leadership as being about the coming together of all. It means "to be faith community in mission — for others — outward-focused rather than what's in it for me." This is about mentoring and coaching and developing relationships with each other. "Leadership is first conversation," said one respondent. Leadership is about "developing one-on-one relationships with potential leaders," said another. The behaviors that are modeled and the language that is used in conversation make a difference. "In our leadership, we practice our language constantly. We are finding good words to help us better define our relationship to the world — and then we practice these words."

It was interesting to note how these interviewees talked about God. While the names "Jesus" and the "Holy Spirit" were used about the Godhead 88 and 20 times, respectively, the word "God" was used 318 times.[52] References to the Trinity, or instances in which the Father, Son, and Holy Spirit were referred to in one response, were limited to 9 times, but this was more than any other system in this study. One respondent talked about the Trinity when referring to Christian classic literature he had read, not to how he understood God to be in relationship with the world. Another respondent used the same phrase in both responses to describe God as "a living God, risen Christ, Holy Spirit." However, no one in either tier of the data referred to God existing in community, in relationship, or as a social reality.

Despite the small amount of theological language concerning the Trinity in this data (and other literature on the Churches of Christ), a significant number of respondents used participation language. For many of these leaders, missional church is about participating in the activity of God and in God's work in God's world. In addition to "participate," words such as "invite," "join," "embrace," and "called" were used to talk about the ways individuals and churches are connected with God in God's mission.

---

52. This was the total number of times each of these words was used, not the number of responses they appeared in.

Conclusions: Churches of Christ

One would assume that a church system that was focused on not being a formally structured denomination would be all over the map in its thinking on leadership and missional church. How can a group of unconnected congregations think consistently about a topic, let alone strive together as a nondenominational system to become a missional church? While some confusion is evident, there was a surprising emergence of some common themes.

Leadership for this system is not hierarchical. Like other systems in this study, members of the Churches of Christ believe that leadership is for all and depends on the gifts and strengths of a community. What that looks like may be a bit fuzzy to them, but it does give them hope and encouragement. Furthermore, this system of congregations, while lacking everyday Trinitarian language about God (at least in the data), used quite a bit of participation language when talking about "missional church." Perhaps this also gives this system hope. "Missional church gave me new language," said one leader. Another said that one of the things that needed to be taught in their system to innovate missional church was to "begin with language — a vocabulary people identify with that brings imagery to mind . . . [and] encourages them to articulate missional language."

Summary

I should note that this chapter only reviews one dimension of the data collected from these four denominational systems. Much more could be done to better understand how these denominational systems understand themselves and their relationship with God, and how they participate as a church in becoming missional. By framing the conversation around leadership within a missional ecclesiology, one informed by a doctrine of the Trinity and shaped by feminist theology, I have attempted to look at the stories and metaphors of the people in these systems. It is through these stories that places of commonalities emerged.

First and foremost, the people interviewed in this project clearly have a passion for what God is up to in the world and how they and their churches can be a part of it. Even where confusion and frustration existed, hope endured. In fact, for many the idea of becoming a missional church, even if they did not clearly understand it, gave them hope for their church and their denominational system.

Second, all of these systems talked about leadership as highly relational. Missional leadership does not occur in a silo, but in and among the many. Missional leadership is about using the God-given gifts of all, in whatever shape and form they come. Ordained leaders, judicatories, national church bodies, and institutions are to teach, create space, and provide opportunity for those gathered to carry out God's mission.

Respondents across the four systems used "participation" language — though to different degrees. For many, the church is to participate in God's mission in the world; but few used it to describe what that participation looked like. For some, participation is to do God's work; for others, it is about working with God in God's work. Even fewer used it to talk about how that relates to our relationship with the triune God.

Finally, all of the data is filled with references to God the Father, Jesus the Son, and the Holy Spirit, though their frequencies varied across the four denominational systems. However, all four systems were consistent in their failure to mention the Trinity and in how their insight related to the mission of God in the world. Perhaps this serves as the missing link. While each of these systems can show an understanding of God as triune in their confessional documents or official teaching, very few of the people interviewed could articulate the implications of this belief in their everyday language when talking about missional church.

Missional church is about an understanding of *being* that leads to *doing*, rather than starting with doing; yet the "doing" language is pervasive in the data. In order to explore what becoming a missional church looks like for congregations and the systems and institutions that serve them, perhaps a helpful way to move forward would be to better understand how people relate to God. Missional church is about being in relationship with God, with one another, and with God's creation. These are interrelated, not separate entities. Yet each system seemed to have developed the first one more than the last one. Clearly, people understand themselves as having *a relationship* with God. But is that different from an understanding of *being in relationship* with God? Perhaps this is where missional leadership can start: by helping everyone better understand what it means to live in community, within the divine community of God, and with each other for the sake of the world.